Why They Did Not Starve

Why They Did Not Starve

Biocultural Adaptation
in a South Indian Village

Morgan D. Maclachlan

A Publication of the
Institute for the Study of Human Issues
Philadelphia

Manufactured in the United States of America

1 2 3 4 5 6 7 8 9 90 89 88 87 86 85 84 83

Publication of this book was assisted by a grant from the Publications
Program of the National Endowment for the Humanities, an independent
federal agency.

Library of Congress Cataloging in Publication Data

Maclachlan, Morgan D., 1940–
    Why they did not starve.

    Bibliography: p.
    Includes index.
    1. Agriculture—Social aspects—India—Yaavahalli.
2. Yaavahalli (India)—Social conditions 3. Ethnology—
India—Yaavahalli. 4. India—Famines. I. Title.
HD2075.Y25M25   304.5   81-20203
ISBN 0-89727-001-0   AACR2

For information, write:

Director of Publications
ISHI
3401 Market Street
Philadelphia, Pennsylvania 19104
U.S.A.

Contents

Acknowledgments vii

Note on Transcription ix

1 *Why They Did Not Starve* 1

2 *The United Temple* 20

3 *Body Dharma* 42

4 *Kashta Kelsa* 83

5 *The Male Management of Agriculture* 108

6 *One Man or More* 140

7 *Coming of Age: The Social Construction of Patriarchy* 159

8 *The Development of Agricultural Intensification* 199

9 *The Evolution of Intensification Fitness* 231

Appendix: Notes on the Social Sciences, Sociobiology, and the Sexual Miasma 279

References 285

Index 289

Acknowledgments

The field research on which this study is based was conducted under Grant MH30713, funded by the National Institutes of Mental Health. I am most grateful to the people of Yaavahalli for their kindness and cooperation. The work of Caryl Abrahams Maclachlan was crucial in the organization and implementation of the fieldwork project. The project required the collection and recording of large quantities of descriptive information. It would have been impossible to undertake without the aid of a number of competent and industrious research assistants. Particularly notable were the contributions of K. S. Gangadriah, K. S. Munivenkatasvaami, K. Shama Rao, Shankar Narayana Rao, and V. N. Srinivasa Murthy.

In the course of writing and revising this work, I was aided by the comments and suggestions of a number of readers: John Adams, Arjun Appadurai, Alan Beals, Lucy Garretson, Stanton Green, Sheryl Horowitz, Mary Maclachlan, Nancy Sedeberg, Henry Selby, and Robert Stewart. They did their best to relieve this book of its flaws; those that remain are my responsibility.

Finally, I would like to note my appreciation for the expertise, sensitive interest, and ample patience of my editors at ISHI.

Note on Transcription

The Kannada terms used in this book were transcribed using, with slight modification, the phonemic romanization developed by William Bright. Readers should pronounce the letter *v* in initial position as the English *w*. Upper-case consonants in the middle of words indicate retroflexing: in pronouncing them readers should turn the tip of the tongue up to the roof of the mouth. Vowel length, which is phonemic, is indicated with single and double letters. Thus the duration of the initial vowel in *beeku*, "it is wanted, I want," is roughly twice as long as that in *beku*, "cat." For the convenience of my readers I have in most cases used the English *s* to indicate pluralization, rather than the appropriate Kannada suffixes.

chapter 1

Why They Did Not Starve

> Famine is a disease of all agricultural countries. India is
> and has always been mainly agricultural under conditions
> peculiarly exposed to famine.
>
> —*Imperial Gazetteer of India*

This study amounts to an argument, a series of related hypotheses,
aimed at explaining how the people of one Indian village managed to
protect themselves against famine and how they acquired this capacity to
defy, for the time being, conditions that might otherwise have starved
them to death.

The village is Yaavahalli, a small, mostly Kannada-speaking farm
community that lies in Kolar District in the state of Karnataka at the
center of the southern tip of India. The argument centers on that venera-
ble Indian institution, the joint family, and bears on a number of general
issues, perhaps most notably these:

To what extent and in what manner do biological sex differences
influence the sexual division of labor?

How does the labor intensification of agriculture come to be organized as a cultural response to increases in population density?

Why do social arrangements in human societies sometimes seem to
vary according to sociobiological principles?

I cite these issues both to give some idea of what the book is about
and to provide a triangular basis for an initial exposition of the rudiments
of my argument. There are, however, certain facts about Yaavahalli and
the region of which it is part that are so pertinent to the argument that
follows that I must call attention to them, even before I explain why they
are important.

Topography. The region lies at an elevation of about 2,800 feet, east
of a place called Nandi Hills and some forty miles north of the city of
Bangalore in the Maidan or eastern portion of what once was the princely

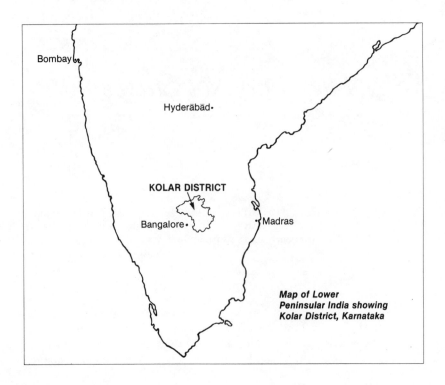

**Map of Lower
Peninsular India showing
Kolar District, Karnataka**

state of Mysore. To the west, massive granitic hills rise as much as twelve hundred feet above the undulating plain below, and in places rainfall flowing from these hills has created seasonal streams and narrow erosional flood plains; elsewhere erosion has left horseshoe valleys. Both of these features have been utilized as sites for the construction of the large number of irrigation tanks that now dot the countryside. Yaavahalli lies near one of these.

Rainfall. The annual rainfall is moderate, averaging about thirty inches, but rather variable. Roughly one year in seven a drought occurs in which eighteen inches of rain, or less, fall. Irrigation is essential if the population is to survive at its current densities.

Population density. According to the 1961 census, the rural population density of the *taluk* (or subdistrict) in which Yaavahalli is located was 307 persons per square mile. This figure is misleading, however, because the *taluk* contains large tracts of eroded, uninhabited, and uncultivated wasteland lying at higher elevations. Yaavahalli is one of nine villages surrounding an irrigation tank and the land it irrigates, and if one were to draw an ellipse around these villages and the lands their inhabitants routinely cultivate, the 1966 population density of the encompassed area would have been over 1,000 persons per square mile. Yaavahalli is a favored village in this respect: were one to add the area of the village site to the farmlands villagers own, and divide the sum, less than half a square mile, by the number of villagers, the resulting density in 1966 would have been about 800 persons per square mile. While such densities are high, there are higher densities elsewhere in rural Asia. However, a comparison between this region and others should include an assessment of soil quality.

Soil quality. Soils are relatively poor here. They are largely hard tropical laterite, through which nutrients and water pass all too freely. This soil does have a redeeming property, however: a well dug in it will usually hold a vertical face for many years, and the soil is so porous that a well, pumped dry, will refill quickly, often in a few hours. These wells are used to irrigate intensively cultivated gardens, and Yaavahalli is, once again, an especially favored village; garden holdings per capita are much higher than in most surrounding villages and are more than seven times as great as those of the rural population of the district as a whole. Garden cultivation seems to have expanded rapidly in this century along with the size of the population.

Population. Population growth from 1921 to 1961 was about 45 percent for rural areas of the *taluk*. There was some rural to urban migration during this period, and so the actual contribution of these areas to population growth in the state must have been somewhat higher. However, Yaavahalli's 1921 population and their descendants had doubled their numbers by 1961. There was, moreover, continued immigration to the village during this period, so that from the time of Indian independence in 1947 until the end of my stay in December 1966, the population rose by 90 percent to 360.

Kinds of villages. Yaavahalli is of about average size among villages of the area. Big villages—those with, say, 600 or more people—are also old ones with large Hindu temples and other datable architectural features attesting to their age. They contain the descendants of the former, mainly Brahmin, landlords of the area and people of many castes, a few of whom follow nonagricultural occupations. There are also tiny hamlets in which people of only one or two castes, usually low-ranking ones, live.

Yaavahalli is a particular kind of village of which I visited several; though I studied only this one, the others seemed similar in size, age, and caste composition. In addition to being middle-sized, Yaavahalli is also young, having been founded in the first third of the last century. About 70 percent of the population is of one caste or *jaati*, the Hosadevaru (also called Morasu) Vokkaligas. In my censuses of the nine villages mentioned earlier, I found that while Vokkaligas were the most populous caste of the area and were found in seven of the nine communities, they constituted only about 36 percent of the total population of 3,608.

Most of Yaavahalli's remaining population is divided between the two *jaatis* whose numbers rank second and third in the nine villages. They are the Naayks (hunters by traditional occupation, farmers now), who make up 13 percent of Yaavahalli's people and 15 percent of the people in the nine villages, and the Holeyas (Harijan field hands), who make up 11 percent of the population in both Yaavahalli and the nine villages.

The little corporate state. Thus, Vokkaligas, who are the dominant peasant caste of the region, are especially dominant in Yaavahalli, where they own most of what is worth owning and dominate village politics as well. More precisely, one lineage of Vokkaligas that accounts for about a third of the *jaati*'s population controls village politics, and this lineage is led by one household, that of the village headman. Metcalfe's famous characterization of Indian villages as little republics is inappropriate here: Yaavahalli is more like a little corporate state. In fact, it was the only village I ever visited that had a party line. On a number of occasions I heard visitors told, "We do not have factions here," and, "We have many progressive farmers here."

But Yaavahalli is also a village where the majority of people are middle peasants by local standards, where to own ten acres, three of which are garden land, may make one a substantial farmer, and where there is only one landless household. Though the headman's household is much wealthier than any other save that of his classificatory father's younger brother, this is chiefly a community of freeholding farm households that are relatively independent units of production. The corporate character of the village derives not from a simple concentration of wealth, but from a hierarchically integrated social network in which wealth and influence with notables beyond the village boundaries are elements of power. Every Vokkaliga in Yaavahalli is, at least by some sort of marital connection, related to every other. Indeed, with only two exceptions among the thirty-nine Vokkaliga households, every household contains at least one person, and usually more, who is somehow consanguineally related to at least one person in every other Vokkaliga household. This occurred because in the formation of the village, women from the headman's lineage were married to men of several immigrant lineages, which in turn gave brides to new immigrants from several other lineages. These marital ties were later reinforced by a number of subsequent marriages.

All the Holeyas and most Naayk families depend on employment from Vokkaliga households to supplement income from the cultivation of their own lands. There is also one prosperous farm family of the Goldsmith caste closely allied to the village headman's household. This leaves the village Brahmin's household, which relies on the largesse of leading families who support the temple and on the income the husband receives working as a tenant of the headman's classificatory father's younger brother.

As you can see, there seem to be few loose threads in the village's social fabric. But this does not mean that there is no dissent in Yaavahalli. A mordant class consciousness, critical of the *sovkaars*, the big peasants or kulaks of the region, and of the government officials who serve *sovkaar* interests, prevails among the *madya jena* and the *badavaaru*, the middle (class) people and the poor. This criticism, however, is kept private for the most part and in any case is not something people in Yaavahalli or other villages can really act on except at election time. Even then, the headman of Yaavahalli can be fairly certain of solid support from his fellow villagers.

So far as the government is concerned, Yaavahalli is but one of ten villages governed by a group *panchayat* or council elected by villagers. There is no longer a headman for Yaavahalli officially recognized by the government. But the headman of Yaavahalli can be sure of his seat on the *panchayat* because he is the *patel*, the village headman of custom, an office he inherited in an unbroken line of eldest sons from the founder of the village.

The party line is right: Yaavahalli does not have factions; it is one. If you look at groups called factions in other Indian villages you will find that, typically, a powerful individual organizes a following of his clients, his relatives, and their clients in order to engage in some sort of political contest with someone else who has done the same thing. This is exactly what Yaavahalli's headman has done. The only difference is that he has used the office of *patel* to organize an entire village as a constituency in a new political community, the group *panchayat*. Often *sovkaars* of the area represent groups with special interests, but none of them represent a place to the extent that Yaavahalli's headman does.

Factionalism within villages often leads to political stagnation as each faction undermines the other's proposals. Yaavahalli speaks with a single voice, and that voice gets the desired results. The village contains primary and middle schools attended by children from larger villages nearby. It also had a veterinary clinic for a few months, until someone in Bangalore discovered that the money spent for this program had not been earmarked for Kolar District, and so the veterinarian was transferred elsewhere. The village-level worker assigned to assist in community development programs in the area also lived in Yaavahalli for a time before I came. But he was a member of a merchant *jaati* who dressed and talked like a townsman and made a practice of delivering lectures on agriculture to Vokkaligas who regard themselves as predestined to be farmers. The villagers had him sent away.

It would be easy to attribute all of this to the genius of a single individual. But the headman was a product of his family, his lineage, his caste, and his community. His parents were uneducated people who sent two sons to college. During periods of price controls prior to Indian independence, a number of his lineage mates formed what was alleged to have been the most accomplished agricultural black-marketeering ring in the *taluk*. His *jaati* was in the vanguard of a class struggle of cultivators against the local landlords, the *joodidars,* a conflict that ended in a legislative land reform.

More to the point at hand, the headman could achieve what he did only because he could rely on the material backing as well as the political support of the village as a whole. The state government paid for the materials to build the veterinary clinic, but the villagers themselves built it in a matter of weeks. The same was true of the schools and the village-level worker's house. Thus, government officials liked to spend money in Yaavahalli because they knew that when they did, the job would get done. No factional dispute would stop construction; no bricks would disappear into a wall of someone's house.

Yet mobilization of public support for these ventures was not always without rancor. Judging from the reports of villagers, a certain amount of browbeating and threatening accompanied the cajoling and persuading used to organize such projects. I had this in mind when I likened Yaavahalli to a little corporate state: according to the leadership, the community is everybody's business whether everybody likes it or not. Moreover, everybody is the community's business too. The village has the practical equivalent of a secret police in the informal group of senior Vokkaliga women who keep a weather eye on everyone's morals. On occasion people not only engaged in but got away with acts of which these women disapproved. But when they said, for instance, that consumption of beef and alcohol was bad, they meant bad for everybody, including the Holeyas, for whom these items are ordinarily permissible.

So if projects were completed on time it was, in part, because threats of public criticism or economic duress were used to keep them on time. Still, the fact remains that Yaavahalli exhibited a notable capacity for collective community effort that distinguished it from other villages. It was, for instance, the only village I knew of that, during 1966 at least, managed to turn out a labor force for *varada kelsa,* "weekly work." This did not in fact occur with anything like weekly regularity; it occurred prior to visits by government officials. Each household would contribute one young man to spruce up the village, a task that mainly involved cleaning its gutters and sweeping its streets.

I do not mean to suggest that Yaavahalli is unique, but merely that it is unusual. As I noted earlier, I visited several other villages in the *taluk* that were demographically similar to it, and they too appeared to have developed some of the economic boosterism I found in Yaavahalli. But it is unusual to find a village where the Harijans are supposed to abide by the dietary rules of higher castes and where young caste Hindus are readily induced to act as village sweepers. It is unusual for a visiting dignitary, such as the deputy district commisioner who came to Yaava- halli in the fall of 1966, to arrive in a small village where his first sight is of a cleanly swept granite street lined with four public buildings of substantial masonry. Because there are over 2,700 villages in Kolar Dis- trict, it is uncommon for the busy deputy district commissioner to visit any one of them. He went to Yaavahalli, rather than to any of a number of other nearby villages, at the urging of subordinates who portrayed the community to him as a model village: there are many progressive farmers there; they have no factions. Such a reputation is a positional good: the value of being known as a model village diminishes as a point of honor with increases in the number of villages so portrayed. For the term "model village" to be taken seriously by a well-informed individual such as the deputy district commissioner, it must be shown that the commu- nity is in fact outstanding with respect to matters he takes seriously. In Yaavahalli he could be shown a relatively young village of modest size that had become a central place: in the local scheme of rural develop- ment, Yaavahalli was one of a group of villages known as Yaavahalli Circle. It was, as we have seen, a place of the new political and economic order in contrast to an old order represented by the older, larger, land- lord villages nearby. He could also be shown scores of well-tended gar- dens in which the latest products of plant breeding were growing: a new variety of maize developed for the region, a hybrid millet that was being urged on farmers at the time, and the new superintensively cultivated fodder crop, a hybrid Napier grass.

He could have been shown these crops elsewhere, but rarely in so great a concentration as in Yaavahalli, and perhaps in no other village nearby could the deputy district commissioner dine with so articulate a proponent of the new order as Yaavahalli's headman. If, moreover, he had been taken elsewhere, he would have seen too much of things his various hosts knew about but perhaps did not wish to show him.

The deputy district commissioner was accompanied on his tour by the block development officer, who was charged with the green revolu- tionary task of stimulating farm production in the area; the *taluk* engi- neer whose supervision of public works included irrigation, electrifica- tion, and other agriculturally relevant projects; and the local Congress Party secretary, the chief political cadre in what amounted to a one-party *taluk*. These men would readily admit that the economic conditions pre-vailing in the *taluk* at any time were not primarily the result of either their best efforts or their worst mistakes. But like civil servants and politicians elsewhere, these men would rather point with pride than view with dismay when guiding a superior around their area of jurisdiction, on the grounds that they might be held responsible, in some measure, for the conditions he saw. As it happened, in 1966 the area was recovering from a very bad agricultural year. In many villages one could see the evidence of this in haggard people and gaunt livestock. One did not see much of that sort of thing in Yaavahalli, and so by concluding the deputy district commissioner's tour of the *taluk* there, his guides managed to emphasize the recovery, which was almost complete in Yaavahalli, rather than the bad year. Which brings me to my next point.

The drought. When I came to Yaavahalli, in the fall of 1965, the village was, like much of the rest of India, in the grip of a terrible drought. In Kolar District it was a drought of the century, the worst in living memory: in 1965 only twelve inches of rain were measured at the weather station nearest to Yaavahalli, only 40 percent of normal rainfall and the lowest rainfall to be recorded since 1876. Yet nobody in Yaava-halli died as a direct result of this drought.

There were only two deaths in the village during my stay of over a year, and neither individual was especially malnourished at the time of death. There were some famine-related deaths in other villages—how many I do not know—but I doubt that deaths greatly exceeded those to be expected in a year of normal rainfall. I believe this because my house-hold became, at the request of villagers and with the advice of physicians in the nearby town, a sort of first-aid clinic treating about twenty cases of minor ailments and injuries a day. Because people from a number of villages were coming to us with their health problems, we had an oppor-tunity to monitor, through them, health conditions prevailing in their communities. We encountered relatively few of the intestinal and respira-tory infections that so often are the proximate cause of famine deaths, and with one exception, patients recovered from those we did encounter. Moreover, I regularly visited and did census work in a number of sur-rounding communities, and few deaths were reported as having occurred in the previous months.

I do not mean to suggest that the situation was not dire. Even in Yaavahalli, which was an unusually prosperous village, diets became perilously poor, for many people some of the time and for some people much of the time. Indeed, my fieldwork was conducted, to a large ex-tent, during a period described by the Western press as a famine, and I was living in a region that was supposed to be especially hard hit. But when I looked around, the people and their draft animals were not dying. In fact, people were busily, and for the most part cheerfully, engaged in agricultural work the whole time.

The great famine. If the fact that the people of the area managed to live and work through the drought of 1965 does not appear to be worth writing a book about, I would call attention to the *taluk*'s past experience with famine.

The failure of the monsoon in 1876 continued a drought that had begun in 1875. Similar conditions prevailed over most of South India, leading to the great famine of 1877–78 in which perhaps four million persons died (Loveday 1914). In 1871 the population of the *taluk* was reported as 59,273; by 1881 it had declined to 41,450. This decline was not due to migration, for neighboring areas also suffered large losses of population, and the only nearby city, Bangalore, grew by fewer than 2,000 people between the two censuses. Rather, it is likely that upwards of 18,000 people, one-third of the *taluk*'s population, died in the famine.

Now, I do not mean to suggest that the conditions I observed were comparable to those leading to the great famine of the 1870s. Then there were two successive years of drought, whereas the 1965 drought was followed by normal rainfall in 1966, though its impact was aggravated by poorer than average crops in 1964. In the nineteenth century the government's capacity to undertake famine relief was quite limited; by 1965 rural areas of the *taluk* were linked to Bangalore by railway, paved roads, and motor transport, and stores of imported food were available, as was the institutional ability to deliver them to rural people. Moreover, the population of 1965 had benefited from a sustained period of technological development and economic growth fostered both by private ventures and by the government's many rural development programs.

Public agencies acted to mitigate the impact of the 1965 drought, and doubtless these actions made a real difference in the well-being of many people. Noteworthy were the free mid-day meals distributed for some weeks in Yaavahalli to children, the elderly and disabled, pregnant women, and nursing mothers. These certainly reduced malnutrition and may well have saved lives among those groups in the population. But the largest number fed in one day was about four hundred, roughly a tenth of the total population of the villages the program served; the average number of persons fed per day was considerably less.

For all these reasons we would not expect the drought of 1965 to have led to thousands of deaths in the *taluk*. But another major factor was at work as well, one closely related to my reason for calling attention to the calamity of 1877–78. At the time of the great famine, villagers of the region were extensive grain farmers who supplemented the yields of their unirrigated land with the products of paddies irrigated from tanks. When a protracted drought occurred, not only did the unirrigated crops fail, but the shallow tanks, which depended upon rainfall and were subject to rapid evaporative loss of water, dried up. Thus deprived of an essential factor of farm production, water, villagers were faced with a period of enforced unemployment: once the drought was upon them, there was little or nothing villagers could do to help themselves. That is why thousands died and many more survived only because of external assistance.

By 1965 the descendants of those who survived had become labor intensive (and substantially commercial) gardeners who ordinarily grew staple crops on the unirrigated and tank-irrigated land they cultivated in addition to their gardens. Although Yaavahalli's tank dried up and the unirrigated crops failed in 1965, the wells irrigating gardens generally continued to fill with water, permitting cultivation—and thus income—to continue. When wells did dry up, their owners simply dug them deeper or hired someone to do the work for them. In 1966 over 21,000 hours of labor were devoted to the renovation of forty-four existing wells, and over 9,400 hours were spent digging a new well for the village headman. When I left the village, construction had begun on another large well. The labor intensity of garden cultivation when I came to the village exceeded an annual rate of 3,000 hours (roughly a man-year) per acre on many plots, an intensity sustained through my stay, and yields were fair to good in spite of the drought. When the monsoon rains commenced in the late spring of 1966, most villagers and their draft animals were in fairly good condition to return to a more normal agricultural cycle.

Thus, the fact that a Malthusian catastrophe did not occur in 1965 and 1966 is due in large measure to the comparatively drought-resistant agricultural adaptation villagers had achieved. Villagers did not starve or require government intervention to prevent widespread death because they had intensified their agriculture. Over the years they had dug more and more wells and had devised ways to employ more and more human energy in the implementation of an increasingly intricate agricultural technology. My task as an economic ethnographer, a political economist of everyday life, has been to figure out how they managed to do this, to determine why they did not starve. The argument that fills this book is a result of that effort.

A science of the mundane, the political economy of everyday life deals with commonplace ways in which people monitor material conditions impinging on their lives, manage responses to those conditions, and thus influence the physical events and circumstances they will subsequently face. These tasks involve symbolic interaction, mostly talk. The countless hours of human effort used in constructing the agricultural system I observed and the many thousands of hours employed in its operation and ongoing construction during my stay were organized with talk; people told themselves and one another what to do. My argument, which is divided into two main parts, is concerned with how and why villagers organized the flow of human energy as they did. The first portion is a synchronic account of the organization of labor in Yaavahalli during my stay. The second is a diachronic account of how the agricultural system I observed may have evolved, couched in a discussion of the general evolution of farming. In the rest of this chapter I will outline both halves of the argument, which will be developed in later chapters.

The point from which the synchronic portion of my argument departs is the observation that the basic units of farm production in Yaavahalli are also units of social reproduction; they are households. This has a number of consequences. For one thing, people who farm together also pursue reproductive interests together. When villagers speak of the uses of the fruits of farming, they often speak of the rearing, provisioning, and mating of children, portraying farming as a villager's way of creating more villagers. This also means that the effort and attention used in running a domestic establishment and that employed in agriculture are both drawn from the same stock of family labor, involving persons who differ in sex and age. That is why my argument deals with sex roles and the sexual division of labor. As I shall use the term, a sex role is a normative doctrine construed from what people say individuals ought to do according to their gender. The sexual division of labor is, by contrast, a statistical matter construed from observations of how women and men in fact allot their time to alternative tasks and described in terms of differences in the frequencies with which the two sexes do the things that get done.

As it happens, sex-role discourse is easy to elicit in Yaavahalli because villagers have a term, *dharma*, "duty" or "right action," that serves nicely as a gloss for our term "role." It is the *dharma* of women, say villagers, to "make families," to do *mane kelsa*, "housework," and much animal care. It is the *dharma* of men to do *kashta kelsa*, "difficult work" or heavy manual labor, and to "do farming," to manage agriculture. Villagers insist that these *dharmas* of women and of men, what we would call village sex roles, have a constitutional basis: the *dharma* of women stems from the fact that they bear children, while that of men, they say, derives from their greater physical strength.

I will argue that the division of labor stipulated by the *dharmas* of the sexes, which essentially describes the division of labor villagers implement, is highly proficient, provided the constitutional grounds on which villagers divide tasks between the sexes are empirically sound. Agricultural proficiency is here defined in terms of two variables: intensity, the amount of useful work people manage to do, and allocative efficiency, measured by the average return on a unit of effort at a given level of intensity. The proficiency of a division of labor, then, is measured by the amount of food and fiber it obtains from a stock of time and energy.

Of the two sex roles, the *dharma* of men is clearly the more problematic. Villagers assign to women those tasks that are most compatible with or closely related to motherhood, which is in turn a cultivation of the biological circumstance created by maternity and the nursing bond. Women's roles in most societies have been built around motherhood in one fashion or another, and it scarcely seems controversial to suggest that, given their maternal role, village women's time is most proficiently used when they undertake tasks conducted in or near the home. For men, on the other hand, the question is more complex. Though village women do a great deal of farm work, certain tasks are always or almost always performed by men, and it is the men who are the managers of agriculture. I shall argue that the proficiency of these task assignments turns on three questions. Are village men systematically stronger than the women with whom they live? Is men's work labor in which greater physical strength provides a genuine advantage? Does performance of men's work convey to men an advantage in managing agriculture?

The *dharmas* of the sexes may be viewed as a model *for* (to borrow a term from Clifford Geertz [1966]) the division of labor, since they constitute instructions concerning what people are supposed to do according to their gender. In proposing that the people of Yaavahalli enhance their agricultural productivity by following these instructions, we transform the *dharmas* of the sexes into a model *of* the division of labor, which may be subjected to empirical investigation.

The *dharmas* of the sexes are, however, but part of a larger body of doctrine that villagers call the "teachings of the elders." These are composed of policies endorsing hypergamous and consanguineous marriages, a later age at marriage for boys than for girls, patrilocal residence, equipartible patrilineal inheritance of agricultural resources, and a gerontocratic division of authority. All these policies, I will argue, have one general goal: to enhance the harmony and stability of the joint family household—the desired household type in Yaavahalli. The villagers say that the joint household, apart from being a good in itself, is simply more productive than the nuclear family households into which it is prone to divide. We can readily test the validity of this belief, and we shall find that, indeed, joint households outproduce nuclear family units by a wide margin.

The question then arises as to whether adherence to the teachings of the elders does in fact help joint household members "work together in

unity" as villagers claim. To continue with the distinction I have borrowed from Geertz, once more the task is to construct a model of
villagers' models for behavior, a rudimentary theory that postulates conditions under which the teachings of the elders might yield the benefits
claimed for them. This aspect of my argument has many deficiencies,
most notably my inability to subject a number of its hypotheses to rigorous empirical tests; the reasons for this inability will become evident as
we progress. But the theory has some merits as well, and one of them is
parsimony. It is mainly premised on three conditions: the *dharmas* of
women and of men and the later social maturation of males, another
phenomenon based in biological circumstance.

The *dharmas* of the sexes are a model for the organization of labor in
the short term; they divide labor among the people a household happens
to have. The teachings of the elders are models for the organization of
labor in the long term. As household composition changes over time, the
changes may be managed to some extent through decisions concerning
marriage and related matters. The teachings of the elders are policies for
making these decisions, and because they are decisions about mating, the
differing circumstances of the sexes influence the way they are made.

As we will see, girls begin to participate in the work of women at an
early age and are often able to do much that women do before the final
growth spurt to puberty. By age fifteen or so, when they marry, they are
fundamentally competent in the *dharma* of women. On the other hand,
boys of this age are just beginning to participate in the work of men.
Until then, they do not have the physical strength that allows them to
become proficient at men's work. Hence the later marriage age of males:
they are not regarded as fit husbands until they have undergone a period
of training in which they prove themselves as workers.

The problem of converting boys into responsible men is all the more
urgent because the strength of young men, guided by the expertise of an
experienced farm manager, is an extremely valuable resource. Moreover,
villagers tend to find that young males are rather unstable persons: they
are less likely to behave as their elders would like them to behave than
their sisters are. Hence the policy of patrilocal residence: villagers would
ordinarily rather keep their sons and build the male-managed family
farm on the bonds of trust and authority established between father and
son and among brothers than take a chance on someone else's son. Once
this basis for patrilocality is established, the remaining teachings of the
elders seem to fall plausibly into line, as we shall see.

With this background, let me more rigorously restate the thrust of
this segment of my argument. The *dharmas* of the sexes and the teachings of the elders constitute a biocultural system in the sense that biological sex differences are culturally amplified in patterns of symbolically

monitored and managed behavior specifically adapted to conditions of labor intensive cultivation. The things people tell themselves and one another to do make biological, political, and economic sense. At least they do from a particular point of view to be discussed shortly.

First, however, let us note that the cultural amplification of biological sex differences should in no way be confused with the biological determination of behavior. In this instance, anatomy is not destiny: it is circumstance. Since we are dealing with cultural behavior, another way of putting the matter is to say that the *meaning* of a sex difference is not necessarily immanent, although it is conceivable that it might be. There is, for example, accumulating evidence indicating that the meanings attributed to certain facial expressions are virtually pan-human, that our proclivity to these expressions and our responses to them have a phylogenetic basis. The meaning of a smile is, to some degree, immanent; it is in the smile.

But this is patently not the case, for instance, with respect to sex differences in physical strength. In some communities the male strength advantage is used in warfare or for bullying women, perhaps to avoid arduous work; in others, the community of scholars for one, it is scarcely used at all. In Yaavahalli it is used for heavy labor, *kashta kelsa*.

Nothing I will say should imply that men do heavy work everywhere it is done. While cross-cultural data indicate, in my view, that sexual dimorphism is a major factor in divisions of labor around the world, the issue is not whether women do or do not, or can or cannot, do heavy manual labor in this society or that one. What is at issue are the circumstances under which men are induced to devote themselves to heavy manual labor. Doing heavy manual labor is not doing what comes naturally for anyone; it is doing what comes hard. I will suggest that the evolution of human food production is, in part, the history of getting men to work.

At any event, in speaking of cultural amplification of constitutional sex differences I am simply noting that physical differences between the sexes may become elements in symbolic interaction in a great many ways; they are subject to amplification in everything from dress to vocal music. Here they are amplified in the organization of work, and in this context they become material conditions of the political economy of everyday life, influencing who is going to do what, and how, where, and when they will do it.

Cultural amplifications of sex differences in the sexual division of labor may enhance proficiency in at least two ways. Direct amplifications occur when members of one sex possess some physical trait that conveys to them an advantage over the opposite sex in the learning or performance of some task, and members of the favored sex are assigned the task. Indirect amplifications occur when a direct amplification places members of one sex in a better position than members of the opposite sex to engage in or to manage some activity, and the favored sex does engage in or manage that activity. This is the basis of my argument that:

1. The *dharma* of women is an indirect amplification of maternity and the nursing bond. The work women do is premised on motherhood, which is a direct amplification of the female reproductive function.

2. The *dharma* of men is a cultural amplification of sexual dimorphism in matters related to physical strength. The assignment of *kashta kelsa* is a direct amplification of this trait, while men's management of agriculture is an indirect amplification of it for reasons that will become evident later on.

3. The remaining teachings of the elders may be viewed as amplifications, in several ways, of the difference in maturation between the sexes. By handling young men and women as they do, the elders who arrange marriages, and thereby regulate household composition, create social situations within households that are more stable and manageable than might otherwise be the case.

Eventually these three rather general propositions will be replaced by six more precise ones. But the bearing of this study on the first of the three issues I mentioned at the outset should be clear enough: biological sex differences may influence the sexual division of labor because such differences are not simply phenotypic traits; rather, they can become material conditions of life to which people respond culturally in attempts to solve practical problems.

To speak of solutions to practical problems implies that recurrent situations are regarded as problematic by *someone*, which leads me to the particular point of view from which the teachings of the elders make sense.

You may have been wondering who the "elders" are; they are parents. The teachings of the elders make sense from the point of view of a married couple who are farming with limited resources in order to rear a family to be farmers who will rear families. If people follow the teachings of the elders (and they do not always do so), what they will accomplish is very simple: they will enhance the life chances of all of their children and grandchildren as peasant farmers who will be bearers of the culture their elders have transmitted to them. That, as villagers say, is their *dharma*: to farm well in order to rear families of farmers. In other words, their purpose in life is the perpetuation of their particular mode of farm production through its biocultural reproduction.

Villagers also say that it is because they have obeyed the teachings of the elders as well as they have—which as far as the elders are concerned is not well enough—that they have been able to prepare for and get through hard times. That is why they did not starve. I am inclined to agree with them, because I have discovered that in the course of following the teachings of the elders they have devised ways of using more and more human energy in the implementation of an increasingly intricate agricultural technology.

The diachronic part of my argument assumes that the state of affairs I observed evolved over time and amounts to an enquiry into how it may have evolved. The reconstruction of the demographic and agricultural history of the *taluk* and the village on which this enquiry will be based is, I am afraid, a good deal more speculative than the first part of the argument. Even so, it provides a theoretical context in which my ethnographic material becomes, for me at least, more fruitful and interesting, for in this second portion of the study we shall address the latter two of the three issues I posed at the outset: how does agricultural intensification come to be organized as a cultural response to increased population density, and why do the social arrangements of human communities sometimes seem to vary according to sociobiological principles?

Those who are familiar with the work of Ester Boserup will have surmised that the people of Yaavahalli provide another test case for her proposition that farm people respond to a furthur crowding of their landscape with labor intensification of their agriculture. While it is true, in general, that the behavior of the people of Yaavahalli has conformed to her predictions, my concern is not with whether farm people always behave as she suggests, but with how and why they may.

I will not argue that people respond to crowding with intensification because they must. There are, in fact, alternative responses. I will merely suggest that the behavior of those who do respond in this fashion will, in the course of time, become the standard of their region through cultural selection. The main issue at stake in cultural selection, as I shall use the term, is simply this: to what extent does a sequence of cultural behavior create conditions conducive to its own repetition?

One way of looking at the matter in this case is to argue that intensification is the reproductively successful response in biological terms: those who engage in it can support more people in greater security on a given amount of land than those who behave otherwise. In the long run it comes to a question of intensification or starvation. That has, indeed, been an issue before the people of the *taluk* in the past, for we know that many people died in the famine of 1877–78, and those were by no means the last famine deaths to occur.

The biological reproductive success of those who intensified their farming would insure a success in cultural selection as well, since the intensifiers' children would live to continue their parents' behavior. But this argument leaves us with a problem. The development of the intensive garden-centered cultivation I encountered in Yaavahalli does not seem to have really gotten under way until the 1920s, *after* the area's population reattained 1871 densities. Once it began, intensification occurred quite rapidly, along with a sustained period of population growth. This suggests that something more than avoidance of malnutrition is at work. In fact, a year or so after my return from Yaavahalli the village headman wrote to tell me, proudly, that once the irrigation wells currently under construction were completed, every household in the village would have at least one. If this was so, there would have been over sixty wells, a doubling in a generation. In a recent visit to the village Caryl Abrahams Maclachlan found that the population appeared to have nearly doubled since 1966 and that large areas of previously unirrigated land had been brought under intensive garden cultivation. Apparently, once begun, intensification stimulated further intensification; when some people tried hard, other people tried harder. It is this interactive phenomenon that I speak of when I ask how intensification comes to be organized as a cultural response to crowding.

What role do the teachings of the elders play in this evolutionary process? I would suggest that the behaviors the elders promote are both the products of and devices for cultural selection, and they persist because they enhance their bearers' capacity to respond to population growth with agricultural intensification.

The general outline of how this seems to have happened in Yaavahalli is simple. Farm households (and villages) exchange members, chiefly through marriage, and when they do so, deliberate choices are made among alternative individuals, families, and villages. For instance, parents will judge whether a certain young man from a particular family and village is a suitable mate for their daughter. The teachings of the elders establish a framework within which such decisions will be made, as well as a set of criteria for looking at other people (and oneself) as potential choices.

Villagers employ criteria of wealth and productivity in making these choices, which means that as population density increases, those who intensify their cultivation practices to prevent reductions in income have a relative advantage over those who do not in acquiring brides for their sons. Those families who can persuade prospective affines that their girls are diligent and cooperative are likewise advantaged. Households that fail to follow suit will pay a price in the marriage market. But most people do follow suit, which accounts for the rapid rate of agricultural growth I encountered. They follow suit because, while the manual labor of young people is essential to intensification, the process is managed by older people who also manage marital choice.

Thus, intensification does not occur just because people recognize that it is a good idea, but because it is enforced through the system of marital alliance. And so a direct connection is made between continued reproduction and the labor intensification of agriculture. That, I believe, is how intensification came to be organized as a process of cultural evolution in Yaavahalli.

Any policy or practice that, when implemented, stimulates a people's capacity to intensify their agriculture may be said to enhance their intensification fitness. This is what the teachings of the elders do when situated in the domestic life of a living village: they stimulate people to intensively cultivate their interest in intensive cultivation.

To some the term "intensification fitness" may seem an unnecessary biologism. My reasons for using it will become more apparent later, but I introduce it now to indicate the approach I will adopt toward the last of the three issues stated at the outset: why do human social arrangements sometimes seem to vary according to sociobiological principles?

My argument should not be viewed as settling the issues that have emerged in the debates between sociobiologists and other social scientists in recent years. It should be understood instead as an example of a biocultural position in anthropology with respect to some of these issues. In a biocultural approach, the culture-versus-biology opposition is rejected as specious: the question is not whether features of the human biogram influence patterns of learned behavior; rather, the central issues are the nature and scope of interactive relations between culture and the human biogram. In this view, the available evidence indicates that we are a biologically generalized species that has evolved the ability to modify its behavior symbolically. Our capability from the neck up is used in the management of our phenotypic traits from the neck down, including those that distinguish one sort of person from another by age and sex. Every society manages human sexuality—some would say hypersexuality—just as each manages the rearing of children from an extremely infantile state through a long period of maturation. Studies in kinship and marriage are, to a substantial extent, studies of alternative cultural amplifications of these traits.

Those who share this position are inclined to greet with some skepticism the "genes-for-this, genes-for-that" variety of sociobiology, which attributes rather specific (though usually unspecified) genetic bases to widespread forms of human behavior. I am quite willing to acknowledge, though, that some of our responses—those to smiles and frowns, for instance—have as direct a phylogenetic basis as our response to a kick in the shins. Indeed, I am persuaded that our sociability, as a general phenomenon, has a phylogenetic basis. There may be a great deal more direct genetic influence on human behavior than we now recognize, but this remains to be seen.

In the meantime, it is well to avoid confusion by pointing out that the issues pursued here are quite different from what I take to be the basic sociobiological question with respect to human behavior, that of whether the human biogram evolved according to the sociobiological principles that have been developed through the study of other species. Rightly or wrongly, sociobiologists look for uniformities in human behavior and postulate phylogenetic bases for them.

The question posed here is premised on the opposite notion: that human arrangements are not uniform and that the variations we observe in them sometimes resemble those we observe in social behavior across other species or, indeed, within the same species in alternative environmental settings. For example, later on we shall find that the male role in farm production varies across societies in exactly the fashion sociobiological theory would anticipate.

I will suggest that the social arrangements of human communities sometimes seem to vary according to sociobiological principles because cultural selection often mimics natural selection. This is especially likely to be the case where one is dealing with variations in subsistence activities, domestic organization, and the sexual division of labor, because in these instances the criterion of cultural selection most closely approximates that of natural selection: reproductive success. In the course of choosing mates for their children, choosing members for households, and allocating work and income among them, and in choosing migrants in the formation of Yaavahalli as a community, villagers created cultural analogues of principles of selection that are central to sociobiological theory.

In short, the people of Yaavahalli short-circuit, through cultural selection, the more ruthless forces of natural selection because village culture is responsive to criteria of reproductive success. As one village mother put it, "How shall we feed all of these children in a time such as this one?" Her children's nutrition was a physical problem she and her husband created for themselves biologically. Let us now proceed to their cultural solutions to it, and discover why the teachings of the elders are regarded as the good argument that ought by now to have driven poorer ones from the field of discourse.

chapter 2

The United Temple

In the next two chapters I want to introduce the people of Yaavahalli and develop further my argument concerning the *dharmas* of the sexes and the teachings of the elders through a discussion of several matters bearing on it.

Ethnographic data are knowledge of a highly personal sort, and one of my aims in presenting the people of Yaavahalli is to describe a situation that affected me deeply. In the last chapter I presented a bare outline of my argument, which, by itself, might be taken for a best-of-all-possible-worlds functionalism in which the institutions of village life fall neatly into place, creating highly proficient agricultural behavior. In fact, I do not mean to suggest that villagers are optimally efficient or rational or anything of the sort. They are ordinary human beings, like the rest of us, who frequently find the conditions they face unpredictable and perplexing and who are often disappointed by the outcomes of their actions. What I do mean to suggest is that villagers struggle for mastery over the very conditions that perplex and disappoint them and that in the course of this struggle they have reached conclusions, many of them the received wisdom of their ancestors reconfirmed in the experience of each generation. Our task is to attempt to discern whether an empirical basis may be found for their conclusions. As we proceed, I think it worthwhile to convey something of the character of their struggle through the translation of villagers' own words, an effort that will commence in the following pages.

A second matter has to do with the way in which I gathered the information used in my account. I have attempted to construct a deductive argument out of these materials, though clearly there are gaps in the data. But however well or badly I have constructed this theory of my field notes, I did not go to Yaavahalli with the argument in mind and then set out to test various propositions there by collecting the relevant data; had I done so, the deficiencies in the data would not be so great. I did go to Yaavahalli to carry out a research proposal that I shall describe presently, but thereafter I pursued a line of heuristic inquiry, attempting to gather data to answer questions as they emerged in the course of my work. This involved a good deal of inductive inference and a great deal of luck. In the years following my return to the United States, I continued to work on the material I had gathered in an effort to arrive at the most observationally adequate and fruitful account of my ethnographic record that I could manage.

The most propitious event to occur while I was in Yaavahalli was the decision by a village elder that my inquiry into their affairs was so misguided that it fell to him to set me on a proper course. That is how I discovered the teachings of the elders. It is important to describe this event and the circumstances surrounding it because it bears on an important methodological question: did I discover the *dharmas* of the sexes and the teachings of the elders, or did I create them? Did I pose novel questions to villagers that prompted them to a rationalization of their affairs in which they would not otherwise have engaged, or was I made privy to aspects of the intellectual life of the community that had gone on before I came and continued after I left? I believe I discovered models for behavior that villagers did employ in their dealings with one another, but I must demonstrate why I believe this is so.

Finally, it must be acknowledged that any ethnographic account is but one interpretation of the materials on which it is based. Critics of an account are bound to offer alternatives, so that it is well to consider alternatives in advance of criticism. In the next chapter I shall take up what appears to me to be the most obvious alternative to the interpretation I shall offer. The alternative is that the teachings of the elders exist to serve male interests.

All these matters bear on the subject of this chapter, the village household. In it I hope to show that villagers regard the formation and maintenance of joint family households as a struggle, a struggle all the more important because it often fails. In retrospect I believe this to be the first matter of real importance I discovered about Yaavahalli, for it is linked to the second matter I mentioned: it leads us to see that the economic superiority attributed to joint households was not a novel rationalization prompted by questions I asked, but the ground on which villagers had conducted their struggle for household solidarity all along. In describing the way villagers talk about joint households, I will also prefigure Chapter 3's discussion of the "male privilege" alternative. Villagers portray the joint household as a collective providing benefits for *all* of its members that none can obtain acting alone or in nuclear families. Thus, it is appropriate to ask each person to contribute to the welfare and solidarity of the group according to his or her age and sex. The teachings of the elders demand individual sacrifices for the common good; they constitute a folk logic of collective rationality. If conditions can be postulated under which this doctrine might yield the benefits claimed for it, and to the extent that these conditions may be shown to occur, then it may be argued that the doctrine not only provides, but is intended to provide, benefits to both sexes. In that event the "male privilege" alternative becomes suspect as an ethnocentric interpretation.

With these matters in mind, let us turn to the subject at hand, the "united temple," the joint household. First I shall describe how I encountered the notion of joint household superiority.

Gangappa's Lecture

I began to study the teachings of the elders because an elder of Yaavahalli told me to do so. This is how it happened.

I went to India to investigate a simple idea I had begun to develop seriously as a student of the industrial sociologist Stanley Udy. In its general form, the idea is that the organization of social relations in groups that perform work and the organization of the work such groups perform are interactively responsive to one another. This was hardly an original idea; Udy had it too, and it was also to be found in the work of a number of other authors in a spectrum from Marx to Homans and in a variety of empirical interpretations.

My variant of this simple idea derived from the notion that the structure of domestic groups and the character and organization of subsistence activities in nonindustrial societies are related to one another. There were cross-cultural studies suggesting this, but these were crude affairs that told us, for example, that matrilocal societies also tended to be horticultural ones. The crudity of these studies lay in more than the fact that they employed gross categories aggregating phenomena across societies that were by no means the same (the term "horticulture," for example, encompasses a variety of practices found on varying landscapes); these categories were also crude when employed to describe single societies.

Detailed ethnographic studies of domestic organization showed that wide variations in household composition often occurred in the same community. Indeed, putative norms, such as a preference for one form of postmarital residence, might be followed by only a minority of a population. Studies of developmental cycles in domestic groups describing longitudinal changes in household composition were also current at the time, and some authors spent a good deal of effort debating whether a society could better be described as having one developmental cycle or many.

It seemed to me, therefore, that a description of a domestic system, if there was such a thing, should require two steps: first one would determine a set of relevant variables, and then one would describe the ways in which these varied and covaried. Leaving aside the question of what these variables might be, the finished description would not depict the domestic organization of a population in terms of a typical household type or a series of types, or even a domestic cycle. Rather, it would consist of a series of characteristic variations or oscillations in these variables, which, as a covarying set, constitute the system. One might then ask what accounts for the characteristic shape of the system apart from the variables' influences on one another.

To return to the other side of my simple idea, it also seemed to me that describing populations in terms of predominant subsistence patterns provides inadequate information about them. In particular, the fact that a group of people are farmers does not mean that they all farm in the same way. On the contrary, an adequate description of farming practices would also require the identification of a series of variables and the determination of their characteristic variations and covariations. Again one could ask what gives this system its peculiar shape. The formulation of the idea would be completed by suggesting that the two systems were in fact one, that variables describing the household organization of a community and those describing the ways in which various groups implemented the available technology would be responsive to one another.

Here is a concrete example of this abstract notion. A couple with several daughters but no sons hasten to find an able son-in-law willing to live with them as soon as their first daughter is marriageable because they believe they will need a young man in the future if they are to fully exploit their farm resources. The decision to conclude a matrilocal marriage, which alters household composition, occurs in response to an agricultural problem, and once concluded, the marriage may alter the household's cultivation practices. Thus, the distinction between the domestic system and the agricultural system is purely arbitrary, the one having to do with living arrangements, the other with the exploitation of the landscape. But when the family farm is viewed as a dynamic ecosystem, this distinction disappears except as a convenient way of grouping variables that are substantively similar.

I have presented this telegraphic account of the idea I took to India to explain why I proceeded with my work as I did. First, my thinking had at the time been cast largely in statistical terms. I set out to describe the domestic organization and the farming practices of a single village with quantifiable variables. Second, I felt that of the two tasks, the description of the organization of farming and farm work would be by far the more difficult. Household composition changes rather slowly, and people could, I believed, be relied upon to report who lived in their household last year or even many years previously. Perhaps I was wrong in that belief, but the point is that I also reckoned, quite rightly I think, that the same people could not be relied upon to report, for instance, how long they spent plowing last week. Data of that sort were best obtained through direct observation.

Thus, when I began work in Yaavahalli, my first priority was to establish a reliable system for observing and recording data on agricultural work and farm production. This entailed mapping the village fields, an ethnosemantic analysis of the nomenclature for crops, tasks, tools, and other matters, and a census of the village so that the ownership of fields and the identity of workers could be recorded. I also had to hire and train high school graduates from nearby villages to patrol the fields and record both who was doing what and the location and duration of work each time they saw work in progress on a plot of land. This procedure not only provided detailed data on the organization of farm labor, but also kept us posted on the state of cultivation of each plot, so that yields (in terms of quantities of food or fiber) could be recorded at the time of harvest. At that time we also asked the owner of each harvested plot to tell us about things that were hard to observe, such as the amounts of various inputs consumed in cultivation of the crop. When cash was spent on these, we recorded the amount spent along with cash expenditures for labor, and if the crop was subsequently sold, we tried to find out how much it fetched.

It took two months to get this system working smoothly because it took that long for me to know what I was doing and for my first group of assistants to learn their jobs (I began with three and eventually employed seven). At that point I began the domestic organizational side of my project in earnest, starting by eliciting the nomenclature used to talk about kinship and marriage and then turning to the collection of genealogies.

I tried to explain my work to villagers in order to obtain the best possible approximation of informed consent. I wanted, I told them, to study the way they farmed and the way they reared their children and conducted their family life so as to write a book that would give people elsewhere a better understanding of Indian people. That explanation was and is an honest one, but it did not serve very well to explain my actions to them. At first they seemed to conclude that I was some sort of agricultural expert, which indeed I was trying to become, and that my formal elicitation sessions were language lessons, which they were after a fashion. I should add that villagers received my wife and me as honored guests and almost invariably displayed the courtly courtesy typical of South Indians, treatment they regarded as a point of village honor. As my work progressed, however, some began to experience misgivings about it. Of particular concern was the collection of genealogies, which followed the census and the land survey, a sequence of events that gave rise to the suspicion that I might be establishing grounds for some sort of land reform.

It took me a while to allay these fears, which in the meantime may have prompted some village elders to take me more seriously in an attempt to determine what my real intentions were. At any event, this problem seemed to compound another that I posed for villagers. Not only was I prying into their affairs, but in the course of doing so I often tried their ample patience with many questions they found vexingly naive. What is more, they were preplexed at my practice of asking the same naive questions of different people. Let me give two examples of reactions provoked by my early interviews.

While eliciting crop categories one day, I asked a man to tell me how many kinds of rice there were, to which he responded by producing a taxonomy containing sixty specific varieties. At the conclusion of this, I asked about varieties of *joLLa,* "sorghum," at which point he turned to my assistant Shama Rao and said, "Why don't *you* tell him these things?" Apparently he found it tedious to sit and produce long lists of items that were, as far as he was concerned, common knowledge (though actually they were not: Shama Rao, a young Brahmin from a village several miles away, did not recognize the names of most of the rice categories this man produced).

I provoked bemused rather than irritated responses in my initial encounter with the *dharmas* of the sexes. After eliciting categories of farm work, which I needed to implement my scheme for reporting work done in the fields, I continued to explore the term *kelsa,* "work," as a semantic domain. How, for example, did *kelsa* differ from activities that were not work? I found that virtually any activity could be regarded as work if it was undertaken with the intent of producing material benefits through nonsupernatural means. Thus, "praying," *puje maaDu,* is not work for ordinary people even if they pray for good crops, but it is for the *pujaari,* the Brahmin priest of the village, because he is paid to do it.

From this point I ventured into the division and specialization of labor, employing such frame questions as "What is the work of——?" and filling in the blank with various social categories, including women and men. Most informants asked which women and men I was speaking of, for their answers depended in some measure, they said, on an individual's caste and occupation. It was when I replied that I wished to know about the work of farming people like themselves that I elicited the explicit models for behavior noted earlier. Women were to "make" or "construct" families and do housework; they were also to do farm work and care for animals, activities informants described in varying degrees of detail. Village men were to do *kashta kelsa*, "hard work," and to "do agriculture," which informants described as selecting which crops to plant, dividing land into plots, deciding when to plant, and other activities that may be summed up as managing farming.

Why were women and men to do these things, I asked. Because it is their *dharma*, their duty. Why is it the duty of women to make families? Because they are the mothers. Likewise, it is the duty of men to do hard work because they are the stronger sex, a point one man illustrated by flexing his muscles in a weight-lifter pose reminiscent of the man shown in an advertisement, commonly seen in the area, for a brand of men's undershirts called Power Banyans. Eventually I asked these questions of several adults of each sex, receiving a number of variants on the replies I have just described. And in most cases when I asked why men and women were supposed to do the things they were supposed to do, I was greeted with laughter or puzzled looks that suggested that my informants found this question astonishingly childish. Finally one man said, "Look, do not the men do the plowing in your country?"

I have included this account of the way I conducted my work in its early stages to illustrate two points. First, by and large I was not asking villagers to justify their institutions. There were some exceptions, notably my request for an explanation of the *dharmas* of the sexes (a matter to which we shall return), but I had spent most of my time counting people, things, and events and finding out how one talked about them. Second, there was evidence that my conduct was provoking some frustration among the people who were giving me their time. Both these factors may have influenced the event that introduced me to the teachings of the elders.

My introduction to them occurred, I suspect, because social relations in Yaavahalli are conducted on the presumption that older people have a warrant to give younger people advice. Thus, one dusty spring afternoon, Gangappa, a man in his fifties, undertook to set me straight about what I should attend to in my research. This is part of what he said:

> Look, you have come to this poor village from your big country asking about so many matters concerning our families. If you want to know why we have all of these troubles, it is because in these days no one knows how to behave. All of these families would be so much better off if they stayed together in one house, but the people quarrel and divide into many different houses. I don't know why they quarrel [in response to my question]. It is certain that a united house is better; these small houses are not good. Many years ago I quarreled with my father and moved to this place. All of my difficulties started from that time.

A *yajaman* of a joint family adopts the dour demeanor of the village elder to pose for the camera during a conversation with his peers. The chief matter on which this particular elder chose to advise me was the poor quality of my spoken Kannada.

Before going further, a Kannada term glossed in this text should be explained. Villagers reckon the population of a village not by the number of persons but by the number of houses, or households, it contains; the word for house is *mane*, the plural being *manegaLu*. The form *vandu* is homonymous in Yaavahalli Kannada. It is the number one, so that *vandu mane* may mean "one house." But *vandu* may also be glossed as "unified," "combined," "at one," or "united." Thus, the term *vandu manegaLu* is grammatical; it means "united houses," in contrast to nuclear family households, called "small houses" or *cikkamanegaLu*.

Now consider the purport of Gangappa's remarks. Earlier one of my assistants had tactfully told me that *bana jena*, "colored people" (that is, people of European descent who call themselves white), were widely reputed to be arrogant and overbearing. He hastened to add that of course I was not like that, but I took this as a warning, for I had noted that villagers despise displays of arrogance, *jumba*, among themselves as well. A salient aspect of *jumba*, as the term is used by villagers, may be likened to an aspect of the Greek notion of *hubris*, the presumption that one is in control of a situation when one is not. When I heard a variant of the "this poor village . . . your big country" contrast used by Gangappa, I often regarded it as an oblique reference to the *jumba* of *bana jena* and as an admonition to examine my conduct. In this case the admonition was followed by the clause "asking about so many matters concerning our families," which I understood to be a description of the genealogies and other materials on kinship and marriage I had been collecting. The sentence that begins, "If you want to know . . . " seems to suggest that this amassing of detail on my part is wrong-headed. Not only was I imposing on my informants' time with lengthy discussions of trivia, but I was doing so to no apparent purpose. If I wanted to know why they had all these troubles, presumably something worth knowing, it was because no one knew how to behave. This explanation implies the existence of a body of knowledge for behaving. He then goes on to tell us about one element in this body of knowledge, namely the notion that people should live in united houses and not be permitted to divide into small houses because united houses are, in some unspecified way, the better kind. But people quarrel, and this leads to household partition; therefore quarreling, we might assume, is not knowledgeable behavior.

Here we see the first of several reasons for believing that I did not create the teachings of the elders. I had not been asking many normative questions, but Gangappa appeared to be saying that I should have been. For him it was the normative issues that mattered, for he initiated a discussion of standards of conduct in apparent frustration with my failure to initiate such a discussion myself, and implicitly offered to instruct me in them if I would listen.

Gangappa went on to describe the circumstances that led to his dispute with his father. It had occurred many years before, when he and his wife and two young children were living with his widowed father in a village a mile from Yaavahalli. As an only son he had anticipated inheriting his father's entire estate. Then one day his elder sister came to visit them in great distress. She and her husband, it seems, had fallen on hard times and faced destitution. Gangappa did not describe the reasons for this in detail, but somehow the sister's husband had lost his land. At any event, the father's solution to the problem was to divide his estate between Gangappa and his sister.

Enraged at the prospect of halving his inheritance, Gangappa refused to accede to his father's wishes. Subsequently the case was heard by the *panchayat* or village council. They told Gangappa that while he might have expected to inherit his father's estate under ordinary circumstances, clearly an exception had to be made in this case, for it was unconscionable that a daughter be left impoverished. His father had given him proper advice, and it was the duty of children to obey the teachings of their elders. Note the construction the *panchayat* appears to have placed on this matter. While they considered the substance of Gangappa's complaint, they treated their role as appellate. Had the father given proper advice? Having determined that he had, the council did not direct a division of property, but told Gangappa to obey the instructions of his elder. Later Gangappa took his case to civil court at the *taluk* headquarters. The court told him that he could claim no more than half of his father's property. By this time Gangappa and his wife had moved to Yaavahalli.

Gangappa concluded his lecture by pointing out that he and his wife had four daughters but no son. Moreover, his oldest daughter's husband had a serious illness that precluded strenuous manual labor. Hence, the daughter and her husband would move to Yaavahalli, where Gangappa would build them a small shop to run (something the village lacked). He saw a divine source for this turn of events; they were the karmic consequence of his actions as a young man, a way of teaching him the appropriateness of the position his father had taken years earlier. Father and son were by this time reconciled, and Gangappa's elderly father was a frequent visitor. Therefore, he said, if people wished to avoid quarrels and the division of united houses, they should obey the teachings of their elders as he had not done.

Verification of Gangappa's Views

Gangappa's lecture was neither the first nor the last time a village elder told me how I ought to behave as an ethnographer, but it was a watershed in my research, for he appeared to have beaten me to my simple idea. If he was correct, the partition of joint households, an alteration in household composition, had a direct impact on the material welfare of a household's members. The degree to which this was due to changes in the organization of farm work remained to be seen, but it seemed reasonable to suspect that the organization of work was implicated somehow. In any case, it also appeared that measures could be undertaken to prevent the division of joint households. To the extent that these measures were premised on the preservation of productive farming practices, it could be said that the organization of farming influenced the composition of domestic groups, just as alterations in the composition of those groups influenced the organization of farming.

Later, I set out to find if Gangappa's views on joint households would be confirmed by other villagers and asked two dozen of them, "Are there differences in wealth between united houses and small houses?" In examining the results of this investigation, we should keep in mind three questions. First, are Gangappa's views reliably confirmed, or are there a variety of responses, some saying there are no differences, or that small houses are better, or that it all depends on the households one is discussing? Second, if responses are in consensus with his views, how shall we judge the validity of this finding? Were informants making straightforward judgments of empirical fact in responding to this question, or were they saying something else—what they believed they were supposed to say, for example? Finally, assuming that other villagers agreed with Gangappa and that there is no reason not to take their agreement at face value, do the advantages enjoyed by joint households have anything to do with the organization of work?

These twenty-four informants were unanimous in their judgment that joint households were better off. This was a random sample of about 10 percent of the adult population, and given the fact that they were invariant in the general thrust of their responses, it seems unlikely that a larger sample would have uncovered many individuals who would disagree with their judgment. Indeed, I subsequently put the same question to a number of other people in the course of interviews on other matters, and never did I elicit a response that contradicted the prevailing view.

Thus, it would appear that these results are reliable, but are they valid? Studies of small nucleated communities may be susceptible to contagion effects: people may tell you what they have heard other people tell you or have heard that other people have told you. Likewise, people may say what they anticipate others, especially their leaders, would approve of their saying. So it could be that in appearing to state a matter of fact concerning households, villagers were really saying something else. Perhaps they were simply refraining from disagreement with Gangappa, a respected man, or perhaps they were saying what they believed other moral arbiters of the village, such as the *patel*'s wife, would want them to say.

I should point out, however, that villagers disagreed about many matters I discussed with them, which suggests that there was no strong general compulsion toward consensus for consensus' sake in responses to my questions. But there are stronger reasons for believing that Gangappa introduced me to conventional wisdom concerning the desirability of joint households.

While informants were unanimous on the main point, that joint households were the preferable sort, their answers were not stereotyped in other ways and often contained illustrations based on personal experience. Here are some examples:

> There is no doubt the united house is better; in these small houses no one works!

> In a united house we can save more money from our farming. If one woman is pregnant, the others do her work. In a single family, if either husband or wife falls ill, there is no one to help.

> In a united house, say one man is plowing, then the other will be free to sell the silk cocoons.

> You see, most of the experts on farming are *yajamans* [male heads] of united houses.

> In a united house you can always find work as a *kuli* [wage laborer] or as a tenant. I divided from my father and elder brother, and now no one wants to hire me.

> The small family has no value. If we live in a combined family, there are a lot of advantages for our livelihood. Now, my elder brother is a lot better off than me. He works hard and gets good crops, and he doesn't put *kulis* in the gardens—he does the work himself. If he has any problems other people help him out. Why? Because he works well and gets good crops and other people need cooperation too, and he gives good cooperation.

You will also note from these examples that informants regularly connected the greater prosperity of joint households with the organization of work, though they did so in varied ways. A young man whose land holdings are small tells us that since his parting with his brother and father, people do not want to hire him, the reason being that wealthier households prefer to employ as tenants families that can offer them a larger stock of labor. The woman who has had to cope with the problems caused by her pregnancy and her husband's illness notes these as exem-

plifying the general principle that people are better off in joint households. Thus, there is no apparent reason to believe that these responses
are anything more than reports based on personal experience and observations of the affairs of others in which it has been found that nuclear
family units of production cannot harness the energies of their members
as effectively as joint households can.

Life Histories

If this is the case, then one would also look for similar reports in other
commentaries on past experiences, and indeed one finds that the life
histories of villagers are full of references to joint households and partitions of joint households. Over sixty life histories were gathered in Yaavahalli. I hedge about the number because some informants were more
forthcoming than others: the longest of these texts exceeds twelve thousand words while the shortest consist of a few paragraphs, and I hesitate
to characterize these as life histories. The shortest ones were often ones I
collected myself.

Early on I found that in narrative interviews my inept Kannada
seemed to interfere with the train of my informants' remarks. Perhaps
they also presumed (correctly) that I might fail to understand them if
they spoke to me as they would to one another. In any case, they tended
to shorten and simplify comments addressed to me. Thus, I found that
such interviews were best left to a native speaker while I retired to listen.
I was fortunate to have among my assistants Gangadriah, a particularly
sensitive interviewer and gifted transcriber of running speech, and it was
he who collected over half of the life histories. Most of the remainder
were collected by Sivanna, a young man who, like Gangadriah, had
considerable experience working with other ethnographers, notably Alan
Beals. A few were collected by Shama Rao, who had worked only for me
but had almost nine months' experience when the life histories were
begun, and by Sidarajappa, who had only two months' experience.

The following procedures were employed. Assistants were in-
structed never to ask leading questions—indeed, to ask only for clarifica-
tions—and never to "correct" any language an informant might use. I
also tried to coach them in what are often called active listening techniques. This was, for the most part, unnecessary because analogous techniques, an orbital nod indicating understanding and assent and phatic
utterances similar to the English "uh huh," are part of the standard
conversational repertoire of South India. Having listened to the advice of
their own elders over many years, all these men were competent in this
South Indian variant of the listener's craft. As an informant spoke, the

assistant made notes from which he later wrote a Kannada text that he would afterwards read back to the informant for corrections. Subsequently the texts were translated, and I have used these translations as guides in examining the original Kannada.

On balance I believe this was as good a procedure as I could manage, but the great defect of these materials, the fact that interviews were not tape-recorded, compounds problems associated with the fact that I was obliged to analyze the results of someone else's ethnographic work. One of these problems is interviewer bias, inadvertent or otherwise. Shama Rao's interviews tended to be somewhat shorter than the others. Villagers may have been less forthcoming with him because he was a *shambog*, a village accountant, and the nephew of the *shambog* who served Yaavahalli. One may be less than candid in talking to the tax collector. But apart from this, I can find no systematic differences in the texts different interviewers produced. There is no recurrent term or turn of phrase that appears in the texts of only one interviewer; no category of event that figures in life histories collected by two interviewers is absent from those of the other two.

At any event, in view of my foreigner's ineptitude with the language and the fact that I was unable to recheck with informants at the time of the interviews many points that I later discovered in the texts, I have tried to exercise caution in interpreting them. Therefore, I shall confine my remarks to gross features of content and to rhetorical elements that occur repeatedly in the texts.

The first thing one notes in these life histories is that while informants were asked to tell their life stories, their responses could just as well be described as family histories. In fact, we also requested a number of family histories, generally one or two for each lineage, and these differed in general content from the life histories provided by the same informants only in their generational depth.

Since the people of Yaavahalli, by and large, do not go away to school or leave the village to take jobs elsewhere, but live and work in the village with their kin, it is hardly possible for one of them to tell the story of his life without saying something about the households of which he has been a member. But I suspect that the fact that villagers live as they do has an important implication for the way they construe themselves as persons. In contrast to the American cult of the unique individual who defies stereotypes, villagers define themselves in terms of conventional relationships to others and in the course of doing so are inclined to say more about other people than they say about themselves.

Thus, an informant typically begins his life history with an account of the origins of his ancestors and their genealogy up to the time of his birth. After recounting the story of his parents' marriage, and those of other couples in his natal household, he goes on to enumerate the children born to each union. Having done this, he may well continue the story of his life by saying something like, "Now here is the story of my eldest sister," in which he notes whom she married, where she married, and the children she had. This information may become pertinent later on when we find that the sister was widowed and has returned to her natal household to live, or that her daughter married the narrator's son. But often such reports on the lives of relatives are not essential to an understanding of later events in the speaker's life; apparently they are presented as being somehow relevant in themselves: to know me you must know my sister. And so by the time a life history narrator reaches the end of his story, he has usually produced a fairly detailed account of the development of the households in which he has lived and of the marital exchanges concluded with other households.

All but two of these narrators described themselves as having lived, at least at one time in their lives, in a joint household. These are, in the great majority of cases, described as particularly good times in which wells were dug, land was purchased, money was saved, and food was ample. Here is an example:

> After the death of my grandmother, my father became owner of the house. At that time my *cikkappa* [father's younger brother] was grazing the sheep and also looking after the farming with my father. While they were working in this fashion, they earned a great deal of money. So my father celebrated his younger brother's marriage to Sonamma, younger sister of H. Byrappa. Then for a few years they lived as a united temple, obeying each other and not abusing the unity among them. In matters of the house they were side by side [i.e., not at cross-purposes]. And my mother and my *cikkamma* [father's younger brother's wife] were unified and cooperating with each other. They maintained the family without misunderstandings. My father and mother were the *yajaman* and the mother of the house at that time.
>
> Before my birth my father and my *cikkappa* had saved and purchased as much land as my grandfather had purchased, four or five acres.

Texts such as these may be regarded as constructions of social reality, and several features of this brief excerpt are of interest, not only because they occur in other life histories, but because they occur in portrayals of the social order that villagers produce in other situations as well.

First, I call your attention to the period in the development of this household described in the passage I have cited. Two brothers have reached economic manhood and, working together, manage to save a great deal of money, suggesting that family income has substantially

Part of a joint family of twenty-six persons (the picture also includes the village priest, third from the right). The turbaned *yajaman* stands in the foreground. A man in his eighties at the time, he grew up in the years that followed the great famine of the 1870s and was the source of much oral history.

increased over the earlier period when the younger brother could not yet do a man's work. Such descriptions of periods of rapid economic growth following the maturation of sons occur repeatedly in life histories, as does the purpose for which a portion of their savings was spent, the marriage of a younger brother.

Following the younger brother's marriage, they lived for some years as a "united temple." The speaker does not use the phrase "united house," *vandu mane,* which we encountered earlier, or *vandu samsaara,* "united family," or the rather Brahminical *vibakta kitumba,* "together family." Instead, he uses the term employed over half of the time in life history texts, *vandu guDi,* "united temple." So far as I can determine, there is no other context in which villagers use the word *guDi* to speak of anything other than a structure set aside for religious ceremonies. Thus, the phrase *vandu guDi* appears to be a rhetorical device that permits a speaker to attribute sacred properties to the joint household. This notion is, as we shall see, supported by other cases in which the metaphor is used.

The informant goes on to characterize the united temple as a place of solidarity as well as prosperity. Different informants use varied locutions, the phrase "working in unity" being perhaps the most common, but the theme of cooperation in working for the common good is a uniform feature of descriptions of this halcyon phase in the development of domestic groups.

Finally, attend to the portrayal of sex roles in this bit of text. At the outset we are told that, "After the death of my grandmother, my father became owner of the house." The term "owner of the house" may be misleading, for he is not an autocrat who can dispose of family property in any way he fancies. He is the designated head of household to the outside world, the person whose name appears on tax accounts and other records kept by village accountants. Ordinarily this person is the *yajaman*, the male head of household, but not necessarily. In this case a widow passed the office to her son, and this was by no means unique. At the time of my stay, five houses were owned by widows; one of them was Sonamma, the younger brother's bride mentioned in this text, by then a woman in her fifties who lived with her two grown sons and their families. Her elder son was *yajaman*, but it was Sonamma's house. She was also "mother of the house," female head of household.

The distinction between male and female heads of household is made explicit in this text ("My father and mother were the *yajaman* and the mother of the house at that time") and is associated with an implicit division of male and female domains of activity:

> And my mother and my *cikkamma* were unified and cooperating with each other. They maintained the family without misunderstandings.
> . . . My father and my *cikkappa* had saved and purchased as much land as my grandfather had purchased.

The land was the men's business; the house was the women's business; there was a hierarchy of authority for each sex, an implicit sexual division of spheres of authority and activity that we shall encounter again.

Unless passages such as the one we have just examined describing a halcyon phase in a joint household's development pertain to a present state of affairs, they are followed by rueful tales of the way the joint household came to divide. First, ominous signs of discord are noted, and then quarreling, declining cooperativeness, work stoppages, and incidents of deceit are cited as the proximate causes of household division. It is interesting to compare such tales to this elicited response to the question "How do households come to divide?"

Say a father has four sons. When they are young they are working well. When they grow older they are not cooperating. Each brother wants things only for his own family. The wives are quarreling too. The husbands and wives are not doing their work. One [brother] does not like the other's wife.

Therefore division [*viibhaaga*] is coming gradually. When it comes the first thing that happens is that the house itself is partitioned. Later the pots and utensils are divided. Then the grain is divided. Then the cash is divided and the loans also. The elder brother tells the others, "Here is your portion, you must pay it." Then the jewelry is divided. The father should have given each bride the same jewels at marriage. Then the animals are divided. Finally the land is divided.

Now consider this example of a life history text from a Naayk family:

Nearly twenty years ago our father and our *doDDappa* and *cikkappa* [father's brothers] and their sons were living in unity. In this village our house was the largest among the Naayks: in total, thirty members. We had forty acres of land and eighty sheep. In those days it was hard to earn money, but we had more food than we needed: poor people came to work and eat and live in our house.

Gradually quarrels began. One reason was our *cikkappa*, Muslappa. He was feeding the sheep in those days. He was not married at the time and would not adjust to living with other family members. . . . He began selling sheep. . . . He used the money in debauchery, giving money to friends and girlfriends. He did not care for his family.

Another reason was Kadirappa, our *doDDappa* [father's elder brother]. He was not doing any work and was talking with the women in the house. He started quarrels among the women, and the women continued quarreling. . . .

There were many reasons for the breaking of our united house; there was quarreling, and little by little, less and less work was done.

Or consider this account by Rangappa of his Vokkaliga family:

After our father's death I became *yajaman* of the house. We purchased ten acres of dry land, we dug one well and fixed an electric pump to it, . . . we earned 10,000 rupees in cash, had many sheep, twenty cows, and three pairs of bullocks . . . then my *cikkappa*'s son married my younger sister's daughter so that soon our family came to be twenty-five people . . . and then we began to have quarrels in our house because my younger brothers [including the father's younger brother's son] began to think I might cheat them.

His younger brother puts the matter thus:

After our father died my elder brother became *yajaman*. At that time quarrels began in our united temple because my elder brother went in errant ways. . . . Then my wife and my brother's wife also began to quarrel.

For the sake of brevity I have cited only small portions of these life history texts, but even so one can see similarities to the response elicited by the general question about how households come to divide. In both cases we encounter descriptions of the halcyon phase of growth and prosperity corresponding to the elicited remark, "When they are young they are working well." I should note that in many instances these descriptions probably overstate matters to some extent. Judging from amounts of land now owned by the Naayks of the first text, their joint holdings were probably no more than thirty acres. And according to other evidence acquired through efforts to reconstruct the developmental history of each village household, the largest this Naayk household ever got was about twenty-five people; the Vokkaliga household numbered at most sixteen. But in their general thrust these accounts are reasonable: these Naayks were, when I knew them, still remembered by others as having been one of the great Naayk families of the area; I have no doubt that under Rangappa's leadership the Vokkaliga household bought the ten acres and dug the well.

Gradually relationships begin to sour in both families. The brothers start to quarrel, as do their wives. Herein we see another guise in which the sexual division of spheres of activity occurs: in most life histories members of each sex are portrayed as arguing among themselves.

In the Naayk case, however, Kadirappa is said to have started arguments among the women. There are other similar cases. But the way in which this aspect of the situation is talked about obliquely legitimates the sexual division of household affairs. Although there were "many reasons for the breaking of our united house," members of this family assigned the greatest blame to the *yajaman*, Kadirappa, for failing to act as a *yajaman* should. Muslappa freely admitted the shameful selling of sheep and his other misdeeds, but as far as most of the rest of the family was concerned, these would not have occurred if Kadirappa had supervised Muslappa properly and begun to search for a wife for him. Instead, Kadirappa would abandon the fields (and his duty) for long periods to idle about the house. Worse still, he had taken a dislike to his younger brother's wife, Nagamma, and criticized her openly, thus undercutting his own wife's authority as the older woman. By criticizing Nagamma he created grounds for her to disrespectfully challenge his wife: "Why does your husband abuse me so?" A proper *yajaman* minds his own business, farming. Once again a specific case parallels the hypothetical case of the elicited response: "One [brother] does not like the other's wife."

Rangappa was accused of cheating his brothers, of favoring his own family over theirs. He met this accusation by offering the office of *yajaman* to either of them. But they declined, and it was determined that the household should be divided. When I knew them, the three households resulting from this partition still lived in apartments created out of the single structure they had once shared. This was part of the settlement arbitrated by the *patel*, who, faithful to the elicited response, assigned each family its share of land, livestock, money, grain, and indebtedness. Each woman kept her own jewelry.

Elsewhere in India the process of partition is sometimes protracted; it takes place in stages, with a long period during which separate units of consumption remain united as a unit of farm production. In Yaavahalli this period appears rarely to exceed a few months. Generally, "trial separations" lead to a clear-cut decision to divide a household, and once such a decision is reached, the entire process, starting with an alteration in sleeping arrangements and concluding with a formal division of land, takes place rather quickly. We shall consider the possible reasons for the absence of staged partition in Yaavahalli later, in Chapter 7. For the present, however, it should be noted that the two examples of household partition we have seen share another feature in common with many others: it is often the actions of men that precipitate household division. Though women are reported in life histories as quarreling as often as men, and indeed are often accused of goading their husbands into conflicts with other men of the household, men are responsible for most of the actions that are so disruptive as to cause irreparable damage to joint family solidarity. Muslappa stole; Rangappa was accused of cheating his brothers. All the women did was to argue. This being the case, no purpose is served by dividing the women's managerial domain, the home, while maintaining intact the men's, the farm.

Thus, while tales of household partition vary in detail, certain predominant themes recur. Indeed, when asked, "How do households come to divide?" an informant can produce a hypothetical case that resembles many real cases. Put another way, he can predict the contents of real cases. It should be noted that the informant whose elicited response I cited was not recounting his personal experience. He was one of two brothers, not four, and his life history was unusual in several respects. For instance, he and his wife had concluded a love match against his family's wishes and had lived with them for only a matter of weeks. They had married with the covert aid of several senior Vokkaliga women, whose stated aim was to prevent the stain of illegitimacy from falling on their *jaati*. This was a *cause célèbre* in the village and the main topic of his life history.

One element found in some tales of household partition, efforts by family elders to persuade younger members not to divide the household, is missing from the texts we have considered so far. Perhaps this is because we have been dealing with joint households that survived for some time after the deaths of both founding parents, for enjoinders to cleave together are most often spoken by a parent whose adult children and their spouses have fallen to quarreling. We shall consider an instance of this in the next chapter.

The great majority of life history informants describe the period following household partition as a time of hardship: "We had many difficulties after the division of our united temple because our children were small. . . . After some years our children came of working age."

Remarks such as this one attributing the economic problems of the nuclear family to the inability of children to contribute to household income are common. Others, like the following example, record the remorse of parents unable to provide for their children in the manner to which they had become accustomed:

> At that time he [the narrator's brother] wished to divide the house. When I heard this I advised him against it, but he would not listen to my advice and so we separated. . . . After the separation we had much trouble. . . . I was not able to maintain the family [adequately], nobody helped us. . . . My children wore old clothes. . . . My brother had a lot of difficulties too. He had to beg for a handful of food and also for clothing. When we were a united family we maintained ourselves and could spend a lot of money; so now he knew the value of money and the advantages of a united family.

Not all accounts of the postpartition period are so grim because in some cases one nuclear family hives off, leaving behind a substantial joint household that continues to prosper. Rather, it is the young nuclear family that appears to be vulnerable. Consider this comment drawn from a conversation with an eleven-year-old girl:

> See, we came from a rich family. Our grandfathers were living in prosperity when they were a united house and also our fathers were [i.e., her father and his younger brothers]. After my father married he separated from his family. He had many troubles then. I did not understand this, but this is what my grandfather has told me.

The United Temple Doctrine

We have now seen that villagers regard the economic superiority of joint family households as a self-evident fact of life. When they tell their life stories, they do so in terms of the developmental histories of households; invariably they praise joint households and bemoan the quarrels that cause household partition. Yet time and again household members do quarrel and divide the estate against their own best interests, behavior that Gangappa describes as ignorant and that villagers in general regard as a serious social problem. Indeed, household partition occupies a place in the life of Yaavahalli rather like that of divorce (an uncommon event in Yaavahalli) in industrial societies.

The teachings of the elders constitute a doctrine for the preservation of the united temple by specifying measures that foster harmony within it. We shall now turn to a more detailed examination of this doctrine and the *dharmas* of the sexes on which, in my view, it is based.

chapter 3

Body Dharma

Village elders say that people ought to live by a moral order they variously call the "teachings of the elders," the "teachings of our fathers," or, when proverbs are used to legitimate a course of action, the "things the ancient people said." At one time or another all sorts of measures may be designated as teachings of the elders by a speaker who wishes to buttress the authority of what he says. But the policies I shall discuss here stand apart to the extent that they are culturally standardized. As best I could determine, all village elders endorsed them. Moreover, they form a coherent set in that they are all measures dealing with household formation and in that all discriminate on the basis of sex. I shall describe the content of these policies more fully in a moment, but first let us consider the way I believe they are best viewed as cultural phenomena.

First, we might note the bearing of villagers' consensus on these matters on the status of the village as a population. Viewed one way, Yaavahalli is just a collection of households conveniently grouped together for study. However, the close proximity of villagers to one another tends to greatly increase the frequency of their interaction, and villagers take an interest in one another's affairs; marriages, notably, are to some extent everybody's business, and to that extent the village is a cultural deme, a unit of population that exchanges members with other such units. The quality of a marriage is not merely the interest of the parties to it; it bears on the honor of the village as a place to marry later, and judgments about the appropriateness of a match are negotiated under a rhetoric of common understandings about marriage. The teachings of the elders are not only shared; they are displayed.

I call the teachings of the elders policies and not cultural rules, however, in order to avoid the misimpression that they are jural rules. They are not. Although people do attempt to jurally enforce some of them in the adjudication of disputes, and though a sort of practical reason emerges when one views the teachings as a coherent doctrine, the teachings of the elders are simply guides for action. People can and do—indeed, must—violate them with varying frequencies.

The question then arises: why do villagers persist in advocating these policies rather than others? One way of answering this question is to look for a motive underlying the elders' advocacy of them. By "motive" I do not mean some diffuse psychological need; I mean a reason for doing things that people state or that may be inferred from the things they say. In describing their affairs and considering alternative actions, villagers, like the rest of us, construct social realities. They designate classes of actors, actions, and the resources and constraints with which and under which persons act in particular settings. They also explain the reasons for things happening as they do, and these reasons include the purposes, interests, or intentions of the actors. These purposes, interests, intentions, are attributions of motive. A motive underlying the teachings of the elders is recurrently indicated by villagers: the teachings are aimed at advancing the interests of one's children, chiefly by fostering the development of cohesive joint family households.

In this chapter I shall urge that the elders be taken at their word, that it is to this struggle for family solidarity that the doctrine is aimed. I shall first say a bit more about the teachings of the elders and then turn to an interpretation of them alternative to the one I shall offer. Having rejected this alternative, I shall proceed to a further exposition of my argument that the teachings of the elders are best viewed as an amplification of the *dharmas* of the sexes and the later and more problematic maturation of males.

The Teachings of the Elders

Of the teachings of the elders listed in the first chapter, one policy is, so far as I could determine, almost invariably followed: girls should marry younger than boys. On the average they appear to marry about five years sooner, with the modal age for females about fifteen and that for males about twenty. But the marriage age for males is much more variable, and it is not uncommon for a poor man to marry in his late twenties. Villagers explain this policy by saying that girls are ready for marriage sooner than boys because they are able to take on adult responsibilities sooner. Moreover, because males marry later, there are always a lot of unmarried males in the village, and if a girl is left unmarried for some time after menarche someone, probably the wrong someone, is likely to become infatuated with her, and everyone, they say, knows where *that* may lead. Thus, almost nobody leaves a nubile daughter unmarried for very long, and it is seen as somewhat scandalous if one does.

The second policy is that postmarital residence should be patrilocal. As one would expect, families with no son bring in a matrilocal son-in-law, but usually only one, and men from poorer families may find such a proposition attractive. These arrangements, however, are regarded as risky for all concerned because villagers feel that a man will not trust and respect a father-in-law (*maava*) as he would his father, nor will a man trust and care about a son-in-law as he would a son. One way to mitigate this problem is to choose a son-in-law (*aLiya*) who is the son of known and trusted kin. Of the five cases of in-marrying grooms I encountered, two involved a nephew (a sister's son) of the male head of household. These cases, then, were avunculocal as well as matrilocal. One other case united a girl with her mother's brother's son; it was amitalocal: the man went to live with his aunt.

The third policy follows from the second: sons should inherit equal portions of the family estate. Of all of the teachings of the elders, this comes the closest to being a jural rule because it is frequently cited in land disputes, and it is enforceable in the civil courts. However, the villagers' endorsement of this as a policy is based on moral and practical grounds, not legal ones, and recognizes exceptions to it as appropriate in some instances on the same grounds. It is the duty of parents to provide evenhandedly for the welfare of their children. Since one ordinarily keeps all sons at home after marriage and provides for one's daughters by marrying them as well as possible, it follows that each son should share equally in the family estate when, unfortunately, it must be divided. But if, as we saw in the last chapter, a daughter suffers some economic calamity, parents should try to provide as best they can for her and her husband as well as for their sons, and if Gangappa's case is any indication, they will be supported in this by other village elders. Likewise, a matrilocally residing son may be asked to forgive a portion of his patrimony to his brothers.

Two more policies follow from patrilocality. If the sons stay at home, one is faced with finding good conjugal homes for daughters and with choosing brides for sons with an eye to the fact that these brides will become members of a joint household. Hypergamy and consanguineous marriage are regarded as serving the interests of both bride givers and bride receivers. Hypergamy may be interpreted in different ways in different places; a woman may be said to marry up in the world in a variety of senses. In Yaavahalli people say that, where possible, it is well for a girl to marry up the *economic* ladder because it fosters her interests and those of her children. Reciprocally, it is well to choose such a bride because she will be pleased with her new surroundings and because she will likely be accustomed to at least as much work as she will be asked to perform in her conjugal household. The worst sort of bride is one who displays *nagarike*, "forwardness," or "haughtiness," or "uppitiness," the sort of behavior villagers attribute to city folk. Such a woman might complain that in her parent's house they had coffee more often than in her conjugal home, and she may disdain farm work. Villagers certainly do not want brides like that; they want practical girls who do not mind getting their hands dirty in the fields alongside the men. The kind of woman they like to recruit helps hold households together; the kind they dislike causes them to divide.

Consanguineous marriages, those that unite cross-cousins or a man and his real or classificatory elder sister's daughter, serve both families because the bride givers send their daughter to known and trusted kin who will treat her well, while bride receivers are getting a girl from the same sort of people, a girl who may be relied upon to be more respectful and cooperative than a stranger might be.

Consanguineous marriage is governed by formal rules. The logic of villagers' kinship terminology is premised on the existence of *gumpus*, "groups," which are exogamous patrilineal clans. *Gumpu* membership is easily determined. Each group has a *mane devaru* or "house god." The great majority of those found in Yaavahalli and environs are Dravidian mother goddesses, each of whom is mistress of a major disease that she uses to punish immoral conduct. But a particular clan is defined not only by the fact that its members are devotees of a certain *mane devaru*, but also by the fact that they are her devotees at a particular shrine in a village that is regarded as the descent group's place of origin. Thus, if people are worshipers of the same mother from the same shrine, they are, *ipso facto*, patrikin.

Marital alliance is viewed as an exchange of brides between such groups. Though these are in principle clans, in practice they are localized lineages. There has been a good deal of migration in times past, and the local members of most *gumpus* live many miles from their shrines of origin. Consequently, the local members of a clan are likely to be the descendants of founding migrants, a lineage, found in one village or in two or three neighboring villages. The members of a local lineage often do not know their kin in distant villages and thus can not consult them in marital matters.

Members of one's *gumpu* are called *bandugaLu*, "people of the same seed." When one's lineage has exchanged a bride with another group, members of that lineage are called *biigaaru*, "people we marry." If one's *biigaaru* have married with a third group, that group's members are called *saddakaaru*, "people who marry the people we marry." Marriage with *saddakaaru* is forbidden. But other lineages that are *biigaaru* to one's *saddakaaru* are *biigaaru* to one's own lineage as well. And their *biigaaru* in turn are also one's *saddakaaru*. Thus, the lineages of a *jaati* are viewed as being divided into bride-exchanging moieties. There are so many named descent groups in the larger *jaatis*, however, that there will be many that stand in no known marital relationship to the local members of a particular group. And so long as a *saddakaaru* relationship cannot be found in the course of marriage negotiations, persons from these groups too are allowable spouses.

Marriages fall into two classes. Those with *biigaaru* who have concluded prior marriages with one's own group are *haLe biigastaana* "old relationships"; all others are *hosa biigastaana*, "new relationships."

The most fundamental marital preference within these rules is that old relationships are better than new ones. Better still are marriages uniting *soodara biigaaru*. A *soodara* relation is a first cross-connection, such as a first cross-cousin. Some 40 percent of all marriages in Yaavahalli were consanguineous in some fashion, and while many of these united moderately distant relatives in genealogical terms, marriages between the children of a brother and sister were common.

The marriage of a man to his elder sister's daughter is the most favored of all choices. While there are few marriages between a man and his own elder sister's daughter because the demographic circumstances conducive to them do not occur often, classificatory variants of this form of marriage are rather common. Hence, for example, a man might marry his father's elder brother's daughter's daughter, a girl who is the daughter of his classificatory elder sister. In fact, tabulated in one way, uncle/niece marriage is the most common form of old-relationship union. Villagers describe marital alliance as bride giving. Following this convention, the *soodara* and classifictory variants of old-relationship marriage may be broken down into five categories, reflecting the fact that villagers use different terms for older and younger siblings. These are: elder sister's daughter marriage, mother's elder brother's daughter marriage, mother's younger brother's daughter marriage, father's elder sister's daughter marriage, and father's younger sister's daughter marriage.

The most common of these is elder sister's daughter marriage. Mother's elder brother's daughter and father's younger sister's daughter marriages follow close behind, with about equal frequency. Father's elder sister's daughter was the least common bride. I should note that in tabulating these data I used the closest relationship between wife and husband; some couples are related in several ways. Moreover, when a girl was both a mother's brother's daughter and a father's sister's daughter or elder sister's daughter, I tabulated her according to the latter relationship because she is viewed as returning to her mother's people. Thus, the method of tabulation influenced the distribution of frequencies.

Another factor in marriage choice—perhaps more important than preference—is demographic chance. Men, we should remember, marry five years later than women, on the average. And there is no difference in this regard between uncle/niece matings and other forms. All recorded instances of uncle/niece unions were first marriages mating young couples whose age differences were about the same as those of other first marriages.

Because females marry younger than males, the chances are poor that a woman will have a daughter younger than her younger brother's son, because the two sets of offspring do not overlap very much in age; hence the low frequency of father's elder sister's daughter marriage. The chances of her having a son who is older than her younger brother's daughter are much better, although he may be too much older. It is fairly likely, however, that an elder brother and younger sister will marry within a few years of one another, creating overlapping sets of offspring and providing chances for mother's elder brother's daughter and father's younger sister's daughter matings.

The high frequency of uncle/niece marriage is likewise accounted for by the discrepancy between the sexes in age at marriage and by the fact that many sibling sets are distributed over twenty years or so of child bearing. A first-born daughter might well have a daughter five years younger than her last-born brother. And the chances of a man's father's elder brother's daughter (his classificatory elder sister) having a daughter of suitable age are quite good. Thus, as a statistical matter, the frequency of uncle/niece marriage may be viewed as an artifact of generational skewing between bride-exchanging groups, a result of the different marriage ages of women and men.

Still, one cannot deny that people state preferences, and uncle/niece marriage is especially favored, at least by older women. There is a pronounced tendency for uncle/niece matings to unite early, often first-born daughters, who are seen as responsible girls, with late, often last-born sons, who are regarded as immature. Thus, contrary to the supposition that uncle/niece marriages might unite domineering older husbands and meek young wives, these marriages are more likely to involve a reliable, practical wife who settles down an irresponsible husband or puts some backbone into an indecisive, unassertive one. That is one reason older mothers of younger sons like the arrangement: it is a way of taking care of the baby of the family. They also like it because their daughter-in-law will also be a granddaughter, a relative who will treat them with affection and respect in their declining years.

Finally, two rare but highly favored marital arrangements bring into still sharper focus villagers' reasons for favoring old-relationship marriages in general. In one, two brothers marry two sisters, a practice favored because girls who were reared together by the same mother are likely to get on well as adults, and therefore a practice that exemplifies villagers' concerns for harmony among the women of a household. The second is called *adalu badalu,* "reciprocal exchange": two households simultaneously exchange daughters as brides. This practice highlights villagers' interest in maintaining the close ties between affinally related households that lead to future marital exchanges.

With this brief description of the teachings of the elders in hand, I would like to dispose of a view of them alternative to the one for which I shall argue. It is that the teachings of the elders serve the interests of males over, and against if necessary, those of females. The practice of marrying boys later than girls could be a device for enhancing the dominance of husbands over wives in this community, which does indeed set store by seniority. Patrilocal residence and patrilineal inheritance could be viewed as the mechanisms whereby males control the means of production so as to control females. And hypergamous and consanguineous marriage might be simply a means of acquiring brides who will be more easily controlled by men.

There are a number of reasons for considering this alternative, and some are sufficiently troubling as to demand consideration. First, societies of plow agriculturalists are often held to be especially male-dominated. Indeed, a complex of patrilineal institutions such as those found in Yaavahalli is sometimes taken, in itself, as a mark of male dominance, regardless of a society's means of subsistence. Second, in Western society we have often been inclined to view relations between the sexes chiefly in terms of social equality or inequality. This is evident in the rhetoric we use to talk about women and men: we speak of equal rights, equal pay for equal work, the status of women, and so on. I have no quarrel with the use of these terms to discuss relations between the sexes, but since I intend to argue that social inequality is not the chief issue in relations between the sexes in Yaavahalli, perhaps I should consider the possibility that it might be, particularly in view of the fact that it was the conventional wisdom of cultural anthropology in times past that all societies were male-dominated in one way or another. This view has now been questioned by many anthropologists, and I would like to show why I believe male dominance is not a fruitful notion to employ in attempting to understand Yaavahalli's institutions.

Third, for a long while I myself regarded Yaavahalli as a male-dominated community, not because I saw repeated instances of men dominating women, but because I went to India with the androcentric expectation that whatever village I lived in would be male-dominated. When I got there, I did encounter a sexually segregated community. This fact, which I interpreted as evidence of male dominance, meant that I, as a male stranger, found it much easier to work with the men than with the women. Moreover, since agriculture, the focus of my study, was male-managed, I had reason to spend more time with the men than with the women. Later, I think, the notion of male dominance served as an instruction to myself that I did not have to worry about the women when analyzing my data, which was convenient since I knew more about the men. It was only when, under the influence of recent feminist ethnography, I began to carefully examine the statistical data on women's work and the life histories and other texts I had elicited from women that I realized how misleading the notion of male dominance had been. Thus, an examination of the question of male dominance in Yaavahalli is useful, if only as a cautionary tale.

The male-dominance alternative has two failings. One of them, the lack of observational adequacy, is quickly evident. Not only does a male-dominance hypothesis contradict the villagers' stated motive for the teachings of the elders, but it is inconsistent with other aspects of their behavior. Perhaps some sort of false-consciousness argument could be advanced in favor of the hypothesis in spite of this, but another failing, which will become evident later, remains: it does not, so far as I can tell, provide the basis for a fruitful theory of the village's agricultural adaptation. The view I shall advocate does; it holds that the teachings of the elders persist because they stimulate an effective agricultural adaptation. And to the extent that this study isolates the cultural mechanisms whereby one process of agricultural adaptation occurred, it contributes to the larger goal of understanding agricultural adaptation as a general phenomenon. Let us now turn to the matter of observational adequacy.

Male Dominance: Genuine and Spurious

The notion of male dominance has a curious history in that it is sometimes not entirely clear what people mean by it. For some it is a temperamental trait: men are domineering. While there is substantial evidence, as we shall see, that males are more prone to aggressive displays than females and that this tendency probably has a biological basis, I do not view male dominance primarily in temperamental terms, because when men systematically display a domineering mien in dealing with women, the habit is probably better viewed as the product of institutions that limit women's alternatives, rather than the other way around. It is because, in many societies, men can get away with social restrictions on women's lives that they arrogantly lord it over women in their personal relations with them.

By my definition, a society is genuinely male-dominated to the extent that men impose external diseconomies on women and to the extent that women are powerless to impose them on men. Though economists

will find this explanation simplistic, as I use the term an external dis-
economy occurs when someone pays for something that someone else
gets. Industrial pollution is the classic example. The public pays for it by
living in a degraded environment; industry benefits because it does not
have to internalize, pay, the cost of cleaning up the mess it makes. Men
impose external diseconomies on women in a variety of ways. I shall note
five important ones and briefly explain why I believe they are not prominent influences on relations between the sexes in Yaavahalli.

VIOLENCE

Historically men have exerted a virtual monopoly over organized
violence, and while men use it to impose their wills on other men, they
use it to impose external diseconomies on women in a number of ways.
Some of these are entailed in warfare. There is a sense in which both
sexes lose wars, but only men win them: any glory or booty devolves
mostly on the male victors. There are also ways in which only women
lose wars: they are abducted and raped. Since organized violence does
not occur in the village, Yaavahalli's women do not have to pay for
protection with subordination.

Wife beating is a common form of violence that occurs in India as it
does in most other areas of the world. Yet so far as I could tell, it did not
often happen in Yaavahalli. Aggression of any sort on the part of anyone
is severely criticized, and physical violence is rare. The few cases of
violence I recorded did involve male aggressors, but all save one involved
male victims too. The exception arose when a man was alleged to have
beaten his daughter and was universally scorned for having done so. It
could be that wife beating occurred that I did not hear about, but I
doubt it. Villagers were quick to criticize one another on other matters,
and the fact is that the ecology of village life is not conducive to wife
beating. Villagers live cheek by jowl with one another, often in joint
families. Worldwide, wife beating is most likely to occur in isolated
nuclear family households. Village men have almost no chance to beat
anybody in private and thus are not free to use the threat of violence to
press demands on women.

MARITAL DESTINY

In some societies men largely determine who shall marry whom, and
they use this power to cement political alliances with other men. Marital
decisions may also serve to obtain women who are easily controlled. In
some areas of North India, women often marry into villages many miles
from home in which they know no one. A young bride in such circum-

stances is likely to be a rather submissive person. Women pay for these arrangements to the extent that they dislike them.

In Yaavahalli the farthest any women had married from home was fourteen miles. Some women marry within their natal villages, and the majority marry within five miles of home. During slack seasons in agriculture, hardly a day passes without some woman's coming or going on a visit to her natal kin.

Moreover, while men do most of the walking and talking in the final arrangements of a marriage, mothers and daughters are regarded as having veto rights over any groom a father proposes, and often it is the mother who proposes a match. I cannot show conclusively that this veto right is systematically enforceable, because husbands and wives so seldom disagreed on marital choices. But in the only two cases of disagreement I recorded, the women won. The *patel* brought a physician to the village as a prospective groom for his eldest daughter. Both the girl and her mother rejected him because he was too old and because they had no idea of who his people were. In the other case a woman obliged her husband to arrange a marriage for their eldest daughter with her youngest brother, of whom she was especially fond. The woman saw her brother as a lonely young man in need of firm feminine guidance; the husband regarded him as undependable and arrogant.

To adequately understand the control women exercise over marital destiny, however, it is necessary to look at their activities in marital arrangements, an examination that will entail a related matter, the way in-marrying brides are viewed as persons. I wish to note two points. First, the advantages ascribed to consanguineous marriage are substantially the product of women's cultivation of affinal ties between households. Second, enormous importance is attributed to obtaining brides with whom other household members can live and work comfortably. The rural Indian bride is sometimes portrayed as a human doormat whom her in-laws may bully in any way they wish. No portrayal could be more radically wrong when applied to Yaavahalli. Consider the remarks of the following two informants. The first was asked to comment on relations between daughters-in-law and their parents-in-law. The second was asked to characterize relations between an in-marrying bride and her husband's younger sisters. Both informants contrast old- and new-relationship marriages in their remarks. According to my records of the interviews, this was entirely their own idea; they were not asked to draw the contrast.

This is what I have to say about relations between *maava* [father-in-law] and *sose* [daughter-in-law] and between *atte* [mother-in-law] and *sose:* In a new-relationship marriage *sose* starts out calling *atte* and *maava amma* and *appa* [as she would her mother and father, a sign of affectionate respect]. But gradually this decreases, and *sose* does not treat them well. She advises her husband not to follow his father. She does not call *maava appa* anymore, and she speaks singularly [i.e., in the familiar form of address] to him. Also, she does not treat her *atte* well. In a lot of families with this type of *sose* in this village this problem happens. Not only in this village; it is a common thing. Likewise, the new-relationship *sose*'s family may not treat their *bii-gaaru* well; they don't adjust well in the relationship. But sometimes in the new relationship *sose* and her family behave well right up to the end. Both families are adjusted, but that depends on the *sose*, and this good type is not common.

See, in the old-relationship marriage, *sose* often treats her *atte* and *maava* very well. In this type of marriage *sose* commonly calls *atte* and *maava amma* and *appa*, and *sose* uses very nice manners. But sometimes there is a hereditary grudge between *sose* and *atte* in the old relationship. In that case there is less respect for *sose*'s family because *atte* knows everything about them. But one thing is very important: in an old relationship there is visiting, and families treat each other like guests. The mothers and fathers talk to each other personally about family matters. In the new relationship the families do not talk things over personally. So mostly when marriages are in an old relationship people treat each other very well. That is why all of the older people search for brides in an old relationship.

See, in the case of a new relationship, *attige* and *naadini* [elder brother's wife and husband's younger sister] don't treat each other well. There is no cooperation. A kind of grudge grows between them, and they argue, in the same way that *sose* argues with her *atte* and *maava*.

This is [by contrast] my own experience with the old relationship. My younger sister married into a house in Keshvara, and I married a girl from Keshvara. Later we married our son to my sister's daughter. That family has treated us well from the start. And our *sose* behaves well with everyone in our house. She behaves as she would in her father and mother's house. She gives everyone respect. She is a good *attige* to our daughter. She gives our daughter good advice about the future; they make jokes with each other and work together happily. That is how it is with *attige* and *naadini* [sisters-in-law] in an old relationship. . . .

See, sometimes too a son does not behave well towards his father. But the old-relationship *sose* will go to her husband and tell him to go back and follow his father's advice. . . .

In the new relationship, brides only give respect at the outset. In the new relationship, *attige* and *naadini* and *atte* and *sose* don't get along. The bride advises her husband to separate from his parents. She does not care for her *atte* and speaks singularly. She does not tolerate the difficulty the family has. . . .

See, if you have money problems, *biigaaru* in the old relationship will help you. In the new relationship they will just say they can't help you. Then you quarrel and thereafter you stop speaking to each other.

Some old-relationship marriages work out badly; some new-relationship marriages work out well. But on the whole, villagers say, old relationships are better, and they describe differences between the two kinds in terms of the behavior of the brides. Brides are spoken of not as submissive persons whom in-laws can order about as they please, but as individuals who exercise independent influence over family affairs for good or ill. The tendency for old-relationship brides to behave well is, I suspect, the result of a self-fulfilling prophecy. Experience has shown that old-relationship marriages are desirable. Therefore, villagers cultivate ties with affinally related households so as to get the marriages they want; the stronger the ties of affection one creates, the less likely it is that some competitor will be able to spoil one's prospects.

Men visit relatives from time to time and, of course, take part in visits by their sisters and other kinswomen. But it is chiefly women who cultivate ties between households. This process begins early in a woman's life, often while she is still a girl. The relationship the second informant describes between *attige* and *naadini* provides an example. Girls are sometimes jealous of their elder brothers' wives, particularly if the wives are not much older than they are themselves, viewing them as interlopers who would take over their role in the household and possibly in their mother's affections. A good daughter-in-law, according to parents, will prevent this by treating her sister-in-law with the same affection she would display toward a younger sister. This appears to have happened in the case cited, establishing the kind of bond that might later lead to a marriage between the two girls' children. Childhood ties seem also to be at work in some new-relationship marriages that mate the children of women who had been close friends as girls.

In the course of growing up, a girl gets to know a wide network of relatives, some of whom she may cultivate later, and is repeatedly exposed to the influence of her female elders, through whom she learns the protocols and skills of visiting. The affinal cultivation process begins in earnest after a woman is married and has children. Early in her married life a woman pays visits, mostly to her natal family, much more often than she is visited; as time passes she is visited more and visits less. Either way, women generally take these visits for granted as something they do because they like to, and the desire to be sociable and exchange news is usually the explicitly stated reason for them. Nevertheless, women begin diplomatic initiatives on behalf of their children's marriages when they are still quite young, and they carefully follow the development of relatives' children who are genealogically appropriate mates for their own. Then, as the children grow, a woman may set apart one or more prospective mates as favorites and begin to cultivate relations with their mothers and with the children as well. Eventually one mother or another offhandedly remarks that it might be nice if their children married some day, and if the other mother agrees, the cultivation of family ties intensifies. If the two mothers continue to agree once the children are nubile, chances are the marriage will occur.

The result is that in many cases a girl joins a family she has known for many years. Her mother-in-law is the woman who made flattering remarks about her in congenial chats with her mother; her husband is the mysterious older boy at whom she was not supposed to stare; the younger children are former playmates or the infants she carried around to show her friends. She knows which uncle is irritable and which aunt has menstrual problems. She is familiar with the food they eat and is acquainted with their neighbors. In short, consanguineous marriage makes good on the benefits claimed for it because, through the visits of the mothers, she has been reared to be a wife of the family.

It is worth noting that the phenomenon I have just described contrasts with studies of marital alliance that view such systems as exchanges of women among men. In terms of its formal rules, the type of marital alliance found in Yaavahalli is what is known as an elementary alliance system. Such systems are distinguished by the fact that certain classes of kin are specifically designated as prospective mates. Some have tried to account for properties of such systems in sentimental terms; people marry with some relatives, and not others, because they like them. Thus, it might be suggested that men in patrilineal societies would want to marry a mother's brother's daughter because the uncle is, in contrast to an authoritarian father, a permissive figure associated with a loving mother. Village men often do marry a mother's brother's daughter (as well as the other sorts of relatives noted earlier), but if they do, it is not because they like their mother's brother. As far as village men are concerned, he is just another village patriarch whom one does not love nearly so well as one's father. Indeed, he is often rather mistrusted because he will probably strike a hard bargain before allowing anyone to marry his daughter. If a man does marry her, the likely reason is that his mother took a fancy to the girl on her many visits home. To make sentimental sense of the system, then, one must adopt the perspective of women exchanging women.

Having said that the notion of male dominance does not get one very far in accounting for the domestic institutions of village life, I do not wish to be viewed as going to the opposite extreme of portraying Yaavahalli as a matriarchy. I merely wish to point out that if you examine the roles of women as matchmakers and as brides, it is difficult to draw the conclusion that they are supine persons whose chief aim is to pander to men's wishes and easy to draw the conclusion that they are decisive adult actors who pursue interests of their own.

If marital choice in Yaavahalli serves the interests of anyone in particular, it serves the interests of mothers, a matter I shall expand on presently. As we shall see, there is a good reason for men to defer to their wives in the selection of brides: the work of women has become so essential to the village economy that women must be able to live in harmony if a joint household is to be a proficient economic unit.

CONTROL OF THE MEANS OF PRODUCTION

A third way in which men impose external diseconomies on women is through economic dependence. A woman who must rely on a man for her living is more likely to defer to his wishes and to fetch and carry for him than one who makes a contribution to family income. It is generally not the case that such women do not work, but they do not do the kind of work that offers real economic power. Men own and/or manipulate the means of production from which income derives, so that a woman's only alternative to her current situation is to find another man. There are usually institutional impediments to this, but most women are inclined to stick with the devil they know anyway.

Men are indeed the nominal owners of most land and livestock in Yaavahalli, though there is no rule against women owning farm resources and some do. Men are also the chief farm managers and do about two-thirds of all farm work. Moreover, patrilocal residence, which is closely tied to the usual means by which men come to own farm resources, patrilineal inheritance, imposes a cost on women. They have to leave home at marriage, and many girls are fearful of this. The boys receive a benefit the girls pay for; they get to stay at home. But in spite of all of this, I do not believe that village men could employ economic dependence very well to control women, even if they wanted to.

The benefits that men receive and for which women pay under conditions of economic dependence often stem from the fact that men's demands on women entail little or no cost for the men's productive activities. In an agricultural community in which women do little farm work, men can demand submission and fetch and carry services from women in the knowledge that their demands will not disrupt other important work because women usually have sufficient time for their domestic tasks, which indeed include fetch and carry services.

In 1966 Yaavahalli's women provided 36 percent of the farm labor force. This means that the average woman was a half-time farm worker by male standards, though there is a strong inverse relation between per capita income and the amount of farm work the women of a household did. Domestic work also consumes much of the women's time, and I found in a sample of daily routines of women, collected during a relatively slack period in the agricultural cycle, that women's work days, for all tasks combined, exceeded eleven hours.

In such circumstances, frivolous demands by men on women's time and attention have serious consequences for the household economy on which men too depend. Put another way, men are obliged by the situation to internalize the costs of their demands.

Moreover, it is important that the women, like the men, of a joint household form a solidary unit in which work is assigned to individuals on grounds of allocative efficiency. As we saw in the case of the *yajaman* who was regarded as having hastened the partition of a joint household by meddling in the women's affairs, the authority to allocate women's time in joint domestic groups is supposed to belong to the mother of the house. Thus, if village women are economically dependent on their men, and they are, the reverse is also true, so that each sex is required by circumstances to respect the demands of the other's work schedules or to pay the price in domestic chaos.

As to the matter of patrilocal residence, the price that girls pay in having to leave home is countered by a price that boys pay. They are not allowed to marry until considerably later than the girls, and they regard this period of enforced celibacy as a burden. Further, during the years following puberty when the girls are settling into a new household, the boys are faced with something of an ordeal, learning the adult male role, which is focused on hard manual labor.

CONTROL OF THE PUBLIC SPHERE

The public sphere is largely in the hands of men in most societies: men make the decisions and create the polity in which women live. And to the extent that men exclude women from positions of power and prestige and make decisions that favor male interests, women pay for something that men get.

At the time of my fieldwork, village women certainly did not play a prominent role in formal public politics. Though women of leading families canvassed voters, and though the group *panchayat* was required to have a female member, the candidates they supported were uniformly male, as were the holders of traditionally inherited offices such as *patel*, village guard, and village accountant. But the prominence of men in public life does not have a strong bearing on the present argument for several reasons. For one thing, few men hold positions of public power: to be a notable one had to be a *sovkaar*, a rich person, as well as a man.

What is more, women seemed to take part in a conspiracy to portray the village as male-dominated to some outsiders. Village women made a categorical distinction between village men and townsmen, a matter I shall note again. In public debates involving only villagers, women had about as much to say as their men, even in disputes involving male strangers from other villages. In fact, when tempers began to flare, men would sometimes fall silent and allow the women to do the talking. But when government officials or town-based merchants came to the village, the women would recede to the background and let the men do the talking. On those few occasions when I heard such an outsider ask a woman a question, the standard reply was "I'll have to ask my *yajaman*."

I suspect women abandoned the public sphere to men when powerful townsmen were present because many townsmen seem to presume that women, certainly village women, are socially subordinate to men, and treat them accordingly. Most villagers are a little awed by government officials and the like, but women tend to presume that such men have come to talk to the men of the village, as they have, and let the men do the talking on the assumption that they, the women, would not be taken seriously anyway.

But the main reason the prominence of men in the public sphere is not a major concern here stems from the fact that we are dealing with the domestic sphere. Within households and in relations between them, women in many ways exercise as much power as men.

MALE CHAUVINISM

Finally, it should be noted that male dominance may occur as an ideological phenomenon, wherin men endorse doctrines of female inferiority. To the extent that men get away with this, women pay for something men get, a patronizing air of social superiority.

Though I will delay a detailed discussion of this until a later section, I can find no indication whatever of such a doctrine in the male culture of Yaavahalli. It may be argued that such negative evidence stems from my failure to ask the right questions or to overhear the right conversations. But there is also a great deal of positive evidence bearing on village men's views of women, and all of it points to the notion that relations between the sexes are to be understood as parallel, not hierarchical. For villagers, women and men are very different beings, but they are simply different; one is not openly regarded as better than the other.

Here again there is a difference between village men and townsmen. So far as village women are concerned, townsmen often "do not know how to behave." Proper behavior, for villagers, involves strict sexual segregation, which ordains, among other things, that a man who is not a relative should not enter a house where a woman is alone. This is a facet of the courtly symmetric respect members of each sex accord the other.

The beginning of the *Hosadevaru Puja*. The woman in the foreground is the mother of the house of the large family pictured in Chapter 2. As the senior woman of the *patel*'s lineage, it falls to her to lead the younger women standing behind her in the ceremony.

It is, for example, a mark of respect that spouses never utter one another's personal names.

Much of this derives, I suspect, from the fact that this crowded and delicately balanced community cannot, or will not, tolerate much sexual competition, certainly none that occurs so publicly as to incur anger and humiliation. Thus, husbands and wives generally portray themselves as totally loyal to one another, even if they are not always, and villagers scrupulously avoid showing evidence of sexual interest in persons in whom they are not supposed to be sexually interested.

Specifically, men should not stare at women. I imagine women are not supposed to stare at men either, but I am sure about men staring at women because that is the rule that is violated. Some village men voiced suspicions, often so intense as to sound almost paranoid, that some other men were out to seduce married women. The alleged transgressors were all men of above average wealth, and the women in whom they were supposed to have shown interest were usually of below average wealth. Since the same men were singled out by various accusers, I was inclined to believe that there was something to the accusations. But if there were a number of attempted seductions, there were few successes. What seems to have happened was that the would-be seducers were caught staring at married women or were said to have gone to see one when no male member of her household was present. Such men are said not to know how to behave properly.

Townsmen are sometimes guilty of the same behavior. When young women and girls go to town, they are sometimes subjected to the sexual stares of high school boys and young men who work in businesses. Village women regard this as extremely objectionable, a kind of visual rape. By taking advantage of women in this way, these men receive a benefit for which women pay. And for the women involved, one sort of male chauvinism seems to be implicit in such acts: the transgressor treats the victim as a social inferior whose body he can violate at will. On several occasions I saw village men fix an intent glare on a young man caught doing this, as if to let him know that his violation of proper sexual conduct had been noted.

Now, it may be that some village women would welcome the advances of some men to whom they are not married. But that is not at issue. What is at issue is the apparent absence of any doctrine of female subordination in village culture, and this includes a conspicuous sexual double standard. In some societies strictures of sexual modesty apply mainly to women. In Yaavahalli they apply to both sexes; the fact that males who violate the code are informally chastised indicates that this is so.

Nothing in the foregoing discussion should be taken as suggesting that village men do not exert more power over village affairs than women. Whether they do or not depends on how one evaluates one domain of power against others, but certainly the fact that men hold such hereditary offices as *patel* and *tooti* (village guard), predominate in the external affairs of households, and manage farming conveys a degree of political pre-eminence to them. Nor would I suggest that antagonism between the sexes is by any means absent from the village. What I do suggest is that notions of sexual competiton, antagonism, and exploitation do not get one very far in explaining why the domestic institutions encoded in the teachings of the elders are perpetuated in the words and actions of villagers.

If, on the other hand, one makes some simple assumptions that are supported by observations of village life, a model of villagers' models for behavior may be readily constructed.

The first assumption is that the *dharmas* of the sexes are the basis of marriage and the family. The tacit assumption underlying the division of tasks they prescribe is that men and women marry and rear children in whom wife and husband share a common interest as a reproductive team, which is to say that the economy is organized for reproductive ends. This assumption is supported by observations concerning marriage as an institution that villagers regard as essential if one is to live a proper life.

Ardha Jena

People who never marry are called *ardha jena*, "half-persons," a statistically rare but pitied and feared sort of person. To never marry is to be incomplete and, to that extent, a member of an impure category. Such persons are to be feared in part because the souls of those who die childless are destined not for proper rebirth, but for an indefinite purgatory from which they may possess the bodies of the living.

An activity in which villagers take pride is *dharmika kelsa*, "virtuous work." One of the more frequently cited forms of virtuous work is contributing to the marriage costs of a poor person who is not a close relative. The religious virtue attached to such contributions stems in part from the fact that they prevent half-personhood and thus reduce the incidence of spirit possession.

So far as villagers are concerned, everyone should marry and have children, and it is the duty of parents to provide for all of their children's marriages. If they cannot, other kin should help out; if other kin cannot provide all of the resources, it becomes the responsibility of others in the community to do so.

It may sound as if many people are forced to marry by social pressure, but this is not so; villagers assume, with ample reason, that their children want to get married, although young people, especially boys, do not always concur with their parents' enthusiasm for old-relationship marriage. As one put it, "Cent percent of the older people want old relationships, but maybe 60 percent of young people want a new-relationship marriage." As it happens, about 60 percent of the young people get new-relationship marriages. But it is not necessarily warranted to suppose that the 40 percent who marry a relative of some sort are marrying someone who holds no romantic allure for them. For although women of affinally related families convivially visit back and forth with their children in tow, potential spouses are supposed to maintain a good deal of social distance between them. This they are to do in spite of the fact that their elders may repeatedly dangle before them the prospect that they might someday marry and become sexual partners. Thus, in the very act of keeping the couple apart, elders recurrently call attention to, and to that extent intensify, their sexuality for one another.

This way of handling prospective spouses is congruent with villagers' treatment of sex generally. They take the view that all nonmarital sex is improper, but their treatment of sex, at least marital sex, is best described as earthy; consider this village proverb concerning wives, which I shall mention again when I discuss men's view of women: "When a woman feeds her husband, she is his mother; when she takes half of the burden of his troubles, she is his friend; when he enjoys her [has sexual relations with her], only then is she his wife."

The proverb employs a euphemism to speak of sexual intercourse, but to use the verb "enjoy" to describe it scarcely portrays sex as nasty. And if this proverb seems to convey a male-centered view of sex, perhaps I should note that villagers regard women as more highly sexed than men in that women are regarded as having an inborn desire to have children. Presumably the wife enjoys sex too.

The proverb also calls attention to marriage as a sexual relationship: only when he enjoys her is a woman actually being a man's wife. The sexuality of marriage is further emphasized in a shivaree that occurs on a couple's wedding night. The female relatives of each spouse sit in parallel rows forming a corridor leading to the house in which the couple will sleep. Then, with gales of laughter and repeated bawdy remarks, these otherwise proper women goad each spouse to present the other with flowers and other articles that are regarded, among other things, as items with which to display sexual attraction. When this is done, the women, with more laughter and more bawdy remarks, shut the couple into the bridal chamber.

This ritual would certainly not be part of the marriage of the daughter of wealthy villagers with pretensions to an urban way of life, but it is a commentary on marriage that ordinary farm people can relish once the Brahmin priest has gone home. I have described the ritual to dispel a myth. Some Westerners of a psychoanalytic turn of mind seem to believe that restrictions on the social situations and relationships in which sexual behavior may legitimately occur inevitably limit the intensity with which individuals can enjoy sex even in legitimized relationships. In short, people who limit sex to marriage are prudes.

This is not necessarily so, and it is important that we recognize that it is not if we are to understand the part played by marriage in Yaavahalli's culture. The fact that marriages are arranged, that economic and other practical considerations are often paramount in marital choice, and that elders strictly control the access of unmarried persons to one another does not mean that marriage for them is an emotionally dreary affair. On the contrary, village culture seems to heighten and focus the sexuality of the young on marriage. This does not mean that the culture always keeps its promises (no culture does); doubtless some young people are disappointed in their mates and in sex. But it is repeatedly made evident to the young that their sexuality is perfectly acceptable, provided they channel it through the marriage system regulated by the elders. To put it another way, villagers assume that people are bound to engage in sex and that arranged marriages provide an economically and reproductively responsible way for them to do so.

Marriages lead to families, and this presents couples with the question of how to rear and provision their children. The *dharmas* of the sexes provide the answer and lead us to a second assumption: the *dharmas* of the sexes constitute cultural amplifications of the reproductive function of women and of the physical strength of men. This assumption is supported by the following observations, which will provide an opportunity to describe the *dharmas* of women and men in greater detail.

In the last chapter I noted that villagers regarded my questions about the *dharmas* of the sexes as odd. Nobody but ethnographers would ask such questions because people—in most societies, one suspects— simply presume that even small children know what women are supposed to do and what men are supposed to do. But this does not mean that the biological rationales villagers offered for their sex roles are not a salient and recurrent feature of their culture, for as we shall now see, villagers cultivate and comment upon them in their portrayals of themselves as men and women.

The Dharma of Women

The chief points I would like to note concerning the *dharma* of women have to do with motherhood: it is a highly elaborate role, it is highly organized, and it may convey to woman a position of genuine power and authority.

ELABORATION

The least elaborate version of motherhood I know of is that of DuBois's unhappy Alorese (Dubois 1944), where mothers wean their children abruptly and devote rather little attention to them thereafter. In Yaavahalli, by contrast, a woman typically devotes copious attention to her children throughout her entire life. The bearing and nursing of them is but a passing phase, for she not only gives a good deal of attention to their development during childhood, but also arranges their marriages, organizes them to joint households, helps to deliver their infants, and arrogates to herself a warrant to give them advice no matter how old they are.

This is what villagers mean when they say that women "make" families. A corollary of the intense interest women cultivate in their children's welfare is that women seem to want their men to produce as much for their children's welfare as they possibly can. That is to say, women approve of men who cultivate the *dharma* of men, a matter to which we shall return presently.

The elaboration of motherhood in village culture is also found in moral and ritual contexts. Villagers glorify mothers as the most virtuous of persons, though some obviously are not. Indeed, villagers literally worship motherhood. This leads to the next point.

ORGANIZATION

It is late evening. A ritual is under way inside a small temple devoted to the *mane devaru*, "house deity," of a Vokkaliga patrilineage. It is the *Hosadevaru Puja* (literally, "new deity worship"), which is conducted annually by women of this *jaati* to insure the continued fertility of all life-giving female resources and beings associated with the lineage, its lands, its livestock, and themselves.

The deity being worshiped is, like almost all other lineage deities of the village, a mother goddess who, like her sisters but unlike the more abstruse male deities of the local pantheon, expresses her displeasure at immorality by visiting a disease upon the community. All of the celebrants in the ritual are women, the wives and unmarried daughters of the men of the lineage. The most senior married woman is the priestess, the other married women are her acolytes, and the unmarried girls are her disciples. These girls must learn the ritual before they marry, for after marriage they will be called upon to participate in the same ritual convo-

cation before the *mane devaru* of their husbands. After they marry they
will also be banished forever from the temple of their fathers' goddess.

Like most rituals these devotional Hindus perform, this one is a
colorful celebration, here a celebration of the reproductive power of
female sexuality; it is also a commentary on relations between the sexes.
While it is true that almost all women live patrilocally, that land and
livestock are mainly owned by men, and that men manage agriculture
and most of a household's external economic affairs, it is women who
manage their internal and reproductive affairs: they construe themselves
as managers of the circulation of women among male-managed patrilocal
family farms. The senior women in the ritual participated in the selection
of the younger ones, just as each mother present will play a central role
in the selection of her daughters' mates. Each daughter will be banished
from the temple of her natal goddess and required to worship the conjugal mother, the new deity, not because she is the chattel of a man and his
kin, but because the women view themselves as sharing a collective
fertility and a collective interest in the life-giving things on which their
children depend. It is in the gift of the new goddess to withhold or
bestow this fertility; to offend the supernatural mother-in-law with worship of one's natal goddess would jeopardize the fertility of all.

I suggest this interpretation of the *puja* because it is a woman's ritual
that only women know how to perform. It is, to my mind, just the sort
of ritual one might expect to find in a society in which women down the
centuries have been recurrently robbed of their children by famine and
disease, and one in which the welfare of children depends in part on the
capacity of women to share resources in households into which they
marry. I note this latter reason because this ritual, like others villagers
perform, requires participants to bury their differences for the time being. It does so because every *puja* must be planned in detail and the plans
must be carried out exactly to avoid sacrilege. Thus, both in its planning
and in the event, the *puja* fosters solidarity among participants.

It also conveys purity, just as most Hindu rituals do. Here, as it
often does, the purity pertains to food. The ritual is but the concluding
ceremony in a series of rituals, others of which involve the men as well.
The series takes some days to perform, and once it has begun, no one
may accept food from the hands of the women until they have completed
the climactic, concluding *puja*, nor may a woman cook food from the
newly harvested crop even for herself. This is inconvenient for the men
and presumably calls their attention to the domestic services women
provide during the remainder of the year.

Thus, the ritual offers a respite from dealing with men and with
children, a time-out from *being* a woman in which to contemplate being a
woman. And in so doing the ritual provides an elegant structural com-

mentary on the *dharma* of women. Women are to children as land is to food, the most important material resource on which the welfare of children depends. In order to secure the welfare of their children, the ritual suggests, women must coalesce in male-managed family farms, the sources of land. Because they do so through marriage, a threefold division or hierarchy among women is produced, and this hierarchy is replicated in the division of roles in the ritual: mother superior, bride, and daughter.

The frequency and timing with which these roles are created in household formation depends, of course, on the demographic features of particular households. But so long as households are formed in the patrilocal mode, they will contain these roles and no others, and these roles define the cleavages along which conflicts among women in households are most likely to occur. That is to say, disputes occur between persons in these roles not simply because these are the female positions characteristically present in households so that any conflict that does occur is bound to involve women in these roles, but because marriage and child bearing, the processes through which the roles are created, produce potentially divergent interests. Let me give a concrete example in which such cleavages are explicitly recognized by parties to a dispute.

It is late afternoon and Shama Rao and I are interviewing a middle-aged couple in their home. Nearby Rangamma, their only son's new bride, is preparing the evening meal. As we are talking, Maramma, their near-nubile daughter, returns from working as a *kuli* in the fields. When Rangamma first came to the village, her name appeared frequently as a *kuli* worker on daily reports of farm labor. As the weeks passed, her name gradually appeared less often, while Maramma's appeared with increasing frequency. Apparently this shift in the assignment of an undesirable task, *kuli* work, corresponded to a reverse shift in the assignment of desirable tasks, such as cooking, in favor of the bride, creating the grievance that Maramma aired shortly after her arrival.

As she entered the house, Maramma's mother asked her to bring a bundle of firewood stacked outside to Rangamma. The girl's face clouded over upon hearing this request, but she obeyed. Next, the mother asked Maramma to fetch water from the well, whereupon the girl burst into tears and turned on her mother, saying, "Those who have been cooking all day should fetch water." A brief, heated exchange followed between mother and daughter, which Shama Rao (and of course I) did not understand. The father then rose in a rage and said, "How dare you speak that way to the mother who bore you? Do you not love your brother? It is his wife who will be mother in this house. Someday you will be mother in your own house. Now, fetch the water."

This was the only case wherein so old a child directly disobeyed a parent in my presence, but it involves a kind of grievance to which village families are commonly heir, a quarrel about a division of tasks between persons of similar age and the same sex. The father's tirade contains instructions as to the proper division of roles among women. The mother is the legitimate authority; it is the daughter's duty to obey her. The bride, not the daughter, is the mother's heir, and efforts to show due respect for her status should not be taken as personal favoritism; eventually the daughter, as bride, will be due the same recognition.

I cannot say that participation in the *Hosadevaru Puja* settles such disputes, but it does require that they be set aside while the threefold division of status among women, noted in Maramma's father's tirade, is reified as the legitimate vehicle for organizing the *dharma* of women. It requires, for instance, that Maramma accept her status as novice in training to leave a ritual congregation of which Rangamma is a lifetime sister, a status difference mirrored in the roles of the two girls in the family. It is, moreover, an explicitly feminist institution that, through the exclusion of males, defines relations among women as the responsibility of women, which brings me to my next topic.

POWER

This ritual is unique to the Hosadevaru Vokkaligas, who derive their name and, to that extent, their identity from it. Nevertheless, the ritual serves as a commentary on the role of women in village society generally. Village women sometimes display the kinds of emotional distress we associate with the disease category "menopausal depression," but they do so most often as brides, not in middle age. A young bride who has not conceived or is unhappy with her new life for some other reason may be subject to periods of depression and tearfulness; villagers sometimes take these for symptoms of spirit possession and treat them with a long visit home, during which the girl can be cared for by her mother and her family's favorite shaman. Depression does not happen among middle-aged women very often, because most of them are in the process of reaping the benefits of family building of which the young bride fears she will be deprived. The menopausal woman is generally occupied with the arrangement of marriages and often with the supervision of new daughters-in-law in her newly won status as mother of the house. If anyone is likely to be happy in village society, she is, because she can look on the past with a sense of accomplishment and to the future with anticipation of security and respect.

In her office as mother of the house, a woman generally arrogates to herself control over all routine household consumption. She budgets food, no small matter in a community with a bitter history of food shortage. Indeed, elderly women in joint households continue as long as they can to prepare food or at least to supervise its preparation and distribution, so as to prevent quarrels among younger women concerning the portions their families receive. Mothers of the house also take a major hand, usually twice yearly, in distributions of clothing, though women in some of the more harmonious joint households seemed to regard their clothing virtually as a collective good and wore one another's apparel almost interchangeably. Perhaps most important, a mother of the house controls the organization of women and girls in the household, allocating tasks among them. I have already described women's influence over marital choice, which some may not view as an exercise of power. I have heard it said that whereas men use power (in the sense of controlling behavior through threat of duress) and hold positions of authority, positions in which the use of power is regarded as legitimate, women merely manipulate social relations to get what they want. It may be true that men have used more ruthless measures; they have certainly had more chances to do so. And those who invidiously characterize what may well be a fairly typical sex difference in political styles may view village women's matchmaking as evidence for their case. But to my mind social power is best defined as the capacity to get people to do what you ask them to do, and authority is measured by the extent to which people will do as you ask simply because you are who you are. In this sense the mother of a house is an authority, though the authority is based on acknowledged competence to manage affairs and not on force.

I have as yet said little about the productive role of women, though it is vital to the economy, as we shall see. I have emphasized the reproductive aspects of the *dharma* of women for a reason having to do with a matter mentioned earlier. Suppose you were a village woman whose lifelong interest lay in enhancing the welfare of her children. What sort of men would you like? I believe you would want men who pursue the *dharma* of men because no other kind would serve the material interests of your children as well, and because such men can do for you things you could not do so well for yourself.

A plausible case for this view can be made by looking at the inner workings of village technology, as we shall do later, but as it happens I have a bit of direct evidence consistent with the notion that village women actually view men as my argument says they ought to.

The Widows' Views of Men

One way of addressing the question of what women want from men is to look at the behavior of women who have no man and set out to get one

on their own, to determine what they try to get. There were at the time
of my stay three sonless widows in Yaavahalli. Each of them owned land,
which they turned over to tenants after they were widowed. Though the
tenants were helpful relatives who took a smaller share of the crop than
tenants might otherwise take, this arrangement still reduced a widow's
income, and she could not look to tenants to make agricultural improvements, or, one suspects, to take the management of her resources as
seriously as that of their own. As a remedy, each woman set out to get a
man. This is what they did.

Bayamma:

> After my husband died I had so many difficulties; I had no son in the house
> to look after the agriculture. After some time I brought Narayanappa [a
> brother's son] to take care of the agricultural work. I protected him for
> some years by working as a *kuli* because he was only seven when he came to
> me. And then he became able to do agricultural work. . . . After he began
> to do the agriculture, we began to get good crops.

Chenamma:

> I had three daughters but no sons, so I adopted [by marriage to her
> daughter] Mudanna [her husband's younger sister's son]. Then, after about
> ten years, Mudanna left his wife and went back to his father's house. Why?
> Because he asked me to register my lands in his name and I refused. I
> wouldn't agree because once he sold gold earrings of mine and mortgaged
> his wife's jewelry in Chikkaballapur for 60 rupees in order to get money for
> his girlfriends. [She goes on to describe her further trials with the scoundrel
> Mudanna, who had since made up with his wife.] Whatever happens I
> won't register my property to anyone else up to the last day of my life.

Tatahalli Sonamma:

> So I brought Kyatamma [her older brother's daughter's daughter] and her
> husband, Malappa, to live with me. Then Malappa [who had no land of his
> own] took care of the fields and he grew good crops. . . . During that time
> Malappa also dug one irrigation well, and he began to work hard in the
> gardens and earned good money. Then, about five years back, Malappa was
> bitten by a snake while working and died in five minutes. After his death I
> had many difficulties and fears about how I could rear these children. [After
> her husband's death Kyatamma ran away, no one knows where, leaving
> Sonamma to care for her three children, one of two cases I recorded of a
> woman abandoning her children. Sonamma speaks of one of these boys as
> follows] . . . Now my grandson is doing so much work in the fields. He is
> only fifteen, but he works day and night. He works as a *kuli* even in the
> rainy season. He has had so much trouble in his life, but he doesn't care.

He is working beyond his strength growing grain in the gardens and in the dry lands also. So now you see Ramappa [the grandson] protects us.

Faced with the problem of running a farm alone, these resourceful women responded by mobilizing kin ties to get themselves a man who could move into the role vacated by a deceased husband. In part, they were simply seeking a male worker to do the heavy work and thus obviate the need for tenant labor. But these women who owned land also reinvented male management of agriculture. Bayamma says she brought Narayappa in to look after her farming, something he began to do after he was able to do men's work. And after he began to "do the agriculture," they prospered. Malappa "took care of the fields" and "grew good crops" for Sonamma. Ramappa, at times baffled by the responsibilities thrust upon him, often turned to older male relatives for advice but was quickly learning to make his own way. Chenamma's inability to get Mudanna to behave did not derive so much from the fact that she was a woman trying to manage a man as from the fact that he had a ready economic alternative—his father's house. Elder men sometimes have similar problems with younger men, especially in irregular households that do not follow the patrilocal norm. Chenamma did not succumb to his wiles regarding registration of the land, though she implies that had he turned out to be a decent man, she might have.

It might be argued that these women got a man to manage their lands simply because they were not socialized to do it themselves. But that is beside the point. What is at issue is the question of why women are not socialized to manage agriculture. To answer this question we must examine the *dharma* of men.

The Dharma of Men

We have now seen that the cultural amplification of the female reproductive function is highly elaborated in Yaavahalli, both in the sense that the maternal caretaker role does not end with a child's maturation but continues into adulthood, and in the sense that motherhood is honored in ritual and, as you shall soon see, in proverb. Motherhood is also highly organized in that women act as regulators of the circulation of women among male-managed family farms and in that women are organized within joint households. The organization of women conveys power to the senior women who regulate it. Finally, I suggested that women want men to pursue the *dharma* of men. They like men who bend their backs to hard work and who manage agriculture proficiently. The men they dislike most are those who "give money to girlfriends." There were

Cooperative voluntary labor is used to build a stone fence for a public building. In speaking of his sister's husband, one informant said, "He was a good worker and a good man; see, in those days education and cleverness were not as important as they are today. People cared only about physical fitness, and that was the kind of groom everyone looked for." Direct comparisons of physical strength are drawn during operations like the one shown, and participants take pains to show their fitness. Note that only the American ethnographer is grimacing.

several men in the village who had been accused of having extramarital liaisons with prostitutes, and what irked women the most about them was not the sexual but the economic infidelity. What women want from men is that they create a secure material setting in which to bear and rear children. Note the way in which Bayamma and Sonamma use the verb "to protect": to work and provide for someone is to protect him or her. That is what women want from men, protection against poverty.

Similar themes of elaboration, organization, and power may be used in describing the *dharma* of men.

ELABORATION

If one spends much time in the fields with village men or talks to men at length about farming, it becomes evident that male strength is culturally amplified, not only in the allocation of tasks, but in a code of masculinity under which an individual's worth is judged by his capacity for hard work and his expertise as a farm manager. As an example of what I mean, consider the following scene:

A group of Harijan men are attempting to remove the stump of a large tamarind tree. Having chopped away the peripheral roots and dug around the main one, they are now attempting to dislodge the stump with long metal bars that they use as levers. Prior to each shove against these levers, they sing a short chant that may be freely translated as "Yo heave ho, what's the matter with you? Have you no mustache?"

The words of the song juxtaposed against the work the men are doing create a metaphor of manhood. Strength is described in terms of mustaches, a secondary sexual characteristic of males. To villagers a weak man is not effeminate; he is no more like a woman than a bullock is like a cow. While each lacks the positive characteristics of maleness—the mustache of a man, the large hump of the bull, the strength of either—they lack also the positive characteristic of female beings, their reproductive power. A weak man is, like a sterile woman, simply someone who is unable to fulfill the *dharma* of his gender.

Because men are stronger than women, villagers say, it falls to their *dharma* to do *kashta kelsa*, hard work. And just as the construction of households flows from the bearing of children as part of the *dharma* of women, it falls to the diggers, lifters, and plowers to manage agriculture.

Two alternative propositions in the literature that might be used to explain why men do *kashta kelsa* can be dispensed with immediately. The first would hold that heavy manual labor is incompatible with child care because it is done away from the home and because it is not readily interruptible. Therefore, it is inconvenient for women to do it, and so they leave it to men (Brown 1970). But village women do a great deal of agricultural work; indeed, women in the poorest fifth of the population spend as much time in the fields as many men, typically the equivalent of well over two hundred full days per year. Much of the agricultural work women do is incompatible with child care, but, as we shall see, very little of the farm work women do is *kashta kelsa*, though villagers would agree with Brown that domestic chores are assigned to women because they are mothers. That accounts for their lower overall participation in agriculture, but it does not explain why they do little heavy work. The other proposition holds that communities assigning dangerous tasks to women are at a reproductive disadvantage because they place their women and children in jeopardy (Burton et al. 1976). But most of the the difficult work men do is not dangerous, or at least men are rarely injured doing it, and so that proposition too leads nowhere in Yaavahalli, though it may hold elsewhere.

Either the men are stronger than their women, and hence are assigned the heavier tasks in agriculture, or the sexual division of labor
makes no sense in material terms at all. So far as village men are concerned, it is self-evident that they are the stronger sex, a point they make
in many instances of masculine posturing, though most are more subtle
than the man described in Chapter 2. For example, a man may, in the
course of discussing farm work, describe a task as "too easy," as boring
because it does not really tax his ability. Likewise, it was not uncommon
to see young unmarried men flexing their muscles in public, displays
village elders regarded as unseemly arrogance, perhaps because they sus-
pected that young men engaged in them to impress the girls.

This behavior is, it seems to me, rather typical of men's culture in
societies where men focus their attention on one or more activities that
are most exclusively male domains in cultures around the world.
Women's roles characteristically require the capacity to shift attention
from one thing to another, to note affect in others, and to deal with the
complex and ambiguous social situations that so often occur in the domestic affairs of human settlements. Men's culture, by comparison, is
frequently riveted on doing some one thing, on doing it well, and on
endlessly redundant commentaries on doing it. As a result male definitions of self are likely to focus on a trait or traits that are adaptive in the
restricted context of this activity, traits such as courage, skill in tracking
and shooting animals, or, as in this case, the capacity to do heavy manual
labor.

So it is that men's culture in many places comes to reflect a morality
of the moment. Men are judged in terms of how well they do some one
thing and the extent to which they display some trait that is useful for
doing it, which is a limited way of judging people. When village men say
that a man has no mustache, or worse, call him a eunuch, it is as if they
are saying that no other feature of his character can redeem him. That is,
I believe, precisely what they mean. If he is a peasant farmer, no amount
of generosity or kindness or religious devotion can redeem a man who is
incapable of heavy toil in the tropical sun. They focus on this trait
because their lives are myopically focused on an enterprise in which it is
genuinely adaptive. As a man matures, however, the worth ascribed to
him by others (and by himself) increasingly shifts to the expertise he
displays as a farm manager.

Men of Yaavahalli pridefully tell the visitor that they are canny,
skillful farmers. But when asked to tell their life history and that of their
forefathers, they spin tales of failure, of ruined crops and foolish decisions. Part of the reason men's work in Yaavahalli, as in many places, is
narrowly riveted on one enterprise is that men's work is often work that
fails. To fail as a social fact is to fail someone, one's self or somebody

else: every man knows that some men have stood in the dock of failure as farmers in the eyes of others. Whatever else happens, a man does not wish to stand in that dock, knowing it is said that he failed because he was weak or foolish or lazy. And so he adopts the dour demeanor that led Buchannan, who walked through the area in the nineteenth century, to write of the farmers of Mysore as the Scots of India. By portraying oneself as canny and frugal and, above all, by working hard, one attributes imminent failure to chance, and not to oneself, before it happens.

Men single-mindedly focus on one enterprise, then, in part because farming is inherently problematic and men are responsible for managing the enterprise. Work is a morally significant act to others and to oneself, and because, as we shall discover, the heavy work men do has a special economic significance in farm technology, it has a special moral significance to those who do it. Men also concentrate their attention on the farm enterprise because the management of other men is one of the most problematic aspects of farming.

ORGANIZATION

In speaking of relations among men of the same household, men's culture employs a dynastic vocabulary. Joint families are portrayed as the descendants of ancestors who created the farm firm through their toil. The Kannada term *vamsharuksha*, generally glossed as "genealogy," is, in the village, interpreted as a mutation record of patrilineal inheritance. When asked why the *vamsharuksha* I had elicited from him contained no female relatives, one man replied, "What has *vamsharuksha* to do with females? *Vamsharuksha* has to do with land!" There are no customary prohibitions against women owning land, nor is the interpretation used in a manner demeaning to women, for what a *vamsharuksha* contains is promises kept between men. A man's authority over his sons is legitimized by his labor on their behalf. Land is lost when families become so financially strapped that they must sell it. It is bought by those who have saved enough money to buy it. Money is saved through unusually high crop yields; by additional labor invested, through tenancy, in the lands of others; or by the construction of a well, which increases the annual productivity of land fivefold. High crop yields come from unusually careful preparation of land, and fields are prepared by men. Tenants are hired primarily because some men own more land than they can prepare adequately themselves, and so they hire other men for the additional labor. Wells, which increase yields, are dug by men. Thus, if a man bequeaths an estate larger and better irrigated than the one he inherited, his sons owe the improvement to their father. And so an intimate connection is made between patrilineal inheritance and paternal authority:

older men tell younger men to obey their fathers because the fathers have worked for them. The father, in turn, tells his sons to cleave to one another and not to divide the estate. As far as men's culture is concerned, a joint family, "a united house," is defined by the fact that two or more men are "working together in unity." Such households come to be patrilocal joint families because men stay with their parents when they marry.

Hence, the organization of males, at least as it is portrayed in the social realities men create in talking about their affairs, is a patriarchy. Just as a woman aspires to become a mother of the house, a matriarch who regulates the lives of younger women, a man aspires to become a *yajaman,* a male head of household who directs the activities of a younger man or men, preferably his sons, in a productive joint family farm, one that will endure until his death and hopefully survive it.

POWER

A man's success in doing this is by no means a foregone conclusion. He faces two basic problems, the first of which is the transformation of boys into men. Whereas girls move gradually into the responsibilities of womanhood and achieve substantial competence by mid-adolescence, the socialization of boys is subject to a marked discontinuity. Perhaps because it is associated with masculinity, village boys seem to romanticize *kashta kelsa;* at least they play games that imitate it. The reality of *kashta kelsa* is aching exhaustion and the prospect of more to come on following days, days that, during the peak plowing and planting season, may stretch into weeks with little remission. A boy must become desensitized to this toil if he is to achieve adult competence.

The modal period from the point at which a boy really begins the work of men to the time of his marriage is roughly five years. The fact that boys remain or are supposed to remain celibate during this period is both a resource and a problem. Boys are told that they must prove themselves as workers in order to marry and that their marital prospects turn in part on agricultural improvements made in the interval. The direct connection drawn between hard work and sexual access to a girl through marriage may stimulate successful adaptation. On the other hand, parents fear that a son may do something rash during this period, that he may seduce a village girl or steal money to visit prostitutes, because some boys do. More realistically, they are afraid that he will simply spend too much time in trivial pursuits with his friends. Fathers therefore try to divert boys' attention from peer groups, in which these bad behaviors are organized, towards the matter of learning to work and manage a farm. This is not always easily done.

The second problem a village father faces if he has more than one son lies in maintaining harmony among them in later years. In examining tales of joint household partition, I tried to determine who was most blamed for the final rupture. Interestingly, in almost all cases a party blamed by his relatives blamed himself in his own life history. Later I asked an American research assistant to judge these texts in the same way. Though we differed on a few cases, she and I agreed on a major point. Cross-sex disputes, though mentioned, were rarely regarded as the proximate causes of household partition. In about half of the cases, partition was ascribed to recurrent quarreling among women. The other half were attributed to disputes among men. This is noteworthy in view of the advantage, as villagers see it, that males usually enjoy of having been reared together. Moreover disputes among males appeared to have smoldered over long periods and erupted into acts of economic violence so serious as to make household partition, itself an act of pyrrhic aggression, inevitable. Early household partitions that lead young, inexperienced couples to establish independent households were particularly likely to be caused by fraternal disputes. Thus, males appear to be the less manageable sex.

Perhaps this is why senior men often employ a sternly patriarchal and rather florid rhetoric in dealing with younger men, a nice example of which may be found in the following bits of text drawn from a family history recounting a grandfather's reaction to the division of his great household:

> From the time of Mare Gauda [a village founder], our forefathers worked in unity. We lived as one house of sixty members. . . . For 170 years our elder and younger brothers were a model for this village. . . . We followed the doctrine of obeying the elders. . . . I tell you, children poured from the vase of one mother should not quarrel; do not divide the united temple into many parts! . . . But a house having sixty *ankanas* [spaces between roof beams] was reduced to powder.

Note the ornate imagery. In an extension of the common metaphor of household as house, the speaker likens household members to an architectural feature (*ankanas*) of the house they share, so that the division of the household may be portrayed as the total destruction of a building. And not only are household members viewed as consubstantial with their home, but the sons who quarrel, while of their father's seed, are a common substance "poured from the vase of one mother," a powerful image in a society in which it is a serious offense indeed to offend one's mother.

I would not for a moment suggest that texts elicited by an ethnographer or noted from conversations he overheard constitute an adequate sample of the utterances of a speech community. But so far as I can tell, pontification of the sort illustrated by the previous example is absent from the dialogue of women. However, if older men regard such sermonizing as necessary to keep younger men in line, they also recognize that quarrels among women divide households too. This brings me to men's view of women.

Men's View of Women

Just as women appear to prefer men to pursue the *dharma* of men, men approve of women who in their view pursue the *dharma* of women properly.

Village men do not talk about women as women; they talk about women in roles. About mothers they say, "A mother's love is greater than a god's." About wives they say, "When a woman feeds her husband, she is his mother; when she takes half of the burden of his troubles, she is his friend; when he enjoys her, only then is she his wife." About elder sisters they say, "Elder sister guards her younger brother like a mother." I asked seven men to rank-order kin terms under four terms of affect: love, trust, friendship, and respect. His mother turned out to be by far the most trusted person in a man's life. Mother is respected as much as anyone else, she is loved about equally with father, children, and spouse, but she is not a friend. The wife ranks high on all terms; most particularly, she is often regarded as a man's best friend. The elder sister ranks above the rank-order mean of all kin, male and female, on all four terms and is especially high on love and trust.

Women in these roles are clearly morally superior individuals in a village man's life. Note that he trusts and loves all of them, his mother most of all, and that the proverbs attribute to all of them an element of motherliness. Note too that the wife role is highly variegated: she is nurturer, ally, and lover.

Such is not the talk of men who regard women as inferior beings. In examining many thousands of words of Kannada text from interviews with men, I could not find a single statement attributing moral or intellectual inferiority of any sort to women in general. One does find, however, references to women's arguing with one another, and the women who are blamed for such behavior are usually other men's wives. The two most *mistrusted* persons in the rank order of kin are younger brother's wife and son's wife. Elder men are simply scared witless of the divisive power of young women. The modest demeanor South Indian village women present to outsiders is in many ways a facade. Observing their behavior among intimates, one is left with the feeling that they are so verbally gifted that they could talk anybody into anything. An older man remembers full well how he looked forward to the end of enforced sexual abstinence that his own marriage brought, and his own wife, in all likelihood, gives him a good deal of advice. Older men therefore have few illusions about the influence junior wives exercise over their husbands.

As a household's resources are strained by the birth of the next generation of children, people have more to quarrel about. Each mother is preoccupied with fostering her own children's interests, even though the women of the house know the advantages of joint family living as well as anybody else. But as time passes and the elders turn over more and more responsibility to junior members of the household, more and more power falls into the hands of persons who have vested interests in the allocation of resources. As noted earlier, the one task mothers of the house reserve to themselves as long as possible is the preparation and distribution of food because it is the one thing young mothers concerned for their children's welfare are most apt to fight about.

Older men's attribution of querulousness to younger women, then, reflects as much as anything else the fact that competition among women for scarce resources tends to involve immediate, everyday interests. A woman can end all of that by becoming mother of her own house, and if matters become bad enough she will press her husband to demand his share of the estate.

Gerontocracy and Collective Rationality

We have now seen that villagers of both sexes are in general agreement about the features of appropriate sex roles but that elders worry a good deal about their ability to control the behavior of younger household members. The principal dimension of domestic power in Yaavahalli is not that of sex but that of age.

The sexual division of labor is the most stable institution of village life, by which I simply mean that it is the most invariant. Not only are certain tasks virtually always performed by members of one sex, but the sexual division of labor is the only materially important institution that is never argued about. Women and men may criticize one another for failing to perform their appointed roles properly, but they never quarrel about the appropriateness of that division of costs and benefits itself. Relations between the sexes are better viewed not as hierarchical, but as parallel and interdependent. The *dharmas* of the sexes provide all of the complementary skills and services needed to farm, to rear children, and to form a joint household under the leadership of the *yajaman* and the mother of the house.

A senior couple's ability to build and maintain a joint household depends, however, on a chain of authority based on relative age. The first principle is that children should obey their parents, even when they become adults. But peace and order are maintained by extending this chain of authority down the hierarchy of relative age to the youngest household member, so that older children are told to give younger ones "advice in the proper manner" and younger ones are told to obey. Because kinship terminology explicitly distinguishes relative age for all reciprocal kin terms, a child quickly learns his position in the rank order of seniority in the family, so that he knows whom to advise and whom to obey. As a result, most children begin to practice elderhood from an early age as parent surrogates who assist the busy parents by looking after younger children. Thus, the very act of obeying one's parents may confer on a child the opportunity to adopt a valued senior role.

This way of legitimizing gerontocracy in family relations also lends legitimacy to models for behavior ascribed to the "ancient people," the "elders," or the "forefathers." The central theme running through these models is the injunction to subordinate private interests to those of the family in support of the united temple as a collective.

Allocations of tasks and rewards in this family collective are made by the *yajaman* and the mother of the house on the principle of "to each according to his need and from each according to his ability," where needs and abilities are defined chiefly according to age and sex. It is difficult to overstress the scrupulousness with which this standard is employed in many families, for food, clothing, and other consumer goods are generally divided in a strictly even way between persons of the same sex or of similar age. Indivisible goods are equally shared by those who may enjoy their use.

Close adherence to these collectivist principles creates a moral order in which self-serving or invidious behavior is uniformly and promptly scorned. What is more, evidence of the wisdom of these principles is abundant in the greater prosperity joint households appear to enjoy. This collective good in which the members of a joint household share is used to justify the policies elders endorse for the continuation of families through marriage and inheritance. The teachings of the elders serve the interest of all; adherence to them is thus a collectively rational act, or so the elders claim.

The dialectics of family development, however, are such that the teachings of the elders carry the seeds of joint household partition, for their ultimate basis is the *dharmas* of the sexes, the parallel productive and reproductive interests of couples, which are newly constructed with every marriage.

The teachings of the elders best serve the nepotistic interest of a married couple in the welfare of all their children and grandchildren. In the pursuit of this goal, they must ask children to make sacrifices for one another that may lead to resentment. This will continue as the grandchildren are born, for the mother of the house will insist that the children of a more fertile couple be cared for as well as those of a less fertile couple. But because the concerns of each couple for their own children are like those that led the senior couple to form the family in the first place, conflicting reproductive interests may eventually divide the household, thus spawning new collectives.

Yet perhaps the elders of Yaavahalli succeed well enough, for the *dharmas* of the sexes and the teachings of the elders provide a highly proficient way of harnessing the abilities of women and men to support continued reproduction, as we shall now see.

Biocultural Materialism and the Teachings of the Elders

Under what conditions might the teachings of the elders guide villagers towards proficient behavior? The thrust of my argument in answer to this question was outlined in the first chapter, and the germs of its substance lie in materials discussed in the past two. In following chapters I shall develop the argument in detail through six propositions that I shall summarize presently. Before I do so, a few further remarks about the general character of the argument may be helpful. It is biocultural in that it treats biological sex differences as material conditions of society. It also falls well within the guidelines of the research strategy Harris (1979) calls cultural materialism. Let me explain.

Harris suggests that ethnographers make four classes of statements in their work. Gangappa's lecture was an "emic/behavioral" phenomenon that I reported: he made an empirical statement about the advantages of joint households that may be operationalized and tested. Moral notions used to justify domestic policy are what Harris would call "emic/mental" phenomena: one cannot demonstrate that a mother's love is greater than a god's; our interest in the proverb lies in the way it is used to control behavior. My exploration of these "emic" phenomena led me to the "etic/mental" proposition that the strategies villagers advocate yield the benefits claimed for them, provided certain conditions are met. Our quest to determine if these conditions are met will lead us into the "etic/behavioral" domain, in which we shall examine the ways villagers were observed to farm and to rear and organize their children.

Throughout I shall argue that villagers employ ideological or "superstructural" elements of their culture, such as the *Hosedevaru Puja,* to justify and comment upon structural procedures used in forming and managing domestic groups. These procedures occur in response to what Harris would label the physical, "infrastructural" conditions that impinge on the process of farming to rear families of farmers. Note that in the last sentence I use the phrase "occur in response to," and not "are determined by." Villagers are not to be viewed as hapless victims of forces beyond their ken or control but as decisive actors who manage their behavior in response to the biological, demographic, and environmental conditions I shall discuss. My purpose is to show that they know what they are doing.

To begin, the *dharmas* of the sexes make little economic sense, as I have already suggested, unless the biological rationale attributed to the *dharma* of men is empirically realistic. If the men are not systematically stronger than the women, then not only do villagers allocate their labor in an energetically inefficient way, but the rationale they offer for male management of agriculture is fatuous.

Therefore, in the next chapter I shall discuss at some length the question of whether the men are stronger than the women with whom they live. This chapter is addressed largely to those who doubt that sexual dimorphism has much to do with sexual divisions of labor. While I can offer no conclusive, direct evidence to support the proposition that village men are in fact stronger, I can establish grounds for regarding this as a reasonable working assumption, and the discussion will provide a way of clearing up some common misunderstandings concerning the role of sexual dimorphism in divisions of labor.

A second proposition holds that men in fact do most of the heavy manual labor for which their greater strength is advantageous. Here we shall find that the empirical evidence, much of it based on direct observations of work in the fields, is rather strong.

The third proposition has to do with the role of heavy manual labor in agriculture. There is no inherent relation between the amount of energy expended in a task and its productivity, but it turns out that heavy manual labor in village farming has a strong bearing on yields per acre. Therefore, its efficient allocation is crucial to farm productivity, which means that the proper allocation of men's time is crucial. Interestingly, this also explains why women's farm work has become so important in Yaavahalli. By undertaking many tasks that do not require so much physical strength, some of them jobs at which women appear more proficient than men, women free men for heavy labor, which consumes about half of men's working time throughout the prime of life.

These propositions lay the groundwork for a fourth, concerning the male management of agriculture. Because the allocation of heavy manual labor has a strong bearing on farm production, and because most of this work is done in the preparatory stages of cultivation, an optimal allocation of heavy labor can be best achieved when decided upon jointly with other factor allocations. Because men do heavy work, they are in an experientially more favorable position than women to make these decisions.

In short, the *dharma* of men is a cultural amplification of their physical strength, which accounts for the fact that women readily cede the management of farming to men; the *dharma* of men, when implemented, enhances the economic security of women and their children.

A fifth proposition states that households containing two or more adult working males outproduce those containing only one by a wide margin. Having shown that this appears to be the case beyond a peradventure of a statistical doubt, I shall consider the reasons it may be so. As it happens, the economic advantages enjoyed by joint family households stem from many factors, but perhaps the most important of these is the fact that men gain expertise in farm management over the years, while their physical abilities decline somewhat. Thus, households containing at least one experienced farm manager and at least one robust younger man to implement his elder's instructions tend to be highly proficient units of production.

At this point only one further proposition is required for the reasons for the later marriage age of males and the preference for patrilocality to become evident, so that the remaining teachings of the elders fall plausibly into line. A later age at marriage for males and patrilocality are both widespread phenomena, which suggests that a variety of factors may favor them. But in Yaavahalli I suspect that the biological circumstances of male development are the key factor. Boys reach maturity later than girls. What is more, the socialization of boys is more problematic than that of girls because boys' peer groups tend to engage in the kind of rough and tumble play that is incompatible with farm work. When boys reach mid-adolescence, therefore, men are faced with the problem of radically altering their behavior if they are to be socialized into adult behavior quickly. Their rapid socialization into heavy work is favored both by the benefits to a household of exploiting the energies of what soon will become the strongest members of the community, its young men, and by the marital criteria imposed by parents of prospective brides, who demand that grooms prove themselves as workers as a precondition for marriage. Thus, the later marriage age of males.

The presence of two or more working males in a household greatly increases farm production, and therefore any factor that enhances the authority of the senior man and the solidarity of the men of a household favors the continuation of this productive advantage. Patrilocality does this. Ordinarily no one is in a better position to effectively manage a young man's behavior than the father who reared him.

Once the biocultural foundations for patrilocality are specified, the remaining teachings of the elders are accounted for easily. Thus, biologically generalized secondary sex differences—dimorphism in physical strength and sexual bimaturism—are culturally amplified in such a way as to ramify throughout the entire order of domestic life, conveying to it its characteristic form for reasons that only become apparent when the organization of village technology is subjected to careful examination.

Let us now turn to that examination.

chapter 4

Kashta Kelsa

In this chapter we will investigate the first two of the propositions just noted. These two propositions, taken together, deal with the general question of whether the constitutional rationale villagers offer for the assignment of *kashta kelsa* to men is empirically sound.

> Proposition 1. *Village men tend to have considerably greater iso-metric muscular strength and aerobic work capacity than the women with whom they reside.*

No direct measures of villagers' physical strength are available, one of the many defects in this study alluded to earlier. Even so, we can examine some of the issues at stake in this proposition and consider data relevant to these issues drawn from other populations. On the basis of this examination, I believe, it may be reasonably argued that the proposition would probably be supported were direct measures of villagers' physical abilities available. At the least, in other words, it is an empirically realistic assumption on which to premise the remainder of the argument.

The issues at stake in this proposition are evident in its wording. First there are the terms "isometric muscular strength" and "aerobic work capacity." For my argument concerning the sexual division of labor to be sustained, I must specify the ways in which village men are stronger than the women with whom they live.

It should be noted that we are dealing here with heavy manual labor in which movement of the worker's entire body mass is a secondary, sometimes an incidental, aspect of the work done. The manipulation of tools and other materials external to the body matters more than walking. That is why the comparisons between women's and men's world records in various athletic events sometimes cited in popular articles dealing with sex differences in physical ability are largely irrelevant for our purposes. To sensibly compare male and female athletic performance, one must use events for which women have received training similar to that received by men and for which there are physical standards of performance expressed, for example, in time, distance, or weight. These restrictions limit comparisons mostly to swimming and running events, sports in which the objective is to maximize the speed with which the body, and the body alone, is moved over a distance.

Such comparisons do not, in my view, sustain the claim of some that sex differences in the performance of these sports are small, or becoming smaller, or due chiefly to cultural factors. But that is beside the point because they do not measure the kind of capacity that is pertinent to doing *kashta kelsa*. Isometric muscular strength and aerobic work capacity are as directly measurable as the acuteness of one's sight or hearing, and they directly influence an individual's capacity to perform heavy manual labor.

Measures of isometric muscular strength gauge a person's anaerobic capacity to lift, push, pull, or squeeze; that is, they measure, for instance, how much you can lift with maximum effort, not how long you can maintain a given level of effort. The devices used to measure muscular strength in laboratory situations may be regarded as proxies for the tools and other objects people encounter in the course of ordinary manual labor.

Aerobic or external work capacity is an estimate of an individual's capacity to consume oxygen in the sustained production of externally applied kinetic energy. Estimates of aerobic work capacity are typically obtained by placing an individual on a bicycle ergometer or a treadmill. These instruments allow the researcher to measure the amount of work a subject is doing while simultaneously measuring his heart rate. Data obtained in this way are used to estimate an individual's maximum oxygen uptake and thus his aerobic work capacity; the more oxygen you can process per minute, the more external work you can do, a reliable index of the levels of strenuous effort you can achieve and sustain in sports or manual labor.

Studies dealing with Western populations indicate substantial sex differences in these two measures, differences that cannot be dismissed as artifacts of cultural conditioning, but that appear to stem from genetically based phenotypic traits. The differences probably occur mainly because men are systematically larger than women, because a greater proportion of their body mass is composed of bone and muscle, because their hearts are larger relative to body mass than women's, and because their blood tends to have greater oxygen transport capacity.

It is often said that populations of Western European origin display a comparatively high degree of sexual dimorphism. I wonder about the empirical basis for that notion, because my review of the literature suggests that sexual dimorphism is among the least studied topics in physical anthropology. Nevertheless, assume that the studies we will now exa-mine do involve relatively dimorphic populations, and entertain two questions. First, is there any reason to believe that Yaavahalli's popula-tion is less sexually dimorphic than Western ones with respect to the ability to perform heavy manual labor? Second, how much less dimor-phic would the people of Yaavahalli have to be in order for men to lose any systematic advantage over coresident women in muscular strength or external work capacity?

One of the few studies of isometric muscular strength in women, by Rohmert and Jenik (1971), involved only ten subjects, but they were all tested for fitness and found to be healthy. They were young (the average age was twenty) and of at least average height and weight for American women, and there is no reason to believe that their participation in the study was not well motivated. The researchers involved them in the study by explaining its purpose and procedures, and the subjects were paid for their time.

While results varied among the eighteen different dynometer mea-sures of muscular strength, the average mean value of the physical strength of these women over the eighteen tests was about two-thirds of male norms of the sort long employed in industrial design. Because the authors did not provide any information concerning the variance of strength among subjects used to establish male norms, the degree of over-lap between the sexes cannot be estimated. However, if variation among male subjects is similar to that found in this sample of women, the overlap is probably not very great. For example, in terms of one-armed pulling and pushing strength, the female mean was 61 percent of the male norm, with a range of 44 to 72 percent. Since the strongest woman in this group was so far below the male norm in this respect, it seems unlikely that she would be much stronger than the weakest individual in a comparable sample of male subjects from the same population.

Studies comparing the aerobic work capacities of men and women have been more extensive than those comparing muscular strength. Not-able among them is that of Irma Astrand (1967). It is notable not only because it involved a large sample (350) of people of all ages, but also because it seems to have been conducted with careful screening of sub-jects and included a large number of highly trained physical education students (and a few competitive athletes) of both sexes. This last feature of the study is important because it offers some control over cultural influences on the physical ability of women and men. It is sometimes said that the greater strength of men is due as much to their greater involvement in sports and manual labor as it is to any constitutional difference between the sexes. Astrand's study suggests that this simply is not so.

The proportional difference between the aerobic work capacities of eighty-six female and male physical education students was actually somewhat greater than that between men and women of similar age in the entire sample. That finding is consistent with other studies suggesting that males are somewhat more responsive to physical training than females. Physical education students achieved much higher maximum oxygen uptake than other individuals of the same age and sex, although it is not possible to distinguish the portion of this difference that was due to physical training from the constitutional advantage these students might have enjoyed over other people even if they had not undertaken a program of training, for it is likely that people who choose to make a career of physical education tend to have better than average athletic ability in the first place.

It also seems likely that the physical education students, whose mean age was over twenty, had long experience with athletic competition, were familiar with the equipment used in the research, and were people for whom physical fitness was an important aspect of self-esteem. Therefore, there appears to be no reason to believe that the women students were intimidated by the experiment or that they were not strongly motivated to do their best. In spite of their physical training and in spite of the likelihood that these women would have been better than average performers even without their training, the mean maximum oxygen uptake for the women students was almost one standard deviation below that of men the same age in the general sample. The age-specific mean for women in general was roughly equal to the mean for males of that age minus two standard deviations.

Until about age fifteen, there were no significant differences between the aerobic work capacities of the sexes. But at about that age, according to Astrand's data, the aerobic work capacity of boys underwent a rapid exponential growth. By the mid-teens the age-specific mean work capcity of boys was considerably above that of girls, a sex difference that was sustained through the later years. While the work capacity of both sexes declined slowly with age, women of a given age had about 70 to 75 percent of the work capacity of men of the same age. There was an overlap between the sexes, but in Astrand's study men aged sixty-five still had an average maximum oxygen uptake equivalent to that of a woman of twenty-five. The greater aerobic work capacity of men is due not only to their greater lean body mass, but also to the fact that their hearts are larger relative to body mass (accounting for their greater oxygen pulse, that is, the amount of oxygen leaving the heart with each beat), and to the greater oxygen transport capacity of their blood. The amount of hemoglobin per unit of blood is a determinant of transport capacity, and women lose hemoglobin through menstruation.

These studies of isometric muscular strength and aerobic work capacity suggest that, in Western populations, there is probably a substantial constitutional difference between the capacities of women and men to perform heavy manual labor.

Other studies of muscular strength and aerobic work capacity in Western populations are consistent with those I have cited. Some, such as Tanner's (1955) measures of the development of muscular strength in adolescence, show greater sex differences; none, to my knowledge, fails to show a systematic male advantage. These data should not be interpreted as indicating the *generalized* inferiority of women as manual workers. In other respects women are superior to men. They mature sooner, are less vulnerable to most diseases, and tend to live longer. In addition to their longer working lives, there is evidence suggesting that women display greater physical flexibility and greater manual dexterity and tactile sensitivity than men. With respect to the capacity to perform heavy manual labor, however, there appears little doubt that males in these populations enjoy a genetically programmed advantage due to morphological sex differences that emerge in puberty.

Are sex differences in physical strength for Yaavahalli's population substantially less than those of Western peoples? The anthropometric literature comparing men and women from the same South Indian populations is rather scanty. Usually the only measures available that have any bearing on this discussion have to do with height. Although the ratio between the mean heights of women and men varies somewhat among South Indian populations, women of the region tend to be about 8 percent shorter than their male caste mates. That finding is consistent with what I observed in Yaavahalli, a sex difference in height that is not much less than that found among Americans.

I could not find adequate data on either body weight or proportion of fat to total weight comparing men and women of the *jaatis* found in Yaavahalli. However, there is no question that the men of Yaavahalli tend to be extremely lean compared to American men. Women also tend to be leaner than their Western counterparts, though the difference appears to be less pronounced. It seems likely, then, that while village women are closer to their men in terms of total body weight than American women are to American men, the ratio of female to male lean body mass is not greatly different from that found in the United States.

Lean body mass is a major determinant of muscular strength. The muscular strength advantage of American men is due chiefly to the fact that they are substantially larger than American women. Thus, if, as I believe to be the case, the lean body mass of village men is considerably greater on the average than that of village women, it is likely that their muscular strength is considerably greater as well, unless some other factor can be found that counteracts their advantage in size.

Research on work physiology is under way in India, and studies have been published dealing with aerobic work capacity in Indian populations. Unfortunately, the studies with which I am familiar employed only male subjects and none dealt specifically with South Indian farm workers. But while there are no data bearing on populations that might be similar to that of Yaavahalli, there are reasons to suspect that the sex difference in aerobic work capacity among villagers is as great as that Astrand found in her study. In addition to being smaller than men, women typically must support more body fat per unit of lean body mass; as I have suggested, villagers appear to be more sexually dimorphic in this respect than Americans. This is merely a guess based on my observations, which could be quite wrong, but one might expect to observe greater dimorphism in this respect where people work hard, often under nutritional stress. Women athletes apparently cannot train off fat as readily as male athletes can, and there may be a straightforward biological basis for this. Reduction of body fat in women beyond a certain point impairs fertility. The physiological capacity to retain enough body fat to insure successful reproduction in spite of exercise and some nutritional stress thus appears to be a basic part of the female biogram. Hence, we might expect to find the sex difference in the ratio of body fat to lean body mass to increase in communities like Yaavahalli much as it does among athletes. This increase would further somewhat the male advantage in strenuous exercise.

I do not know that village men's hearts are larger relative to body mass than those of village women, but since this sex difference appears to be typical of populations elsewhere, there is no reason to believe that it, with the advantage in oxygen pulse it conveys upon men, does not occur among villagers.

Finally, there are reasons to believe that the difference in the oxygen transport capacity of women's and men's blood is greater in Yaavahalli than in better-nourished populations. One of the most common complaints heard in our first-aid practice was of *sustu,* a general lethargy that local physicians attributed to anemia and vitamin deficiencies (those individuals to whom we provided sustained doses of vitamins and iron reported an improvement in their condition). While *sustu* was an endemic problem in the community for both sexes, only women complained of faintness during periods of exertion so severe as to force them to discontinue their work.

I do not believe this difference in the effects of *sustu* on women and men was due to a temperamental difference between the sexes. Everyone is reared under an extremely puritanical work ethic, and both men and women continued to work with injuries and ailments that would have immobilized many Westerners. The very fact that occasionally a woman would work until she felt she was about to faint, or actually fainted, attests to the psychological capacity of village women to endure hardship. Thus, there seems to be no reason to believe that women complained of severe symptoms more often than men because their culture had made complainers of them. What seems more likely is that when an already anemic individual experiences further hemoglobin loss through menstruation, the effect on the oxygen transport capacity of her blood can become rather serious. Therefore, a sex difference that is of relatively minor importance in well-nourished populations in terms of its impact on work capacity may be more pronounced in communities where anemia is endemic. It is possible, then, that the sex difference in aerobic work capacity among villagers may be somewhat greater than that found in Astrand's study because of this prevalent nutritional problem.

Our chief concern, as I noted earlier, is whether it is reasonable to assume that when villagers say men are stronger than women, they are speaking of a material condition of society that would be confirmed by independent measurement. I can see no reason to believe that the sex differences in isometric muscular strength and aerobic work capacity are not sufficiently large to make the average village man substantially better suited to heavy manual labor than the average village woman. But a question remains concerning the possible overlap between the sexes in the distribution of these capabilities. The specification in the first proposition that village men tend to be considerably stronger than the women *with whom they reside* has a strong bearing on this issue.

In an industrial society in which jobs are filled from pools of applicants, nonsexist employment practices would dictate that some women be given preference over some men in jobs requiring substantial physical strength because some women will be stronger than some men. Moreover, the amount of overlap between the sexes in the distributions of muscular strength and work capacity may increase as one draws workers from ever larger and more heterogeneous pools of applicants.

But in communities in the domestic mode of production, people work in and for domestic groups. Thus, the degree of overlap between the sexes with respect to physical strength in the population at large is much less germane than the question of whether men are stronger than the women with whom they live. I have no doubt that Venktamma, the wife of the strongest man in the village, was stronger in every way than elderly little Nagappa, probably the weakest man among the village's active farm workers. But this fact is irrelevant because, given the way village farming is managed, no one would ever be faced with a choice between Venktamma and Nagappa in assigning *kashta kelsa*. In Venk-

Above and on facing page: Bridal couples displaying a range of height differences typical of spouses. The two brides are about the same height. One groom is of below average height; the other is unusually tall. Note the couple holding hands: though the groom is not much taller than his wife, his right hand is much larger than hers. Grip and forearm strength are important in using heavy implements.

tamma's house, work is divided among her husband, herself, her teenage
son, and her younger children; in Nagappa's house, the choice is between him and his tiny wife.

Thus, we are concerned less with the degree of sexual dimorphism
in the population as a whole than we are with sexual dimorphism within
domestic groups, and sexual dimorphism appears to be more uniform
within households than it is among persons drawn at random from the
general population. It seems to me that the degree of overlap between the
sexes in physical strength would be greatest when individuals of divergent genetic and economic background were compared to one another.
Big women tend to come from families of big people, small men from
families of small people. And the likelihood that big women and small
men would be members of the same household is further reduced because marriages tend to occur between persons who are similar to each
other relative to members of their own sex. Villagers say that a couple
should look right together. Desirable people of both genders are *dappa*,
in contrast to *sana* people, who are less desirable. Osgood (1964), in his
cognitive differential research, used Kannada as one of his test lan-
guages. *Dappa* and *sana*, which were translated as "fatty" and "slim"
respectively, were one of the test pairs of terms employed in his inquiry
into how opposites were cognitively related to one another. He was astonished to find that informants regarded "fatty" as "faster" than
"slim." As villagers use these terms, this is not astonishing at all. Applied to people, *dappa* means "robust"; *sana* means "frail." Of course
robust people are faster than frail ones. A *dappa* man among villagers,
however, is what we would call husky, whereas a *dappa* woman is volup-
tuous: she looks like an Indian movie star, with fatty deposits in female
places. In Yaavahalli the *dappa* generally marry the *dappa* and are
pleased, while the *sana* tend to marry the *sana* because that is what the
process of marital selection leaves them. Likewise, the tall marry the tall,
and the short marry the short. As a result, not only do the women of a
household tend to be smaller than their men, but one finds that inter-
marrying lineages, and endogamous castes, tend to run to physical types,
each displaying systematic stature differences by sex in a particular way.

Indeed, there was only one woman in the village who was clearly
bigger than her husband. This couple, the stout and jovial Putamma and
her wiry little husband, were figures of covert fun to village children for
the curious image they presented when walking together. On the preceding pages are photographs of two bridal couples that indicate the range of
stature differences typical of mated pairs. In one case you will note that
the husband is very much bigger than the wife. The second case shows a
couple whose stature difference is about as small as one would ordinarily
find among village spouses. He is only a bit taller than she is, and there

is little facial dimorphism. But if you compare the two right hands, you will see that his is almost twice the size of hers. Thus, there is not the slightest reason to believe that husbands are not systematically stronger than their wives. But what of comparisons between other household members; might not young women be better suited to *kashta kelsa* than older men? I shall return to this matter later, but I would simply say now that the sex differences in physical strength found in Yaavahalli would have to be a good deal smaller and the decline in physical ability with age more rapid than in Western populations for this to be the case.

Proposition 2: *The age/sex division of labor is organized in such a way as to exploit the greater physical strength of adult males.*

This statement involves three issues. First, we must specify the conditions under which, taken singly or in combinations, muscular strength and aerobic work capacity become important criteria for the assignment of workers. It is entirely too vague to say that strength is required for a task; we must specify the senses in which variations in physical capabilities influence work performance.

Second, a reasonable basis must be established for assigning degrees of difficulty to the various agricultural tasks villagers perform. How do we know that one task is more difficult than another?

Finally, it must be shown that the degree of difficulty of tasks is the primary basis on which work is assigned to men rather than women. This means both that villagers must say that difficult tasks are appropriate for men but inappropriate for women, and that they must, in fact, assign tasks in that manner. That is, we must rule out the possibility that the constitutional explanation for the sexual division of labor is not a charade. For example, it could be that men reserve for themselves tasks that are somehow more interesting, while calling upon women to perform equally difficult but, in other ways, more unpleasant work. Thus, the sexual division of labor in theory and practice must be a system premised on maximization of energetic efficiency in order for villagers' views on the matter to be taken seriously as an empirically based strategy.

When Is Strength an Advantage?

Described simply, manual work is movement organized in space and time. Some technological procedures involve two or more persons doing the same thing or coordinating different things simultaneously. Other procedures require that one worker do several things in a specific sequence or that a sequence of acts be divided among two or more workers. Why specific procedures are organized in one way rather than another is not of immediate concern. What is of present interest is the role played by muscular strength and aerobic work capacity in the organization of technological procedures.

Under at least four circumstances, muscular strength and aerobic work capacity are critical work performance criteria.

Absolute demands on isometric muscular strength. If a technological procedure is organized as a series of sequential tasks at least one operation of which requires a certain level of muscular strength, then persons who are not strong enough to perform that operation cannot do the job, even though they would be capable of performing other operations. Often it is the case that a technology involves the movement of large objects and is organized in such a way that it is not feasible to pool the strength of several weaker persons. Thus, only relatively strong individuals are suitable for the task.

Relative advantages to increases in isometric muscular strength. An example in this category would be hunting or warfare with hand-held weapons. An individual is likely to be presented with single opportunities to throw a harpoon or swing a club. The greater the force he is able to exert behind the weapon, the greater his chances for success. Thus, weaker individuals can do the job, but they cannot do it as well.

Absolute demands on aerobic work capacity. Isometric muscular strength may also play a role in circumstances of this kind, but here the question is whether or not an individual has the aerobic work capacity to sustain enough effort to meet the demands on oxygen uptake that are built into the technology. The treadmills sometimes used to measure physical fitness provide an example. When the instrument is set at a particular angle and speed, the subject will have to generate a certain level of energy just to stay on the treadmill. Likewise, technological instances usually involve some energy source external to the worker that sets the pace of work; draft animals are an example found in Yaavahalli.

Relative advantages to increases in aerobic work capacity. Demands on aerobic work capacity are not always built into the technology involved. The rate of work can be continuously varied by the worker by increasing or decreasing his load or pace. However, in some circumstances, there may be decided advantages to assigning to a task workers who can maximize the work rate. Labor intensification can mean any of several things, but in this case it means compressing as much work (defined as energy) as possible into a unit of time. For example, while almost anyone can chop down a tree eventually, shifting horticulturalists facing narrow seasonal windows for land clearing may find it advantageous to assign that task to the fastest choppers available, assigning less demanding jobs to others.

How Do We Know How Difficult a Task Is?

No direct physical measurements are available concerning the energetics of work in Yaavahalli. There are, however, good reasons for believing that villagers know how difficult tasks are relative to one another, and the question can be approached by analyzing what they said about the work they did.

I asked sixteen men who had for years been full-time agriculturalists to rate all the labeled agricultural tasks I had encountered on a five-point scale from very easy to very hard. After eliciting an informant's ratings, I then asked him to tell me why various tasks were hard or easy. With few exceptions, the criterion they utilized was the degree of physical exhaustion a task brought about, often specifying the particular muscle groups that were most tired by a particular task. Not only were they unanimous in saying that exhaustion was their main criterion and nearly unanimous in their specifications of the muscles most tired by each task, but they were also generally in consensus in their exceptions to this rule. Sugar cane cutting, for example, is hard work in part because the worker gets cut fingers and dust in his or her eyes while doing it. Thus, the noxiousness of some tasks figures into their difficulty ratings.

Out of 93 separate tasks that were rated, the range of the sixteen informants' ratings exceeded one point on only 20 items, and of these the range exceeded two points on only three. This degree of consensus across informants might seem remarkable but for the fact that it is quite consistent with carefully controlled experimental studies in Western societies of perceived exertion. These studies vary somewhat in their methodologial details, but they all measure a subject's ability to rate accurately the degree of difficulty of work done on a bicycle ergometer or treadmill, while exertion is gauged in terms of an independent physiological measure, typically heart rate. Regardless of the subjects, the rating scales, or the types of work used, these studies, reviewed in Borg (1971), have uniformly shown that people can tell you how hard they are working with a high degree of accuracy. Correlations between ratings of perceived exertion and independently measured exertion display values such as 0.84, 0.85, and 0.94. It seems plausible to suppose that this accuracy is achieved because subjects are monitoring the same physiological variables the experimenters monitor. What is notable is that such ordinary language categories as "very light" or "moderately hard" provide subjective measures of a high degree of observational adequacy; if you want to know how hard someone is working at a simple repetitive task, these studies suggest that asking him can provide data almost as reliable as those provided by laboratory instruments, once subject and experimenter have agreed on the verbal categories to be used.

The verbal categories used in my ratings of work difficulty were those used by villagers in ordinary parlance, and no one expressed any hesitation to use them in rating the 93 tasks on my list. Hence, there is reason to believe that the experienced farm workers in this sample were also reporting perceived exertion in a manner likely to be replicated by independent physiological studies of work energetics.

How might the four circumstances wherein strength is critical to work performance have influenced my informants' ratings of the 93 tasks? The things that make *kashta kelsa* hard in Yaavahalli usually do not include heavy absolute demands on muscular strength, like those that occur in certain building trades in the United States. Rather, the usual question is whether an individual can do something well enough, fast enough, or long enough to make it worthwhile to assign him a difficult task instead of a less demanding one. Thus, the other three circumstances, often in combination with one another, figure prominently in many tasks.

For example, a preferred way of preparing garden lands for planting involves digging them up by hand with an implement called a *gudali*, which consists of a transverse blade about two inches wide, ending in a heavy metal collar at the top through which a short, heavy wooden handle is hafted. The blade is perhaps two feet long and is bent back at an angle to the axis of the handle. In digging gardens, the worker leans over, raises the *gudali* with both arms to a point slightly above his head, and then swings it down so that the blade pierces the earth a bit in front of him. He then pushes forward on the handle, tearing a large clod of earth from the ground. Finally, he turns the tool over and swings again, breaking the clod with its collar. Informants rated this task as quite difficult, as the remarks of one of them indicate:

> Digging is very difficult because it gives great pain to the arms, hips, and legs. It gives pain to the whole body, but the arms and legs must be very strong for this work. We must use strength when we pull up the clods of mud. Also, experience is very important in this case. Without experience we can't dig properly; we use experience to turn the soil quickly. For this work we want men, seventeen to fifty. Oh, and also this gives a lot of pain to the chest.

Farmers use this technique in lieu of plowing because the soil can be cultivated to a greater depth and because it leaves the soil completely pulverized and level. That purpose will be defeated if the worker cannot swing the *gudali* hard enough to drive the blade far into the ground. Thus, there is a relative advantage associated with using workers who are strong enough to maximize the depth of cultivation. There is little absolute demand on aerobic work capacity built into the use of this imple-

A plot is plowed for either the second or the third time. Note that the share of the plow is buried well below ground surface. These bullocks are rather small by local standards.

ment, since a worker with the muscular strength to do the job properly can, in principle, control his pace of work. There is, however, a great relative advantage to increases in aerobic work capacity. Garden plots can be cultivated all year round, and farmers try to minimize the time that they remain fallow. The higher the individual's sustainable oxygen uptake, the faster he can dig, and thus the fewer the hours of labor required to complete the job.

Bear in mind that a household is likely to have a number of jobs that need to be done on any given day. Therefore, given a choice among workers from a fixed stock of labor, that is, from a stock of family members or members of tenant households, individuals unable to sustain the exertion necessary to dig rapidly will be used in less physically demanding tasks. The same is true of *kuli* workers hired for daily wages. *Kuli* work is the most complained-about category of labor; employers claim that *kulis* slack their pace of work when left unsupervised, and *kulis* complain that employers ask too much of them. An individual who cannot sustain a level of exertion comparable to other workers creates problems for everyone. Other workers complain that he is not pulling his weight, and employers are loath to hire someone who they believe must be constantly supervised.

Absolute demands on aerobic work capacity can be seen in tasks involving the use of bullock-drawn implements. The standard pace of the bullocks coupled with the effort necessary to control the implement makes it imperative that the worker sustain a certain level of oxygen uptake. Individuals with relatively strong legs, arms, and shoulders find it easier to control the implements, so there is a relative advantage to muscular strength as well.

All traction animal tasks done in the fields were rated as of greater than average difficulty. Though plowing, which consumes more time than any of the others, was rated as among the least difficult, consider what one man said about it:

> See, plowing is also somewhat difficult work because we must hold the plow strongly. Without that, the plow simply goes up out of the soil, and we want to plow deep. This gives much pain to the hands, and the legs hurt also because we must walk behind the plow. Also, we want to plow each *saalu* [furrow] side by side, leaving no space in between. So you need some experience also. For this males over sixteen and under fifty are the good people.

Almost any healthy adult could plow for a while, but plowing is often done in eight-hour days. The demands on the worker are built into the technology; the plow typically weighs 40-odd pounds, and the draft power the bullocks exert is about 180 pounds, though this will vary depending on the size and strength of the bullocks and the texture of the soil. With that plowing machine, a farmer can cover about an acre a day during which he will walk roughly twenty miles (Indian Council of Agricultural Research 1960). But walking is the least of the work, for the plowman must manage to keep the furrow straight and the point of the share well underground. Adolescent boys begin learning to plow before they have reached their full physical stature. Those I observed were all able to plow adequately at first, albeit at a slower than ordinary speed due to the fact that they were often given a young, untrained bullock yoked to an older one; but as they tired, the plow began to wobble, furrows began to wander, and the plow would begin to buck up out of the soil. It was not skill that they lacked, although surely experienced workers used their strength more efficiently; they simply could not endure the physical demands of the task for more than an hour or two.

The labor intensification of agriculture is frequently defined simply as a matter of increasing labor time per unit of land. But that definition fails to take account of the fact that farming is a sequential set of tasks, each of which is subject to time constraints. Thus, the intensification of a particular task often depends upon how much energy can be usefully expended per unit of time. The more urgent a task in terms of the time constraints under which it must be completed, the greater the incentive to increase the pace of work, and the greater the incentive to choose workers who will be able to sustain a high rate of work. Therefore, if my hypothesis concerning the sexual division of labor is correct, the men's work should also include tasks that are regarded as urgent.

As an illustration of this proposition, consider the problems involved in the most difficult of the tasks involving bullock-drawn implements, driving a thinning rake (*guntive hoodiyoodu*). The *guntive*, or rake, is used to thin and cultivate staple crops on dry lands, and farmers say it is quite urgent that this be done as soon as the seedlings have reached a certain height so that the further growth of the plants left behind will not be retarded. Since the objective is to achieve an optimal density of seedlings, it is critical for the worker to have an acute eye for what a properly cultivated plot looks like. He must also be careful not to damage the delicate seedlings he leaves behind. The implement itself is made of a heavy beam of wood pierced by a number of long metal tines. A wooden handle is provided to grasp the tool, which is yoked to the oxen by two poles. Because little draft power is required to pull the thin tines through the soil, the bullocks can work at a very brisk pace. The worker's problem is to keep up with the pace the bullocks can maintain because he must lift the weight of the beam much of the time to prevent the tines from piercing too deeply. The exertion required to drive a *guntive* may be imagined by thinking of walking many miles holding a heavy weight in front of you, with your arms partially extended, staring intently at the ground all the while. One American visitor remarked that this looked like an easy job. In fact, informants report agonizing pain in the forearms and frequent cramping of the pectoral muscles. This muscular pain, coupled with nervous exhaustion brought about by the intense concentration the job requires, make this one of the most disagreeable of tasks. The American's remark is indicative of how easy it may be to misconstrue the physiology of work in a technology in which one has never taken part. Consider what someone who had driven a *guntive* over many hundreds of acres in his lifetime said about the task:

> That is very hard work to do. It gives most pain to the arms and legs, and sometimes chest pain comes also. We must hold the *guntive* up when we want to remove a few *pairu* (seedlings) and push it lower to the ground when we want to remove more. We must be very careful of the *pairu*, and it is difficult to see what you are doing. Look, after driving the *guntive* we

can't sleep for two nights because of the pain in our body. See, it requires experience too, because we have to be careful not to damage the crop. Also, in some places there are many *pairu* and in others there are few. You have to know how many to remove. For this work it is best to have a man over twenty but under forty.

There must be easier ways to thin a crop; one could use a smaller rake, for example. But farmers feel that the task is so urgent as to warrant the use of as wide a rake as they can manage. This is typical practice: villagers have devised many ways to exploit male strength to solve their agricultural problems, for as we shall see now, the physical difficulty and the urgency of the work are the primary grounds on which tasks are assigned to men.

How Is Work Assigned in Yaavahalli?

For convenience the mean ratings for the 93 tasks were rounded to the nearest half-point on the five-point scale. Then a nine-point scale was constructed in which tasks falling halfway between points on the five-point scale became even numbers on the new scale. That is, a mean rating of 1.5 on the five-point scale would be 2 on the nine-point scale, just as 4.5 would become 8, and so on. Tasks of greater than average difficulty, then, would be those with mean ratings of 6 or more. After asking informants to rate the difficulty of the 93 tasks, I also asked for a number of additional ratings. Eleven informants were asked to specify the appropriateness of each task for each of eight age/sex categories—people over 50, 17–50, 12–16, and under 12 for each sex—on a three-point scale designating an age/sex category as being "very good," "acceptable," or "not good" for each task. A three-point scale was also used to rate the degree of urgency of each task from "important to get done quickly" to "not important to get done quickly."

A task was judged to be men's work if at least seven of the informants said that men between 17 and 50 were very good for the work *and* if seven said that women between 17 and 50 were not good for it. Likewise, if seven of the informants said that it was important to get a task done quickly, that task was rated urgent. In both cases, informants tended to show a greater degree of consensus in these ratings than they displayed in their difficulty ratings. Indeed, they were unanimous in rating most forms of *kashta kelsa* as men's work.

Of the 93 tasks, 39 received ratings of greater than average difficulty (ratings of 6 or more); of the 39, only 9 were regarded as very difficult (ratings of 8 or 9), while 36 were rated as urgent.

Table 1   Sexual division of labor by difficulty and urgency of task

Type of task	Tasks for men only	Tasks for men or women
Urgent and difficult	17	4
Not urgent but difficult	11	7
Urgent but not difficult	6	9
Neither urgent nor difficult	7	32
Total	41	52

As Table 1 indicates, the more difficult and urgent a task, the more likely it is to be assigned to men, with difficulty being the more powerful of the two determinants. Of the 9 very difficult tasks, 8 were assigned to men only. The one exception, carrying head loads of dirt, occurs in practice only in conjunction with the very difficult task of digging the earth to fill the baskets. Men do the digging while women do the carrying. Among the urgent and difficult tasks assigned to both sexes, at least one, cane cutting, clearly involved criteria other than exertion in the difficulty ratings. Tasks assigned to men that were neither urgent nor difficult tended to be associated with skills used in work that was difficult. Driving bullock carts is not difficult, but men do it because they are familiar with the handling of draft animals.

Let us now turn to the question of how degree of difficulty influences the age/sex division of labor in work actually performed. While most difficult tasks are normatively assigned only to men, it could be that those assigned to both sexes consume much more time than exclusively male jobs. That is not the case.

Some years ago I computed a sample of approximately one hundred thousand hours of labor based on direct observations of work in the fields. These data were cross-tabulated by degree of difficulty on the nine-point scale and the age/sex categories. Children under twelve account for only 8 percent of the labor in this sample, and the production functions I have computed from the cultivation of specific plots indicate that their real contribution to production is so small as to be unmeasurable. Often they were taken to the fields simply to watch or assist their elders as part of their socialization. Their work will therefore be omitted from the following discussion, although the low frequency with which children from six to twelve were even present in the fields while work was going on is a subject we shall return to later.

As a relatively wealthy village, Yaavahalli imports a substantial amount of its labor. Because I wanted to compute mean hours worked per person, the labor of the many different workers from other villages

Threshing grain. These bullocks are larger and stronger than those shown in the previous photograph. Note that the man controls the animal by grasping its tail. Though cattle are venerated and often treated as pets during leisure time, they receive firm, even rough, handling during work.

was also subtracted from the total, leaving a sample of 73,960 person hours. Table 2 provides data on the age/sex division of these hours of effort in terms of the difficulty of work performed.

The interpretation of Table 2 should begin with two technical caveats. First, chronological ages of villagers are at best approximate, a factor that is of some importance in the 12–16 age group. Seventeen was taken as a best guess of the age by which the great majority of girls are married and most boys have begun to perform the work of men regularly. The boys in this sample, however, are an extremely heterogeneous group, those at the upper end of the age bracket performing much more difficult work than those at the bottom. Perhaps the most realistic position lies in recognizing that adolescence is a period of rapid transition in the work of boys, so that there will be cases where the decision as to whether an individual should be classed as 12–16 or 17–50 is fairly

Table 2   Division of labor by sex and age based on sample hours of effort

	Males			Females		
	over 50	17–50	12–16	over 50	17–50	12–16
Number of individuals	28	71	28	27	67	23
Sample hours per person	335	374	408	120	246	300
Work hours as percentage of total work hours	12.7	35.9	15.4	4.4	22.3	9.3
Percentage of work allotted to tasks rated 6–9	40.0	49.0	30.0	2.0	6.0	4.0
Percentage of work allotted to tasks rated 8–9	5.0	9.0	4.0	—	—	—

arbitrary. Second, I have included only those individuals who were actually observed to work in the fields. There are a number of aged persons of both sexes who were not included for that reason. However, women drop out of the agricultural labor force at an earlier age than men, so that there are several women who are otherwise physically active who have not been included. Likewise, the wife and daughters of the village headman never set foot in the fields and are not included. Thus, we are dealing with 244 people who may be called agriculturally active in a population of about 360.

Is this an energetically efficient division of labor by sex that one might expect in a population where age and sex differences in work capacity were comparable to those found in Western populations? I believe it is. Starting with the oldest age group, recall that a man aged 65 has the aerobic work capacity of a woman 25 in Astrand's study. In all likelihood a village man in his fifties still has greater muscular strength and aerobic work capacity than a woman in her twenties. When the motor skills acquired over a lifetime of heavy work are also considered, there would appear to be no reason to substitute a younger woman for an older man when assigning difficult work, especially if the work requires considerable muscular strength, as many of the very difficult tasks do. By contrast, a woman of 65 has the aerobic work capacity of a 12-year-old, and in fact one finds that the per person contribution of women over 50 who work in the fields at all is similar to that of big children. I suspect, however, that older women who do work are far more productive than children because of their greater psychological capacity to work steadily and skillfully. The real reason they do so little farm work lies in the fact that their time is better spent elsewhere. The social and technical skills and the moral authority of older women are the focus around which the domestic life of joint households is centered, so that these women have strong positive reasons for not spending much time in the fields. When they do work in the fields, it is physically and, from the villagers' point of view, morally inappropriate to ask them to do much heavy work.

Turning to persons in the prime of life, those aged 17 to 50, we find that men spend about half of their time doing relatively heavy work. They also perform about two-thirds of the relatively small amount of very difficult work that is done, with older men and adolescent boys dividing almost all of the remainder. These are precisely the individuals one would expect to bear the brunt of heavy labor if work was assigned on the basis of physical ability.

But why do women perform so little difficult work? Women from 17 to 50 spend only 6 percent of their field labor at difficult tasks, which comes to about 15 sample hours per woman in contrast to about 185 hours per man of this age group. Recall that women were rated as at least acceptable workers by many male informants on 11 of the 39 difficult tasks, and yet they, in fact, do hardly any difficult work.

The explanation for this is quite simple. Most of the difficult tasks for which women were rated acceptable do not occur very frequently in comparison to those performed exclusively by men. Tasks involving the use of traction animals, plowing, harrowing, seed-drilling, thinning, and the like account for a very large proportion of all difficult work, and there is a special reason for their being exclusively performed by men.

As elsewhere in India, investment in traction animals often poses a serious indivisibility problem: how many pairs of bullocks should a household maintain given its land holdings? Villagers try to minimize the amount of land devoted to fodder crops, preferring to maintain their livestock on weeds and those parts of domesticated plants that people do not eat. Thus, there is an upper limit on the number of animals a holding can feed without setting aside land for fodder crops. Although there are some economies of scale associated with the labor necessary to care for livestock, the time spent caring for each additional pair of bullocks is almost as great as the time spent on the previous pair. Moreover, the initial price of bullocks is sufficiently high, and their depreciation is sufficiently rapid, to make the purchase of a second or third pair a very serious investment decision. Consequently, no household, with the exception of the village headman's, owns more yokes of bullocks than it has men to drive them. Even if a woman had the skills and strength needed to perform tasks with bullock-drawn implements quite adequately, there would rarely be an occasion to call upon her services so long as the men of her household were better suited to the work than she was. There simply would not be enough bullocks to go around.

When tasks with the bullock-drawn implements are subtracted from all difficult labor performed, much of what is left consists of very heavy manual labor believed, correctly or not, to be unsuitable for women. That leaves a relatively small proportion of difficult work for which women are even considered as workers.

In the meantime, there is much work to be done that is not difficult, jobs women are believed to do as well as, or better than, men. Villagers said that women are more supple and dextrous than men, and for that reason are better suited to tasks, such as the transplantation of grain seedlings, where those abilities are important. Such jobs can be tiring, especially in the hot sun, but no one has sufficient eye-hand coordination to transplant rice seedlings fast enough to really tax his or her aerobic work capacity. Thus, there are a number of essential tasks consuming a great deal of time where the greater strength of men is literally useless.

In practice, then, there are many occasions where there is more difficult work to be done than the men of a household can readily manage, but where it does not make sense to send the women to assist them because they have other things to do that employ their time more productively. In fact, women in the prime of life spent somewhat more time per person than men in farm tasks of up to average difficulty in spite of the demands of domestic work on their time.

When there is more work to be done than a family can manage, workers from other households are employed chiefly in two ways: sharecropping tenancy arrangements and *kuli*, or daily wage, labor. For reasons that will become clear shortly, land-rich households employ tenants to acquire workers for tasks that occur early in the cultivation process. Because those tasks involve a great deal of heavy work, tenant households assign difficult labor by sex, according to the same intrafamilial comparisons of physical strength utilized when a landowning household allocates its fixed stock of family labor to its own lands. Only when workers are hired for cash wages would interfamilial comparisons of the strength of various men and women become a criterion of employment. Women in the poorest fifth of the population spend as much time in the fields as most men. About 85 percent of that time is spent in *kuli* work, so that a relatively strong woman might seem to have many opportunities to compete with relatively weak men in seeking employment for difficult work. But, in fact, the available *kuli* employment for difficult work is almost entirely taken up by robust young men. Digging gardens is the most common heavy task for which *kulis* are hired, and employers are so concerned with finding strong, energetic individuals to do this work that even men in their late thirties tend to be at a competitive disadvantage. In any case, women from the poor households that provide the bulk of the *kuli* work force tend to be the smallest adults in the population. That is not a disadvantage in the kinds of work for which they are routinely hired, but it is very unlikely that an employer would actually be presented with a female *kuli* who was as strong as any number of men available to him.

Finally, consider the work of adolescents in this sample. Boys of this age group do far more heavy manual labor than their sisters, and yet probably the younger males of this cohort are no stronger than their female counterparts. Recall that boys begin their training for men's work before they are physically able to sustain it for a normal working day. This training begins during the spurt of growth in which boys rapidly approach adult stature, and it provides them with an initiation into the skills and work habits of manhood. In a period of a few years, a boy proceeds from a set of tasks little different from his sister's to a set comparable to his father's. By contrast, there is no such change in the tasks set adolescent girls. At age twelve they are physically capable of doing the things women ordinarily do in the fields and simply spend increasing amounts of time doing them as they leave childhood and enter adolescence. It seems reasonable, then, to suppose that the absence of a dramatic change in the work patterns of adolescent girls mirrors the fact that they do not undergo a dramatic change in physical strength that suddenly fits them for the adult activities of their sex, such as that their brothers experience.

In concluding our discussion of this proposition, I would note a methodological problem with the data we have just examined: I did not ask female informants to rate tasks. I decided not to do so because women do not do a number of tasks men perform and would therefore have no experiential basis on which to rate them, whereas my male informants had been observed to do a wide range of farm work, including tasks more often than not performed by women. Still, this was a mistake, for women informants might have responded differently from men in rating farm work, raising serious substantive and methodological issues for my argument.

I see no reason, however, to expect that women's responses would have contradicted those of male informants. As I have noted, there seems to be no competition between the sexes where work roles are concerned, and both sexes describe the male role in the same general way. If women say men do *kashta kelsa* because they are the stronger sex, why should they say that many specific tasks that men perform almost to the exclusion of women were not *kashta kelsa?*

On the contrary, it seems more plausible to suppose that both sexes behave as if they were implementing a sexual division of labor whose appropriateness they take for granted. While the management of labor in Yaavahalli can, from the perspective of managers, become rather complicated, the organizational outlines of the sexual division of labor are utterly simple. If a task is done around the house, women tend to do it; if greater physical strength is advantageous in the performance of a task, men tend to do it; remaining tasks are divided between the sexes about equally. Women not only behave as though their interests were served by ceding heavy work to men, but they also seem to readily concede the management of farming to men, as we shall see in the next chapter.

chapter 5

The Male Management
of Agriculture

In this chapter I will try to describe what I believe to be the empirical connection between the male performance of *kashta kelsa* and the male management of farming, a connection that stems from the peculiar status of hard work in farm production.

> Proposition 3. *Because the tasks performed only or largely by men mostly occur early in the cultivation process and because they are subject to variable intensification, which has a strong impact on subsequent productivity, the management of male labor tends to be economically problematic.*

There is no necessary relationship between the physical difficulty of work and its productivity, that is, the value of what it accomplishes. This proposition states, however, that in technologies like Yaavahalli's heavy labor has a special significance deriving from what it does and from when and how it is carried out. Work that taxes the strength of men and the power of bullocks to pass the heaviest of tools through soil and manure is the high-energy component of village technology, the supply of which is limited by the number of men and bullocks available. Men's work tends to be the first work that is done on a plot of land, and it is the kind of work that villagers do more or less of per acre, where more or less is defined in terms of the actual physical changes in plants and land that work brings about. To say that these factors make the management of male labor problematic simply means that deciding how much male labor to use, when, where, and how is a tricky business if you want to maximize your farm income.

As you will recall from the last chapter, the problems entailed in the allocations of men's time to heavy labor cannot be disposed of very well by allocating more of women's time to such tasks, provided I am correct in believing that women would be physically less suited to these tasks than men. Often it is not so much man-time as bullock-time that is in short supply, and once time consumed by tasks requiring draft animals is subtracted from the *kashta kelsa* men do, much of the remaining work involves very difficult tasks. But perhaps most important are the opportunity costs that would be incurred by using more of women's time in heavy work. It is not as though we are speaking of women who are otherwise unemployed. In addition to the domestic work and livestock care women provide, much of which must be treated as an overhead, there are so many other kinds of work that are just as essential to farm production as heavy work, and for which women are at least as suitable as men, that a marked increase in the heavy work women do could be undertaken only at the expense of other vital activities.

Before proceeding further, two other points should be noted as well. First, we have been and shall be concerned primarily with routine farm work, which consumes the bulk of villagers' productive effort. But it must be borne in mind that the agricultural system we are examining depends upon the construction and maintenance of irrigation works. Virtually all of the labor required to construct and maintain these works is *kashta kelsa,* and women do a lot of it. As I have indicated, men do the digging and women carry away the dirt. This is an effective arrangement because digging is a task that is greatly speeded as the muscular strength and aerobic work capacity of workers increase, an especially important consideration in view of the fact that digging often occurs in confined spaces that limit the number of workers who may be used. Though carrying basketloads of dirt is regarded as heavy work, the weight of basketloads can be adjusted by the diggers to suit the physical abilities of those who carry them away. Thus, I do not wish to convey the impression that shortfalls in the availability of male labor for *kashta kelsa* cannot ever be relieved by using women in heavy work. If one extrapolates from the data I gathered on the construction and maintenance of wells and tanks during my stay, it would appear that over the years women of the region have contributed millions of hours at heavy manual labor to create and maintain the irrigation works on which village agriculture depends. By serving as sod-carriers, women release men to be diggers.

A similar relationship obtains between the heavy work men do and the work women do in routine cultivation. One of the goals women accomplish by taking on over half of the farm work that is not difficult is to release more of men's time when it can be used advantageously in *kashta kelsa*. In other words, women help to relieve some of the problems encountered in allocating men's time to heavy labor in farming, but they do not do it by undertaking heavy work themselves; they do it by providing other essential work, which has the effect of increasing the supply of male labor available for *kashta kelsa*.

With these qualifications in mind, let us turn to the main question: why is the allocation of men's time to heavy labor in farming economically problematic? To answer this question a more rigorous description of village farming is required.

Cultivation Opportunities

A cultivation opportunity occurs every time there is a chance to do useful work on the land. Because of the sequential and seasonal nature of agriculture, the exploitation of a cultivation opportunity is subject to a time constraint, or seasonal window, during which the work must be done lest the opportunity be lost or one's ability to exploit another opportunity be impaired. Clearly, one objective of land management involves the manipulation of cultivation opportunities so as to acquire the best ones possible at times when they can be exploited most fully.

By definition, some value is attached to every cultivation opportunity, for to say that work is useful is to say that there is likely to be a material return on it. Because of the sequential nature of agriculture, however, no cultivation opportunity is sufficient in and of itself to produce income. Viewing a single cultivated plot in isolation from others, all that can be said of any cultivation opportunity, save harvesting, is that its exploitation creates the material basis for the next opportunity in the sequence. So long as farmers cultivated all of their holdings in a single crop as a unit, and assuming that the quality of the soil was relatively homogeneous, decisions concerning labor allocations would be fairly simple. They would try to exploit every opportunity as fully as possible and then wait for the next one to come along. But that is not the way things are done in the rather complex technologies of Indian villages.

As we have seen, three types of land are cultivated in Yaavahalli: paddy lands irrigated from tanks, unirrigated lands on which subsistence crops are grown, and garden lands irrigated from wells. But because the drought in 1965 that almost completely dried up Yaavahalli's tank was followed by heavy flooding in 1966, those crops that were planted on paddy lands (and a large area was not planted) either failed or produced very low yields. Since we have no idea of the outcomes of alternative labor management strategies in more ordinary conditions, these lands will be omitted from detailed discussion. The fifty-six households of the village cultivated 230.0 acres of unirrigated land and 68.5 acres of gardens during 1966. I calculated the yields from those lands in terms of an accounting procedure villagers use themselves, one that results in a measure I call village product. Village product equals gross yield minus cash inputs, save those for labor. This measure ignores the value of manure, seed held out for future crops, and depreciation on bullocks and tools, all of which are real costs but ones that villagers treated as an uncosted overhead. So, village product equals available disposable income to villagers, some of it expressed as wages and tenants' shares, leaving out an overhead (which I found impossible to cost realistically). The average annual village product yield of all unirrigated lands was Rs. 256 per acre, or Rs. 59,000 total, while that of gardens totaled almost Rs. 100,000, for an average of Rs. 1,460 per acre. Thus, 23 percent of the arable land accounted for about 63 percent of all income from field cultivation; omitting paddy lands.

Investment in an irrigation well increases the potential annual production of an acre of land by a factor of about five. Not only can garden plots be cultivated year round, but crops otherwise grown on dry lands grow much faster and more abundantly under irrigation, and there are many crops that cannot be effectively cultivated at all without irrigation. Most important among these latter crops are vegetables and bush mulberry, used in the production of silk cocoons. About 45 percent of the total village product was sold for cash, and garden lands accounted for virtually all of those sales. Ancillary sources of cash income from dairy and livestock production amounted to only Rs. 12,140. While far more labor per acre was invested in garden lands (an increase of about six to one over dry lands), average returns on labor were not much lower, in part because farmers could regulate crop selection in gardens to take advantage of seasonally strong markets.

In managing their garden lands, farmers sought to maintain many tiny plots of land at varying stages of cultivation. This practice tended to minimize the maximum amount of labor required to exploit fully the cultivation opportunities available to a household at any given time. The practice also avoided slack periods when there was little useful work to be done.

On dry lands, farmers have far less control over the timing of cultivation opportunities because all soil preparation and planting must be completed within a seasonal window dictated by the Southwest Monsoon. That window is sufficiently wide, however, to permit some sort of cultivation to take place on all of the village's dry lands, and it can be manipulated to some degree through crop selection. The standard subsistence field consists of an interculture of finger millet (*raagi*), a bean fairly rich in protein (*avare*), and a variety of sorghum (*kaki joLLa*) used only for fodder (accounting for about 5 percent of the seed rate). This mixture must be planted fairly early, as must unirrigated rice, which is also commonly grown. Grams and a hardy millet called *haaraka* can be planted somewhat later. Cultivation of paddy lands commenced immediately after the preparation of dry lands.

In cultivating their dry lands, farmers did not simply start at one end of a holding and plow to the other end. Rather, they tended to subdivide holdings into plots that were treated as quite separate entities. Starting with their best soils, they would prepare fields for *raagi* interculture or dry rice and then proceed to the poorest, which would be planted in *haaraka* if the plowing occurred late in the seasonal window. If a plot of *raagi* or rice did not emerge properly because of poor germination, a farmer might plow the plot again and plant it in gram. Throughout this period decisions had to be made regarding the number of times each plot would be plowed (from one to four), whether or not it would be harrowed as well, and whether the seed would be sown by broadcasting or by the more effective but more time-consuming use of a seed drill.

Farmers could influence to some extent the times at which different plots would mature, permitting demands for labor in crop thinning and harvesting to be spread more evenly over time. They might also try to intensify their preparatory labor on those fields where they believed it would do the most good, but the seasonal window severely limited managerial options in cultivating dry lands in comparison to garden lands. Thus, it was much more difficult for farmers to fine-tune the timing of cultivation opportunities on dry lands.

By manipulating cultivation opportunities, farmers are manipulating the flow of labor over land through time. This practice may be thought of as a dynamic control process whose objective functional is the maximization of household income, subject to security constraints aimed at producing some food even if weather conditions are poor. The manipulation of labor flow over land through time involves finding an optimal joint trajectory in the allocation of the time of different kinds of workers.

Employment Opportunities

An employment opportunity occurs each time useful work can be found for any person in a household's stock of family labor. Employment opportunities must be kept distinct from cultivation opportunities, both because labor is bought and sold among households and because the age/sex division of labor dictates that a cultivation opportunity offering employment to one sort of person may not offer it to another sort.

Now, a landowning family will, other things being equal, attempt to manage its lands in such a way that cultivation opportunities maximize employment opportunities for family members, unless it has determined that allocation of time to activities other than farm labor is worth more than the wage needed to replace family members in the fields or the income lost from leaving work undone. Other things are by no means always equal. The nine richest households of the village hired 70 percent of the labor they used, and because so much labor was utilized as a variable cost, their decisions regarding allocations of labor were reached somewhat differently. The people they most often hired were those from the thirteen poorest households, who spent 85 percent of their labor time working for other people and had so little land that they had relatively few problems in organizing the cultivation of their estates so that all cultivation opportunities could be well exploited by family members, though they did sometimes have to choose between working for themselves and the immediate payment offered by *kuli* work. These two categories of households, the *sovkaars*, or rich, and the *badava*, or poor, each constituted about 20 percent of the population. The remaining 60 percent spent the great bulk of their time working for themselves and hired relatively little labor, so that the organizational problem they faced was pretty much the one stated: to manage land so as to maximize employment opportunities for family members. Once a basis has been established for understanding how these households go about doing this, we can return to the case of the rich and the poor and show that their labor organization strategies are largely special cases of the general model of farm management.

For the short term, land is not a commodity in which villagers invest money in hope of a return; land is simply a resource that they have and in which they invest labor. Thus, whatever the value attached to a cultivation opportunity, so long as its exploitation is undertaken by household members, the returns on exploiting the opportunity may be thought of as the wage value of the employment opportunities it creates for family members. But because the cultivation of a plot requires the exploitation of a *series* of cultivation opportunities, at least some of them necessary but none sufficient to produce income, it is inappropriate to say that any person produces any portion of the crop as an individual. The family produces the crop as an organization, which means that the productivity of any unit of labor—that is, the value of the physical changes the labor brought about in terms of its impact on final crop yield—is contingent upon the physical changes brought about by prior and subsequent labor. In that sense, an external economy pertains among the efforts of various members of the organization: the productivity of one individual depends not only on his or her own efforts but on the efforts of other individuals as well. We shall return to this point in a later chapter.

Since we are concerned with the allocation of labor as a fixed stock rather than a variable cost, the question, then, is not one of whether or not to use labor but one of finding its highest and best use. That labor stock may be portrayed as a matrix of P persons over D days of the year. This labor stock matrix establishes two dimensions of all alternative

Transplanting rice seedlings in a tank-irrigated paddy. These young women are household members working on family land. Groups of *kulis* are often used on larger plots. Women almost never transplant alone because it is important to complete the work promptly and because they like one another's company to relieve the tedium of the work.

allocation matrices, which assign each unit of labor to a particular task on a particular plot of land. Now, while it is not sensible to attach a value to a unit of labor in isolation, it is possible to attach a value to any cell of a given allocation matrix; this value is expressed as the income lost as a result of the withdrawal of that labor, with the remainder of the allocation matrix held constant. Labor withdrawn from one plot might, in principle, be added to another. Thus, the trick is to find an optimal allocation matrix, of which, in theory, there may be many.

Income may be lost due to the withdrawal of a unit of labor in various ways, depending upon the nature of the cultivation opportunity involved. Some cultivation opportunities are essential to farming (every plot must be planted in some way or other); others are optional (thinning a dry land grain crop improves yields greatly but is not absolutely necessary). Certain cultivation opportunities are exploited in a fixed manner, while others are subjected to variable intensification.

In years past, villagers sometimes planted grains in irrigated lands by broadcasting the seed, the easy way, and sometimes by carefully transplanting thousands of seedlings from nursery beds. Over time, the easy way has been determined out of the technology because it insufficiently exploits the opportunities created by the many hundreds of hours of other work invested in an irrigated plot. When a farm family mobilizes the labor to transplant a plot, not only can they fairly accurately estimate the labor required to do it, but they also know that whatever the ultimate yield of the plot is to be, the average and marginal products of the labor spent transplanting seedlings will be about equal. That is so because the physical product of the first unit of labor will be the same as the last, a seedling planted. One simply starts at one end of the plot and works until the entire area is planted. Since planting is essential to cultivation, the withdrawal of one person-day of labor would reduce the area of the plot. By reducing the size of the plot, the scope of later cultivation opportunities in terms of their capacity to usefully absorb labor would also be reduced, but the per unit productivity of subsequent labor would not be affected. There would simply be less area to irrigate, weed, and harvest. The productive role of such tasks performed according to a fixed procedure, like transplanting, may be thought of in terms of a linear or an input-output production function. With other labor inputs per acre held constant, the more you do such a task, the more you get at a relatively constant rate, because the size of the plot must increase along with increases in the labor devoted to the task.

By contrast, to say that a cultivation opportunity is subject to variable intensification is to say that there are better or worse or more or less thorough ways of doing something. Poorer or less thorough techniques have not been eliminated from the technology because there are costs in labor time, or perhaps other factors, associated with the better techniques that make it unfeasible or undesirable to use them on some occasions. It is also likely that the better techniques, which consume more time per acre, produce higher yields at a declining rate. While each additional plowing of a field, after the first essential one, improves the texture of the soil, the impact of the third plowing on yields is greater than the fourth but less than the second. Thus, the productive role of cultivation opportunities that are subject to variable per acre intensification is better described in the logarithmic terms of the Cobb-Douglas production function so commonly found in analyses of farm production.

Whereas allocations of labor to input-output opportunities determine plot size and hence the absolute availability of subsequent cultivation opportunities (but not the per unit returns on the labor invested in them), allocations to Cobb-Douglas opportunities have the reverse effect. Investment of time in these activities, above that essential to bring a plot of given size under cultivation, influences the per unit returns on all other labor expended on the plot. A garden plot that has been carefully dug by hand rather than plowed will produce more abundant crops. Consequently, while each unit of labor spent transplanting yields the same physical product, a planted seedling, the ultimate value of that product—how well it will grow—is influenced by how well the plot has been prepared. That, in turn, has a bearing on the benefit to be derived from sending an individual to transplant in that plot relative to other employment opportunities that might be available to the person at the time.

As it happens, there is usually no reason inherent in the technology that makes one cultivation opportunity subject to variable intensification and another not. The planting of irrigated grain once was subject to variable intensification, though it is no longer. When the exploitation of a particular cultivation opportunity is subjected to a wide range of intensification, it seems reasonable to consider it a particularly problematic aspect of the organization of work. For one thing, this may indicate a bottleneck in the demand for labor that cannot be overcome by manipulating the timing of cultivation opportunities—there is simply not enough labor to fully exploit an opportunity within the available time.

But there is another important sense in which this aspect of labor organization may be problematic. Early in the cultivation process, decisions regarding allocations of labor are made under conditions of considerable uncertainty and risk. As the productive process continues from initial preparation of the soil to final harvesting, the farmer's ability to estimate the probable yield of his crop increases. The rate of crop failure in Yaavahalli is quite high; even in average years as many as a quarter to a third of the plots planted in certain crops will produce such low yields as to be regarded as failures. The bad weather and plant disease that cause crop failure are difficult to predict and impossible to control, but careful soil preparation can, to some extent, counteract the impact of poor rain. In response to this, farmers sometimes contemplate the outcomes of alternative labor allocations under various weather conditions when deciding how much labor to allocate to the preparation of different plots being brought under cultivation at about the same time. We shall return to this matter presently.

Men's Preparatory Labor

Now we can begin to see why the management of male labor is so problematic. In the first place, one would want male workers to really exert themselves in those preparatory tasks, like digging, leveling, and bund building in gardens, where there are great returns on the maximal utilization of aerobic work capacity. The faster they work, the more quickly the plot can be turned around for another planting. Because cultivation opportunities for heavy work sometimes come in sequences of days at a time, especially during the preparation of dry lands and paddy lands, one would also want workers who would stick at these tasks in spite of the hardship involved. We will turn later to the interpersonal aspect of the problem—how to get men to work hard.

But another critical problem in allocating men to hard work is knowing when to stop work on one plot and move on to the next. What one wants to do, in the long term, is maximize the average product of this work over different plots. Because different crops are planted, because soils vary somewhat, and because both irrigated and unirrigated lands are cultivated, the optimal solutions to this problem—and, in theory, there may be many—amount to more than just spreading labor time evenly across plots of land. As we have seen, the manipulations of plot size and of the timing of cultivation through crop selection permit farmers to exercise some control over cultivaton opportunities. In the best possible situation, a farmer could fully exploit the opportunity to prepare a plot of land thoroughly at no opportunity cost to other plots. In practice this usually cannot be accomplished. Generally a point is reached at which the devotion of additional labor to a plot must draw labor away from another plot unless the farmer is willing to hire workers to perform the additional work. This problem is especially pronounced in the preparation of dry lands due to the narrow seasonal window within which the work must be done. And as we have seen, allocations of labor to garden lands must be made with the long-term utilization of the plot in mind, not merely in terms of returns on the crop under cultivation, because a delay in the planting of a garden plot delays the time at which it can be prepared for the next crop. Therefore, an allocation that increases the yield of the current crop might, in the end, reduce the plot's annual yield.

While a detailed analysis of the ways farmers address the issue of allocating male labor to the preparation of plots would be an extraordinarily complex computational problem (if it could be realistically computed at all), some general rules they employ can be described. Generally speaking, the amount of labor expended on cultivation opportunities subjected to variable intensification per acre is linked to the amount of other labor that is to be used in the remainder of the cultivation process; this, in turn, is related to crop selection and the type of land being cultivated. Consider the implications of this policy for a hypothetical middle peasant who is seeking to maximize the employment opportunities available to members of his household. Maximizing the productivity of the male labor used in the early stages of cultivation, expressed in terms of maximizing the value of employment opportunities for family members over the year, amounts to two things: creating a lot of employment opportunities spread evenly over time, and increasing the average product of all labor expended, viewed as a unit. If a crop requires a great deal of labor, the returns should be worth the effort; low-yield crops are invariably low-effort crops. Hence, as we would expect, there appears to be a fairly close fit between the average labor inputs and average yields per acre for alternative crops when land type (irrigated or dry) is held constant. Moreover, in contrast to the common notion that average returns on labor decline sharply with the shift from unirrigated to irrigated farming, we find that in this community, where the two types are mixed, the decline is not very great at all. In investing in irrigation wells, villagers greatly expand the scope of cultivation opportunities available to them, but in allocating their time between the two types of land, villagers have been so successful in fine-tuning the management of cultivation opportunities that they are often working for roughly similar wages wherever they work. This relative parity in the average returns on labor over plots of different types planted in different crops is sustained by the practice of allocating labor to preparing plots for planting that is proportional to the other work to be invested in them. If one has *already* decided that a plot is to be cultivated according to a package of technology that requires a great deal of other work, then that plot should be prepared very carefully. When a low-yield, low-cultivation opportunity crop such as *haaraka* is selected, then considerably less labor is expended on the preparation of the plot because experience has shown that the marginal return from increased intensification is so low that the labor could probably be better spent elsewhere.

Table 3   Results of regression analysis of labor inputs on net yields for twenty-one plots of irrigated *raagi*

Type of labor	Regression coefficient (B)	Beta	Standard error	F ratio
Male preparation of soil	0.395	0.797	0.095	17.390
Other male labor	0.082	0.101	0.139	0.351
Female labor	−0.045	−0.092	0.093	0.234

Multiple $R = 0.794$; $R^2 = 0.631$; R^2 adjusted with 3 and 17 degrees of freedom = 0.566.

Thus, decisions regarding crop selection and plot size need to be made jointly with a determination of the degree of intensification to be utilized in the preparation of the plot. While the village as a whole seems to be doing a fairly good job of managing land through the management of labor, in that the average returns on labor do not change radically with changes in crop and land type, a plot-by-plot analysis in which crop and land type are held constant should display the following results: if the amount of male labor time tends to be insufficient to completely exploit all early cultivation opportunities (but not so insufficient as to warrant the purchase of additional bullocks, a shift of labor from other plots, or the allocation of more of women's time to these tasks), then we would expect a significantly positive marginal product to be associated with increases in preparation time per acre. We might not expect similar results for inputs of other forms of labor per acre for reasons that will be discussed shortly.

I have tested this hypothesis with data from a sample of thirty-four garden *raagi* plots on which very detailed day-by-day data on labor allocations were tabulated from observations in the fields. Of these plots, thirteen were judged by the farmers to be crop failures because they were damaged to one degree or another, chiefly by *kandava rooga*, a stem borer endemic to wet *raagi* cultivation. The failed plots were omitted from the following analysis because we are concerned with the physical contribution of different kinds of labor to successful cultivation. Likewise, labor used in harvesting fields was also omitted on the grounds that it simply reflects the conversion of standing crops to edible grain and fodder, and we are interested in the labor that produced those standing crops in the first place. A regression function was computed by regressing the logarithms of male preparation labor per acre, all other male labor per acre, and all female labor per acre on the log of village product yield per acre. The results of this analysis are reported in Table 3.

It would be inappropriate to attribute great precision to a statistical analysis of a single data set like this one, but these results suggest that per acre yields are extremely responsive to increases in the amount of time men spend per acre in the preparation of land. The correlation between the log of male preparation labor per acre and the log of output was 0.789, or almost the same as the multiple correlation for all three independent variables. Moreover, the size of the F ratio for this variable, 17.39, indicates that the results are extremely unlikely to have occurred by chance. It is not the case that the other work done, whether by women or by men, was unproductive. All these data indicate is that variations in the amount of time spent performing those other tasks per acre were not reliably associated with changes in yields per acre. The same lack of association was found when the regression function was computed in linear form as well. When *total* labor inputs are correlated with *total* yield, there is a good, roughly linear, fit between the two, mainly because both yields and labor inputs increase with plot size.

The lack of association between per acre yields and labor inputs per acre for tasks other than soil preparation has two sources. First, transplanting, which consumes a large proportion of women's work, is best described as an input-output opportunity, but it simply took some people in our sample more time than others to transplant an acre of *raagi*. Perhaps those who took more time did a more careful job, but if so the additional benefit was not big enough to measure. In weeding and irrigation, the physical work accomplished per acre differs from plot to plot. However, that variation is not reflected in yields per acre in the case of weeding, because while some plots are weeded better than others, it is also the case that fewer weeds grow in some plots than others. When a plot is dug by hand in lieu of plowing, the rhizomes that produce the most persistent weeds are carefully removed by the diggers. This may account, in part, for the small negative value of the coefficient relating women's work per acre to yields per acre. Women who weed a lot may be making up for deficiencies in the preparatory work of their men, deficiencies they cannot completely overcome. The amount of time per acre spent watering a plot is influenced both by the amount of rain that falls during cultivation and by the care with which the soil has been prepared: if it is very level, well pulverized, and divided into many small bunded squares or *patas*, a given amount of water does the crop more good than would otherwise be the case.

So when male labor time was intensified in the preparatory stages of the cultivation of the plots, not only were yields increased, but the returns on all of the other work that was used to produce the crop were increased as well. The women who transplanted a poorly prepared plot were doing the same thing as the women who transplanted one that was well prepared, but because each seedling the women planted on the well-prepared plot grew better, each was worth more than those on the poorly prepared plot. Likewise, while more time was required to harvest a high-yielding acre than a poor one, the increase in time was less, proportionally, than the increase in yield. That is because the difference in yield stems not from the number but from the growth of the plants harvested. And while weeding and irrigation are performed in varying amounts per acre, the amount of labor required to fully exploit these cultivation opportunities declines as the land is prepared more thoroughly.

Plowing and Weeding

I do not mean to suggest that there are no tasks in which the variable intensification of women's farm work did not in the past or at the time of my fieldwork influence yields and the productivity of prior and subsequent labor. What I do mean to suggest is that villagers do not appear to encounter managerial problems in the variable intensification of women's labor comparable to those encountered in organizing the efforts of men in *kashta kelsa*.

As I have noted, villagers had uniformly adopted the practice of transplanting seedlings in plots of irrigated grain, but they remembered a time when they broadcast seed in such plots. Thus, there must have been a period of transition when both techniques were employed, a period during which the intensification of women's efforts in using the superior technique was associated with sharp increases in per acre yields. But the uniform adoption of transplanting would also indicate that villagers were able to solve any managerial problems that arose from its use. When they needed labor for this purpose, they were always able to mobilize it.

At the time of my fieldwork, the weeding women did in unirrigated lands was perhaps the most notable of the variably intensified tasks they performed because it consumed a large portion of their time and the amounts of time women invested in different plots varied enormously.

In contrast to gardens, in which careful soil preparation sharply reduces the problem of weeds, plowing in dry lands, no matter how thorough, cannot remove rhizomes as well as diggers can. Although careful preparation did seem to reduce the number of weeds that appeared in the first month or two after planting, the same measures that aided the growth of crop plants also seemed to benefit the remaining weeds. Hence, it is reasonable to suppose that the weeding efforts of women in dry lands (which were much greater than those of men) would prevent weeds from crowding crop plants and increase the soil nutrients and moisture available to them.

The problems of managing weeding on dry lands, however, are quite different from those encountered in managing the preparatory labor of men. First, whereas preparatory labor is subject to a severe time constraint, weeding is virtually an ever present cultivation opportunity; the weeds that are here today will, unfortunately, be here tomorrow. To be sure, weeds allowed to grow for a long time would cause irremediable damage, but in practice villagers are able to find the time to keep most unirrigated fields reasonably free of them. For instance, a sample of forty-six *raagi*, *avare*, and *joLLa* interculture plots received an average of 182 hours of women's weeding per acre and an average of 110 hours from men.

The casual way in which weeding is done contrasts sharply with the hectic atmosphere that prevails in the plowing and planting season for dry land crops. In 1966 the perceived seasonal window for this work, the period within which villagers seemed to believe the work had to be done, was unusually narrow. The drought had left the land so dry that a greater amount of rain than usual had to fall before the soil was workable, and the Southwest Monsoon was late in coming. Consequently, most of the work of getting dry land crops into the ground was completed in a period of about five weeks, whereas in more normal years farmers might have allowed themselves a week or two more. Estimates from sample plots suggest that village men spent almost 20,000 hours in plowing, bunding, leveling, manuring, harrowing, and planting the village's dry lands. The average man who actively participated in this work put in weeks of roughly 60 hours at heavy labor during the period of peak activity.

In the weeks prior to this season, farmers repaired implements and tended carefully to the condition of their bullocks. Some bought new tools and new bullocks. In joint households men held discussions to plan their work, like generals mapping a campaign. But in spite of all this preparation, plans sometimes went awry; implements broke or animals became lame or exhausted, forcing farmers to alter strategies in mid-stream.

The careful deliberation with which this work is planned and the alterations in plans required by unforeseen circumstances may have a pronounced effect on the ultimate yields of plots. To understand how these plans are made, one must first recognize that farmers tend to be more risk averse in the cultivation of dry lands than they are in the cultivation of gardens. This aversion derives both from the fact that dry lands are viewed as a source of food rather than money and from the fact that, unlike gardens, they can be cultivated only once a year. Farmers seem more preoccupied with the specter of having little to eat than they are with the prospect of bumper crops, and they employ conservative strategies to enhance the security of their diets. The rationale for these strategies is most easily described by regarding soil moisture as the most important determinant of yields. Soil moisture, in turn, is strongly influenced by two factors, one natural, rainfall, the other cultural, the work men do in preparing fields and the amount of manure they spread before planting. In order to simplify our conceptualization of the roles of these two factors in farmer's strategies, let us make several assumptions. Soil quality is not uniform from one field to the next, but for a moment let us assume that it is. Second, while it is certainly the case that the distribution of rainfall, as well as its total amount, influences yields, let us ignore the distributional factor or, alternatively, imagine that the value of the rain that falls in a year can be judged as a unit, somehow taking into account both its quantity and its distribution so that there will be good, bad, and middling years. Finally, and this assumption is fairly realistic, assume that the amount of manure spread on a plot per acre is proportional to the intensity with which other preparatory work is done.

Now suppose that a plot has been cultivated with a given degree of intensity. As rainfall declines or changes in value from good towards bad, yields decline. Eventually a point is reached at which the plants grow, producing some fodder, but provide no food for their owners. That is what happened in 1965 on most, but not all, dry land plots. The farmer who wishes to stay above this critical threshold of some fodder but no food increases his chances of doing so by increasing the intensity of cultivation, which enhances the moisture-holding capacity of the soil and thus reduces the level of rainfall at which the critical threshold occurs.

The problem is that the amount of preparatory labor available to a farmer is more or less fixed, so that efforts to decrease the level of rainfall at which the critical threshold will occur on one plot will increase the level at which it will occur on at least one other. Thus, as long as one could be assured of at least middling rainfall, the sensible course would probably be to spread one's efforts evenly over all the land. Every plot would be above the critical threshold and the average, and thus total, returns on one's land and labor would be maximized. But farmers cannot be assured of at least middling rainfall, and if rainfall was poor, the evenhanded strategy might lead to an outcome in which every plot failed.

Earlier I noted that farmers tended to begin plowing their best lands first and turned to the poorest last. Moreover, the intensity with which a household cultivated different plots often varied substantially. Now we understand why this was so; villagers were building a measure of drought insurance into their labor allocations. By starting with the best fields, one could be sure that these at least would be well cultivated and produce something even in a year of fairly poor rain. If a farmer started with the poorer fields, a broken plow or a sick bullock might mean that the best fields could not be cultivated well enough to insure some food in a year of poor rain, and the greater efforts devoted to the poorer plots might not be enough to insure a crop on them either. By varying the distribution of his preparatory efforts over fields, often giving the most to the best, the farmer increases food yields in years of poor rainfall. The price of this strategy, it seems, is to accept less than the maximum attainable income in years of ample rain.

In short, farmers are, in preparing their dry lands, playing a lottery, and after the drought of 1965 at least, most tended to play it conservatively. To allocate one's labor is to make a bet on the weather that, once made, cannot be altered. By contrast, weeding is managerially simple; if a field has a lot of weeds in it, you try to find the time to pull them out.

This is not to say that finding the time to weed poses no problems. The distribution of women's weeding time per acre over plots of land was extremely variable because plots close to the village received a great deal of time, typically over 300 hours per acre, while those far from the village received very little. Women's domestic work days contain many slack periods that may be used for weeding, provided efforts are concentrated on plots a few minutes' walk from home. There are in the data scores of instances in which women weeded for periods of fifteen minutes to an hour during such breaks. This tendency to concentrate on plots close to home is less pronounced in the weeding efforts of men; indeed, we find in the sample of forty-six *raagi* interculture plots that the weeding times per acre of the sexes are almost uncorrelated ($r = 0.13$). Although it was my observation that women were more persistent and proficient weeders than men, some of whom spent as much time at their favorite sport of hurling rocks to drive marauding birds and monkeys from the fields as they did at weeding, the fact that men's work allows them to spend more time farther from the village evens out the distribution of weeding over fields somewhat. Nevertheless, the problem of working weeding time into busy days may lead to suboptimal distributions of effort over fields.

The fact that weeding, unlike the work men do in establishing dry land crops in the ground, is virtually an ever present cultivation opportunity is related to two other distinctions between these two forms of labor. Because of the seasonal constraint to which it is subject, preparatory labor on one field is undertaken at a cost in labor to other fields, gardens as well as other dry land fields. Weeding, by contrast, is the closest thing one finds to a form of labor with zero opportunity cost; people do it when they have little else to do. Villagers do not plow or transplant or irrigate a field in a series of short intervals spread over a number of days, in part because such a practice would lead to uneven cultivation, and in part because it would waste time. It takes a while simply to get these tasks organized and under way, efforts that have to be repeated each time the work is done. To weed one simply has to pick up a basket and a digging tool and walk to the fields, which is why women can splice short episodes of weeding between other tasks.

Finally, the average return on an hour spent weeding is probably not very high in comparison to average returns on preparatory labor in dry lands. However, my efforts to measure the productivity of weeding statistically, relative to the productivity of other tasks, have been hampered by problems in the data. Because *raagi, avare,* and *joLLa* interculture plots are by far the most common sort of dry land field, they offer a plausible data set from which to work. A number of plots had to be deleted from this population because an inexperienced research assistant did not follow observational procedures properly when gathering labor input data for them. When plots that failed because of poor germination are also omitted, we are left with the sample of forty-six plots mentioned before. The chief problem with these data is that farmers cultivated most intensively the fields that they said were their best. This association between intensity of cultivation and soil quality, a factor that I have no way of measuring apart from the general assessments of villagers, would have the effect of amplifying the apparent impact of intensity of cultivation on yields. Thus, while there is a strong *linear* association of both the preparatory work of men and the weeding efforts of women per acre with per acre yields for the forty-six cases, I suspect that this result is spurious. However, per acre inputs of these two forms of labor are also highly correlated with one another ($r = 0.74$), and this may counteract the influence of soil quality so long as we are only concerned with arriving at some notion of the productivity of the two forms of labor relative to one another. When a multiple regression analysis in logarithmic form (like that we examined for the garden *raagi* data) is computed for the forty-six plots, we find that the regression coefficient (B) assigned to the total package of male labor (per acre) invested early in the cultivation process, from first plowing through planting, is 0.352. That of women's weeding per acre is 0.166. The values of F indicate that these findings are not very reliable; there is a roughly 5 percent chance that this sample was drawn from a population in which increases in neither form of labor had a reliable impact on yields.

As I have said, these data present perplexing problems. In addition to the soil quality factor, the statistical distributions of labor inputs and yields per acre were extremely heterogeneous. I believe that labor inputs per acre really were highly variable (certainly those for weeding were), but it is quite likely that the margin of observational error incurred in gathering data on dry lands was much greater than that we encountered in gardens. The small area of gardens forms a continuous ring around the village, whereas the tracts of dry land are much larger and, in some instances, separated from one another by areas of wasteland or groves planted in *honge* (an oilseed tree) or casaurina. The size and discontinuity of dry land tracts both increased the variability of the soil quality of these fields in comparison to gardens and presented us with technical problems in data gathering. Garden plots were so small that we could measure their boundaries with a tape; dry land plots were so large that we had to step off their dimensions. Using one of Shama Rao's steps as the unit of distance, we plotted each field on graph paper (angles were measured with a transit) and asked the owner to estimate its area. This provided a basis for estimating the absolute area of the squares on the graph paper map of each plot. We took the average of these estimates, which amounted to an average of the estimates of the length of Shama Rao's steps by a variety of observers, as our unit of area. Given the constraints of equipment, expertise, and time, this was the best survey we could manage, and the hope was that errors would be randomized. But while this technique may have been adequate to produce a roughly accurate estimate of the area of dry lands as a whole, inaccuracies in the estimates of individual plot sizes could sharply bias estimates of labor inputs and yields per acre.

Because of the larger areas involved and because a research assistant's view from one tract to another was sometimes blocked by trees, we also found it more difficult to monitor labor accurately on dry lands than on gardens. An observer who spent the day in a tract of gardens could easily note the coming and going of workers on his watch. On dry lands we missed some episodes of work altogether, and in many cases an observer would come upon workers he had not noticed before or would find, upon returning to a field, that workers had left. In such cases we had to guess starting and ending times from information provided by the workers involved.

In retrospect, I believe that it would have been better to observe a sample of dry land fields rather than the entire population. Under the circumstances all that may be said is that it looks as though the average return on a unit of male preparatory labor is substantially more than that on a unit of women's weeding labor. But it is also the case that the mean amount of time women spent weeding among the forty-six plots, 182 hours, was about twice the time, 89 hours, that men spent in establishing the crop on an average acre. Thus, the total contribution to crop yields of the two forms of labor was about the same. The weeding efforts of men made no contribution to yields that I could measure.

The hypothesis that the intensification of women's weeding may make a substantial difference in yields, but that each hour of such work makes only a small difference, is supported by village women's view of this task. They uniformly described it as "gathering weeds for cattle food," suggesting that the value of the weeds as fodder is at least equal to the value of the weeding as a measure aimed at producing more abundant crops. This, of course, reveals another reason for women's willingness to devote so much time to weeding and another standard against which its productivity must be judged. It is not farfetched to say that a portion of the village's livestock was kept alive on weeds during the worst months of 1965. And while I have no quantitative data on the proportion of weeds in livestock diet, I have no doubt that they were an essential resource for many households even in good years. No one ever paid anyone to weed; that was not necessary; there were women who would weed fields for others simply to get the weeds for their cattle.

In summary, weeding is a variably intensified task, performed largely by women, that in all likelihood has a substantial influence on crop yields in addition to providing a wild food resource for cattle. But managing the labor consumed by this work does not pose problems comparable to those encountered in managing the *kashta kelsa* of men. Weeding is an almost constantly available cultivation opportunity, and the fact that it may be exploited at almost any time, even if one has only a little time to devote to it, means that an investment of effort in weeding occurs at little or no cost to other farming activities. Decisions about where to weed are fairly simple: if only a little time is available in the domestic work day, a woman weeds close to home; otherwise she simply looks for plots where there are lots of weeds. And the low average return in terms of crop yields on a hour of weeding labor means that if an inexperienced girl does not pick the best field to weed, it probably will not make much difference.

Rich and Poor

We have dealt thus far with the majority of the village population who are more or less self-sufficient farmers, for whom labor is not a variable cost but a stock for which they seek the highest and best use. Let us now turn to the richest fifth of the population, in terms of per capita income, which employs 70 percent of the labor it uses, and to the poorest fifth, which devotes 85 percent of its labor to the lands of others. Do the practices of utilizing so much labor as a variable cost and bartering so much of one's labor as a tenant or selling it as a *kuli* alter the special status of the heavy work men do in the organization of farm production?

Of one thing I am quite sure: when labor is treated as a commodity in Yaavahalli, the social psychology of the organization of work is fundamentally changed. There are occasions, to borrow the Marxian phrase, when a quantitative difference becomes a qualitative difference; this is one of them. To become *substantially* the client of a patron (or a patron of clients) is to become *essentially* the client of a patron (or a patron of clients). In Yaavahalli and surrounding communities, clientage is a condition that restricts even the remarks one may safely make in casual conversations. A *sovkaar*, by contrast, is not simply someone who is richer than other people; he is someone whose *obiter dicta* will be greeted as law (though not always followed) by sycophantic clients. The obsequiousness of some clients and the arrogance of some *sovkaars* are easily understood from the perspective of the poor. The object of the poor is to maximize minimum annual income by any means necessary. One seemingly necessary means is to play a courtly game with the powerful, the purpose of which is to maximize annual employment by persuading them that one's continued employment is to their continuous advantage.

The ground rules of the game turn on the distinction between the two main employment practices: *kuli* or daily wage labor and sharecropping tenancy. For workers the advantage of *kuli* work lies in its offer of immediate income; tenants must wait for the harvest to receive their share, though, as we shall see, this disadvantage is outweighed by the fact that tenants, on the average, receive a higher return on their labor than *kulis*. From the employer's perspective the immediate payment of *kuli* wages means money lost if the crop is poor. A landowner owes tenants nothing for their efforts if the crop fails. On the other hand, if the crop is good, tenants' shares rise accordingly, whereas the wages of *kulis* one has hired remain constant.

For workers the issue in both forms of employment is who will get work. Although *kulis* are usually hired a day at a time and paid on the spot, relations between workers and employers usually are not casual. If one walks into a field in which a number of *kulis* are at work, chances are that the majority of them are people who rely heavily on this form of employment, and it is likely that the field is owned by someone who employs *kulis* frequently. Thus, it is important for those who need this work to stay in the good graces of those who offer regular employment. One need not be a tenant to be substantially a client.

Tenancy arrangements have been altered by changes in the political economy of the larger society. The land reform that ended the economic domination of the *joodidars* (landlords) some eight years before my arrival relied on the establishment of tenancy records. If it could be shown that a household had been tenants on a parcel of land for many years, that family was allowed to purchase the land for a very low price (Rs. 25 per acre for dry land), which was used to indemnify the *joodidar*. The fact that lengthy tenancy was used as the basis for this reform made an indelible impression on the *sovkaars*, who were often the measure's greatest beneficiaries. Even though the keeping of tenancy records ceased after the reform, larger landowners recognized that in the future another reform could target their holdings. In response, *sovkaars* began speaking of their tenants as "partners" so as to convey the notion that tenants were not clients tied to parcels of land but peers of the landowner who had joined him in a business venture. This was not the only nice turn of phrase used to reconstrue the social relations of production. Indentured servitude had been made illegal, but the practice continued under another name. Well-to-do people no longer called their servants (of whom there were a number, mostly widows and boys) by the traditional term, *jiita;* they called them "salaried employees."

In order to prevent the creation of a tenancy record that would stand up in court, landowners rarely allowed a tenant to cultivate a plot for more than two successive crops. Indeed, most *sovkaars* regularly shifted tenants around from plot to plot to prevent the establishment of regular tenure, and although some tenancy relations were to all intents inherited, *sovkaars* sometimes exchanged tenants. One month A would be working for B while C was working for D; the next A would be found in the fields of D while C worked for B. This game of musical fields created a situation in which tenants tried constantly to anticipate the intentions of landowners so as to be first in line for the more lucrative plots and crops.

In this context, the basic tactic of rational poverty employed by workers was to try to use current employment to gain further employment. Note that in doing this the poor, like their middle peasant neighbors, were trying to find the highest and best use for a stock of family labor. The difference between the two classes of villagers lies in the fact that where self-sufficient farm families manipulate cultivation opportunities, the land-poor manipulate social relations.

This manipulation of social relations is best described in light of statistical data reflecting the choices employers made in employing women and men as *kulis* and tenants. Table 4 is a matrix whose horizontal rows are quintiles of the population divided in terms of per capita income (a measure described in detail in the next chapter), from the top

Table 4   Mean sample hours worked by wealth category and sex

Wealth quintile	Men	Women
1st	272	132
2nd	367	171
3rd	405	249
4th	393	302
5th	455	393

20 percent, the *sovkaars,* down to the bottom quintile, the poor. The vertical columns divide labor by sex. The numbers were derived from the sample of 100,000 hours of farm labor in the following way: sample hours worked were cross-tabulated by wealth category and age/sex category. Then the total hours worked by men 17 to 50 and by women 17 to 50 in each wealth category were divided by the number of persons in that category. Thus, the fourteen men in the poorest fifth of the population worked an average of 455 sample hours.

Note that there is a sharp and systematic decline in the participation of women in agriculture as land wealth increases. The richest women work only one-third as many hours as the poorest women, who work as much as most men. A few of these women, incidentally, live in households containing no man, though they receive support from male relatives. Although the poorest men work the most, there is no marked decline in the work of men with increases in wealth until we reach the top quintile. Even then, the richest men work about 60 percent of the amount of time put in by the poorest.

This association of work, wealth, and sex influences the sexual division of hired labor. Wealthier families compensate for the lower participation of their women in farm labor by hiring poor women as *kulis.* This compensation further skews a distribution of employment opportunities for *kuli* labor that might favor women somewhat anyway. Households in the top quintile of the population own so much land that they would have to hire a large portion of their labor even if household members did as much farm work as the poor, and the cultivation opportunities for which *kulis* are most often hired, planting and harvesting, involve tasks in which women are heavily employed. In addition to the transplanting of grain seedlings in gardens and tank-irrigated land, there are a number of vegetable crops planted by hand, and here again women are favored over men because of the greater manual dexterity attributed to them. And though men contribute a bit more time to grain harvests than women, women are preferred for harvesting vegetables that are picked from bushes, such as beans and chilies. Consequently, women, who contributed 36 percent of all hours worked in the 100,000-hour sample of farm labor, accounted for 53 percent of the *kuli* labor in the sample. When *kashta kelsa* tasks are subtracted from the sample hours of *kuli* labor, women account for 69 percent of the remaining work. *Kuli* labor was employed for one-quarter of all farm work, and so female *kulis* do about 13 percent of all farm work done.

For tenant labor the sexual division of employment is reversed. Men do 76 percent of such work in the sample. Tenants account for about 17 percent of all farm work done, which means that the work of male tenants is also about 13 percent of the total.

Landowners hire *kulis* to plant and to harvest because these tasks consume a great deal of time and must be completed promptly. In employing tenants they have other considerations in mind: they want strong backs to perform preparatory labor, they want assistance in managing the details of their farming, and they want workers who have a stake in the outcome of cultivation because their income is a portion (half for dry land, one-third for irrigated land) of the net yield.

Regardless of the form of employment, it is a fact of life that employers hold considerable power to dictate wages. The poorest households need employment simply to eat, and there are enough people in this predicament that they must concede monopsony power to the wealthy in the knowledge that if they refuse an employment opportunity, there are likely to be others, perhaps in nearby villages, who will take it. The only time *kuli* wages rise noticeably in response to increases in the demand for labor is during the harvest of dry lands. Even then, the rise takes the form of meals provided workers, a device that preserves the notion that there is a relatively fixed money wage attached to each agricultural task. Daily wages for adults ranged from Rs. 0.75 for transplanting to about Rs. 2.00 (sometimes less, occasionally more) for the hardest work. It seems doubtful that the average wages of *kuli* labor, overall, exceed more than a moderate fraction of the average returns on the work done, so that in the long term *sovkaars* do not face a severe risk in employing workers in spite of the fact that wages equal money lost in the event of crop failure. For example, all of the male labor required to prepare and plant an acre of dry land in *raagi*, *avare*, and *joLLa* at an average level of intensity could have been hired for as little as Rs. 20. The average village product yield for the 46-plot sample is Rs. 387 per acre.

Still, even the wealthiest households encountered recurrent cash flow problems in an economy in which short-term credit is quite expensive. Thus, in spite of the low level of *kuli* wages, *sovkaars* rather frequently made sharecropping arrangements with tenants, especially when the other cash costs entailed in cultivating a crop were unusually high, in order to hold down the immediate expenses of production and to reduce their loss in case of crop failure.

As I have intimated, however, landowners are doing more than contracting for a package of labor to be used in cultivating a plot when they take on a tenant. Because tenants have a stake in the crop, they are counted on to approach their work with greater zeal than *kulis* and thus require less supervision. Indeed, tenants are often used to supervise *kulis*. This is particularly important at the preparatory stages of cultivation, when it is important that work be both thorough and quick and when the landowner's knowledge concerning ultimate yields is poor. He can anticipate that male tenants will exert themselves much as they would if the land were their own, and he knows that he will owe them nothing for their efforts if the crop fails.

Thus, in practice, tenants often become a part of a landowner's productive establishment, a stock of labor he can exploit almost as if they were family members. On a number of occasions we found that men of tenant households were asked to work on plots other than those for which they had contracted. In private, tenants regarded this practice as exploitative (they were, as they said, working "for free"), but though they resented these demands, they did the work. To refuse to do so would have jeopardized their continued tenancy.

Moreover, in spite of this device to drive down the effective hourly wages of tenants, they were still higher than the average wages of *kulis*. I calculated a wage index for the poorest quintile of the population in the following way: I took the total net income these households received from the cultivation of their own lands and divided it by the total number of hours they worked on their lands in the sample of 100,000 hours of farm labor. This ratio was treated as numeraire, 1.00. Then I totaled the income these households received from tenancy and *kuli* labor and divided each sum by the sample hours they worked in that form of employment. In this way I found that the effective wage of tenant labor was 49 percent of what the poor earned in working for themselves, while the return on *kuli* labor was only 36 percent of the self-employed figure.

So it seems clear that the goal of the poor should be to get as much tenancy labor as they can, and in fact it is. Tenants try to ingratiate themselves with a patron by industrious work and by making him as dependent as possible on their managerial and supervisory expertise so as to retain their position. For instance, while the *patel*'s written accounts were kept in order with the assistance of his eldest daughter, much of the information that went into the books came out of the head of his chief factotum, Krishnappa, a young Holeya who had been a client of the *patel* since childhood.

Not only may one employment opportunity as a tenant be used to secure others, but tenancy may place one in an advantageous position to acquire *kuli* work as well. The extra work men do can be used as a moral lever to acquire *kuli* work for the household's women. Tenants have advance information concerning a patron's plans, and they can, by calling attention to their past loyalty and effort, secure favored treatment for their women when there is transplanting or harvesting to be done.

This situation places poor households who are not tenants at a competitive disadvantage. There will be a substantial amount of *kuli* work available to them, but much of it will involve tasks for which comparatively low wages are paid. The *kuli* work for which the highest wages are paid, *kashta kelsa*, accounts for only about 6 percent of all farm work done, and there are about as many men competing for these opportunities as there are women available for the more ample supply of *kuli* labor at less difficult tasks. Hence, the more problematic aspect of employment for such households is finding hard work for the men to do. As I have noted, employers regard *kulis* as less well motivated than tenants, a view that tenants are quick to promote. So long as *kulis* are working for someone who does not employ workers very often, or for a *sovkaar* whose tenancy positions appear solidly booked for the foreseeable future, I suspect that the work rate of *kulis* left unsupervised does tend to fall below that of other workers. If one looks into the history of many tenancy arrangements, however, a recurrent theme emerges: tenancy relationships are preceded by periods of regular *kuli* employment. Through a demonstration of their industry in the heavy work for which they have been employed as *kulis*, men induce landowners to add them to their staff of tenants. Several new tenancy relations were established during my stay in the village, and in each case the men who obtained these positions were, in the parlance of American industrial labor relations, rate-busters; they outworked the competition.

Earlier I likened relations between patron and client to a courtly game in which arrangements perpetuating economic inequality are portrayed as arrangements of mutual advantage, which, in the context of prevailing property institutions, they are. The game is most often played out in relations among men, not only because men manage agriculture, but also because of the peculiar status of the heavy work men do in the cultivation process.

The preparatory work of men is the first work done on a plot of land, and the manner in which it is done is likely to influence the productivity of all work done later. The peculiar status of this work figures no less prominently in the deliberations of the rich and poor than in those of the self-reliant farm family.

In closing this segment of my argument I would like to return to points made at the outset of this chapter. By attributing special prominence to the *kashta kelsa* of men, I am not relegating the female farm labor force to the status of a women's auxiliary. As we have seen, the lower a household's income, the more of women's time it allocates to farming, even to the point at which women become full-time farm workers. Examining the behavior of the poorest quintile of the village, we find that they acquire the highest average return on their labor by working on their own land. This way of looking at familial labor is justified by the fact that from the short-term perspective of villagers, land is not a commodity in which they invest money, but a resource that they have. Thus, though conventional economic analysis would regard a portion of this familial labor "wage" as a return on the land, from the point of view of the worker this is irrelevant: the question is, will he get more from working on his own land or from working on the land of others? He gets more from working on his own land. For the poorest quintile, familial labor is also the form of labor that consumes the least time. More time is spent on tenancy labor, which yields the second highest return, whereas the most time is spent doing *kuli* labor, which provides the lowest average return. *Kuli* labor is also the kind of work to which women make the largest proportional contribution: *kuli* labor constitutes a quarter of all labor time, but over a third of women's labor time. In a crude sense, then, the poor receive sharply declining marginal wages with increases in the amount of farm work they do. Once they have exploited opportunities on their own land, they turn to tenancy; once the supply of tenant work the wealthy are willing to make available is exhausted, all that remains is *kuli* work. And it is largely through the efforts of women, who have been willing to leave their homes to work long hours at low wages, that the additional rupees that make the difference between dietary stress and a measure of dietary security are squeezed from a stingy labor market.

I have returned to the subject of women's increased participation in farming in response to increased crowding of household resources because this synchronic patterned variation across households seems to have been recapitulated in the population as a whole over time. Though a more detailed discussion of the matter must be postponed to a later chapter, it appears, as I have said before, that women's participation in agriculture, both absolute and relative to men's, has increased as the region's population density has grown.

While the expansion of garden cultivation, which has been largely responsible for the general increase in the labor intensity of farming, has increased per capita incomes in years of poor rain, dietary incomes per capita in most years do not seem to have changed much. Over the years rural people have been doing more work for about the same income; increased efforts have produced declining marginal returns, a process that has been coupled with the increased contribution of women to farm labor. This co-occurrence did not take place because women were any less productive than men in the tasks to which they were customarily assigned; it happened because, beyond a certain point, women's time was the only stock of labor from which additional workers could be obtained.

This situation may seem familiar to many Americans. One of the many reasons for the increased participation of women in the paid labor force of the United States is inflation. As the buying power of a husband's income declines, or at least stops growing, the wife takes a job. In a general sense, the same sort of thing happened in Yaavahalli. As the capacity of men to feed families on an ever more crowded landscape declined, women stepped up their efforts in primary production.

But there is a vital difference between their situation and ours that stems from the difference in the way labor is organized in the two societies. When income is won by individuals who seek and secure jobs in a large labor market, wives and husbands work and earn independently of one another. To be sure, one spouse's job may prevent a couple from moving to a place where the employment opportunities of the other might be better. But from the immediate perspective of a couple, the fact is that she gets her check and he gets his through actions conducted independently. If she works hard she may obtain a raise, but her hard work will not help her husband get one.

In Yaavahalli, where households are the basic units of production, there is an interactive relationship between the productivity of the women of a household and that of the men. By increasing their contribution to farming, village women are not simply performing a rough equivalent of getting a job. Because women and men of the same domestic group work in the same productive organization, the increased participation of women both releases more of the men's time for *kashta kelsa* and retrieves a fuller value for the heavy work men do. For instance, during the plowing of dry lands, women virtually took over a number of ongoing tasks, such as the irrigation of gardens, to which their men had been making large contributions. Had they not done so, this work could have been done only at a cost to preparatory labor. Likewise, as we have seen, standardization of the transplanting technique on irrigated land and the weeding women do on dry lands both enhance the productivity of carefully prepared land.

Thus, if it may be said that the *kashta kelsa* men do occupies a special place in farm production, the same may be said for the farm work of women, which has been the single most important factor in the increasing labor intensification of village agriculture. The special role of male labor, however, places men in a more favorable position to manage farming.

> Proposition 4. *Because the tasks performed only by men are economically problematic and because decisions regarding the allocation of farm labor are reached analogically, men are in an experientially more favorable position to manage agriculture than women.*

Our examination of the last proposition provides most of the supporting evidence for the present one. What remains to be done is to explain its meaning.

Before turning to this explanation, I might note in passing an alternative view on the male management of farming that may have occurred to readers familiar with the literature on psychological sex differences. In their magnum opus on this subject, Maccoby and Jacklin (1974) cite four sex differences found so reliably as to suggest an underlying biological basis for them: males are more aggressive than females; females have greater verbal ability than males; males display a greater ability to conceptualize spatial/visual relationships than females; and males show greater mathematical ability than females, a difference that may be related to spatial ability. There is, moreover, some direct evidence indicating biological foundations for these differences. The differences in verbal and spatial/visual abilities, for instance, may be due to differences in hemispheric dominance in the brain.

Farm management in Yaavahalli amounts to a sort of folk engineering in which the capacity to conceptualize relations among objects and activities in space over time is essential. If men, on the average, inherited a greater capacity for manipulating spatial relations than women, it would make them better able to manage farming.

I have not, however, incorporated this line of argument into my account of village farming for two reasons. First, the biological foundations for this sex difference are scarcely established; we know a great deal more about the physiology of work capacity than we do about that of conceptual ability. Second, this factor is not necessary for my argument. If males did have a systematic advantage in spatial ability, farm management would be a cultural amplification of it, but that advantage would simply be another reason for men to manage farming that would be congruent with the reasons we shall consider. Those reasons have to do with the experience of being an adult male.

The meaning of the term "experientially favorable position" is illustrated by Alan Beals's research on social interaction within the crews of B-29s (Beals, Spindler, and Spindler 1967). In these World War II vintage bombers, the most highly skilled positions, such as pilot and navigator, were assigned to officers, while the putatively less skilled gunner positions were filled by lower ranks. If one of these planes came under attack by enemy aircraft, it fell to the gunners, particularly the central gunner, to tell the plane's commander how best to evade the attack. Situated in a plastic bubble atop the plane, the central gunner was in the best position to see what was going on; that is, he was in a favorable experiential position to make decisions about evasive maneuvers, even though that meant a sergeant would be telling an officer what to do.

An illustration of analogic decision making is provided by Miller, Gallanter, and Pribram (1960) in another example involving aircraft. One of the authors was taking flying lessons, which required the learning of a good deal of specific technical knowledge. But as it turned out, that sort of information was not all that he needed to know to fly an airplane. Suppose, for example, that during a landing approach, his instructor told him to give the plane a little left rudder because they were in a cross wind. When asked how much left rudder, the instructor could only reply, "Enough." The amount of left rudder was supposed to be proportional to the strength of the cross wind, and that was something one learned by experience to judge from the feel of the aircraft in varying situations. Decisions of this sort are made analogically, in contrast to digitally reached decisions made through the manipulation of some metrically organized calculus. Perhaps one could develop for any aircraft a function specifying the degrees of rudder appropriate for any cross wind measured in miles per hour. But pilots of light planes do not need such information, because they can land just as well working with an analogic calculus based in trained senses. Just as the differential of a car allocates power to its wheels proportional to their traction, so the pilot knows what conditions look and feel like when the aircraft is in the correct position.

What is true of airplanes is true of peasant farming. I was once told by an engineer of the Public Works Department that he estimated the number of workers required for the construction of irrigation works by first calculating the cubic meters of earth contained in, say, a ditch to be dug. Then he divided that number by 1.75, the number of cubic meters of hard laterite a man could dig in a day. Villagers do not make very many allocative decisions this way, but that does not mean that they make decisions based on poor information. Recall that experimental subjects could estimate their degree of physical exertion with a very high degree of accuracy. When making decisions about the allocation of manual labor, an experienced worker may, through a retrospective examination of other situations, come up with a solution that is better than any one could obtain at acceptable costs using a digital calculus like that employed by the engineer.

I recall speaking to a village farmer in the fields after the first heavy rain of the Southwest Monsoon. The soil of the village dry lands appeared soft and moist to me, and so I asked him if plowing could begin. He squatted, felt the soil for a moment, and said that, no, the ground was still too hard and dry. One night shortly thereafter it rained again, and at dawn the fields were full of plowmen. The texture of the soil is somehow related to the effort required to plow it, so that until some critical texture is reached, it is not worthwhile to try to plow.

Because so many allocative decisions are made in this fashion, the effectiveness of farm managers depends on how acute they are as analogic computers. People who measure environmental conditions with experienced eyes and hands in order to determine how much of some input is enough can tell you a good deal about the decisions they make, but often their remarks are expressed in proportional—that is, analogic—terms, of more and less, better and worse.

Perhaps almost anyone provided with appropriate numerical data, such as some of the statistical materials I have discussed, could make sound digital decisions regarding farm management, if he or she had the necessary mathematical skills. But since villagers do not have or even attempt to get data of that sort, the question is, whose experience puts them in the best position to make allocative decisions in agriculture? The answer is men, especially senior men, not only because men participate in all phases of farm work and spend about twice as much time in the fields as the average woman, but also because of the economically problematic status of the work that only men do. If someone has not done a good deal of plowing, he will not be able to make the kind of determination my neighbor made that spring morning. And because allocations of male labor over alternative cultivation opportunities are so critical, and because they must be made jointly with decisions regarding plot size and crop selection, the experience men have with men's work places them in a position more favorable than that of women to make decisions about farm management.

Moreover, their position provides them with experience concerning more than environmental conditions. Senior men have worked alongside their brothers and sons and many other men of the village. Unlike the Public Works engineer, for whom every man is equal to 1.75 cubic meters of laterite, village farmers make fine distinctions among individuals according to their reputations as workers. The *sovkaars* who hire tenants believe they know who has a mustache and who does not. And poor men who have been tenants for years know which *sovkaars* tend to be devious and stingy and which tend to be generous.

These economic personalities men construe in one another derive from ongoing patterns of interaction determining who is going to do what for whom. For example, experienced tenants know how to contrive situations in which their labor becomes what may be termed a Giffin input—something that is not supposed to exist according to economic theory. A Giffin commodity is one, like potatoes during the Irish famines, for which demand increases with commodity price and declines with increases in income. During the famines, real income went down and people increasingly substituted potatoes for other foods. As they did so, potato prices increased, to which they responded by trying to buy more potatoes. Giffin inputs are not supposed to exist, because firms are not supposed to be subject to the kinds of budgetary constraints that constrain households (Intrilligator 1971). What experienced tenants try to do is to make themselves an indispensable part of the patron's labor force. Then they present the patron with a pressing need, such as the cost of a child's marriage, and imply that their worry over this problem is so grave as to interfere with their work. If done with enough craft, this stratagem will yield a loan that may never be fully repaid. Thus, the tenant is able to contrive an increase in his net wage—the cost of his labor—while at the same time insuring a continued demand for his services, for he will not be fired so long as he is in debt to his patron. Indeed if the patron's fortunes decline he will be the last tenant fired.

Sons use the same tactics on their fathers when the father is reluctant to arrange a marriage for them. By appearing distracted and truculent in their work, and by spending a great deal of time with their peers in highly suspicious circumstances, they may goad their parents into arranging the marriage they want, thereby securing an additional benefit from their continued effort in the fields.

Fathers and *sovkaars* have their stratagems too, and we shall return in the next chapter to the matter of knowing how to manipulate one's relations with other men. We shall see that farm management has perhaps more in common with coaching an athletic team than with running a business for profit.

chapter 6

One Man or More

In the last chapter I endeavored, through a detailed discussion of the mechanics of village farming, to describe the role of *kashta kelsa* in cultivation and the connection between that role and farm management. Although the plot-by-plot statistical analyses I presented supported my thesis concerning the role of male preparatory labor in production, they were of limited scope and, in one case, of suspect reliability. Thus, while we may have succeeded in isolating the material reasons for the great importance villagers attribute to the high energy component of their technology, the case is scarcely conclusive.

In this chapter, however, we shall examine more comprehensive data concerning the annual production of households. These data indicate that a simple difference among households, whether they contain only one man or more than one, makes a large and systematic difference in productivity. These data, then, strongly suggest that, whatever the mechanics of the phenomenon, variation in the organization of male labor has a strong impact on farm production.

The data also confirm what villagers say they know: that the partition of joint households, which generally creates households containing only one man, exacts a high material price.

> Proposition 5. *Households containing more than one man have higher crop yields and higher per capita incomes than those with only one.*

Because a number of factors are associated with measures of household productivity and income, some care must be exercised to control for these other sources of variance before this proposition can be tested.

In order to measure annual yields per acre for a household's entire estate, criteria must first be established for estimating a farm's estate size. Using unirrigated lands as numeraire, garden holdings were indexed at five times their absolute area because median annual yields from garden lands exceeded those of dry lands by about that ratio. Tank-irrigated paddy lands were indexed at only 0.65 of their area because the median yield was only 65 percent that of dry lands. During a better year the relative status of these lands (and of farmers' decisions regarding their cultivation) would be quite different. Two households with extremely large estates were dropped from the sample because both owned lands in other villages for which I was unable to acquire data that I believed to be reliable. Several female-headed households and that of the village Brahmin were also dropped from the sample because they did not manage their own lands and thus did not constitute household firms in the same sense as other households. (The reader should bear in mind that these omitted households, some of the very rich and some of the very poor, were included in the quintile data cited in the preceding chapter.) What remains is a sample of forty-eight owner-cultivators with estates ranging from 1.5 to 66.3 standard acres.

Household size was taken as the sum of the Lusk coefficients of consumption of all household members. This coefficient estimates the nutritional needs of different age/sex categories, using adult males as numeraire. The measure is thus sensitive to the fact that most village households have a high, though unmeasured, propensity to spend increases in income on food. The smallest household in the village, a man and his wife, has 1.83 consumption units, while the largest, a joint family of twenty-six persons, has 17.37 consumption units.

Annual crop yields were totaled from the village product yield of each plot cultivated. Thus, "yield per acre" means total village product per standard acre. So calculated, annual yields per acre ranged from Rs. 37 to Rs. 473. Likewise, per capita land wealth is taken as the number of standard acres owned per consumption unit.

Annual household income is the total of village product yields from land minus the cost of hired labor, plus income received from *kuli* wages, tenants' fees, and ancillary sources of money income such as dairying. Per capita income is thus annual income per consumption unit, which ranged from Rs. 95 to Rs. 1,315. If one wonders how anyone could live on Rs. 95 per capita, the answer it that no one could. This elderly childless couple received support from the husband's brothers. Nevertheless, they were included in the sample because they were a working farm firm and because excluding them made very little difference in the statistical results. Moreover, their inclusion indicated what happens to childless people with little land; if they had a son, their yields would have increased.

With these measures in hand I found that per capita land wealth accounts for 49 percent of the variance in per capita income, but only 2 percent of the variance in yields per acre. Thus, a test of the proposition must control for the influence of per capita land wealth on income, but we can be fairly sure that land wealth will not exercise a spurious influence over yields per acre, the other variable of interest.

On the assumption that the remaining variance in per capita income is accounted for by variations in yields per acre, by variations in the difference between expenditures for and revenues from hired labor, and by variations in income from other sources such as dairy and livestock production, I computed a variable to measure residual income, that is, the portion of a family's income not accounted for by per capita land wealth or by the yields they received from cultivation of their own lands. To do this I first calculated a value of predicted per capita income for each household, using the regression coefficients for per capita income associated with per capita land wealth and yields per acre. Residual income was taken as the difference between predicted and observed income per capita for each case. A household having a high value on this variable will be one that enjoyed a favorable balance of payments between expenditures for and revenues from hired labor, compared to other households at similar levels of per capita land wealth, or it will be one that received substantial income from ancillary sources, or both. By contrast, households with low values (or, as it happens from the computation procedure, negative values) on this variable will be those with comparatively poor balances of payments and no ancillary income. The proposition is thus revised to state that households containing two or more men will have higher yields per acre and higher residual incomes per capita (over and above the income they would be expected to have, given their yields and land wealth) than households with only one man.

Discriminant function analysis, the statistical technique used to test this proposition, may be thought of (for those unfamiliar with it) as a distant cousin of factor analysis. To employ it, we choose a discrete "group" variable, here the two types of households, along with a set of independent "discriminating" variables, which are, or are treated as, continuous. With this technique we first calculate a linear function from the discriminating variables that is maximally powerful in distinguishing the (in this case two) groups from one another. Where the groups are very different from one another in their distributions over a given independent variable, that variable will receive a large coefficient in the final function. If the groups are relatively similar to one another with respect to some other variable, that variable receives a small coefficient.

Having computed this discriminant function and measured its power to discriminate the groups from one another, we then attempt to predict the actual group membership of each case in the data. Table 5 displays the results of a discriminant function analysis in which yields per acre and residual income were used to discriminate between the two types of households.

Table 5   Discriminant function analysis of households with one and more than one man by yields per acre and residual per capita income (actual minus predicted per capita income)

A. *Means of discriminating variables*

| | Type of household | |
Variable	One man ($N = 21$)	More than one man ($N = 27$)
Yields per acre (Rs.)	152.05	276.32
Residual income (Rs.)	−55.06	42.74

Canonical correlation = 0.672; Wilkes lambda = 0.548; chi square = 27.07; significance level = 0.001.

B. *Prediction of group membership*

| | Predicted group | |
Actual group	One man	More than one man
One man	18 (85.7%)	3 (14.3%)
More than one man	4 (14.8%)	23 (85.2%)

Cases correctly classified = 85.42%

In over 85 percent of the cases, the computer correctly "guessed" the number of men in a household on the basis of the two discriminating variables. The values of the canonical correlation coefficient and chi square indicate that the distinction between the two groups of households accounts for a large proportion of the variances of yields per acre and residual per capita income (about 45 percent of the discriminant function's variance) and that these results are very unlikely to have occurred by chance (significance better than 0.001).

Moreover, there seems to be no viable alternative explanation for this phenomenon. For example, the absolute size of holdings, which increases with increases in the number of men in a household, is not associated with yields per acre. The first-order partial correlation of estate size with per acre yields, holding the number of men constant, is only 0.07. Because the average number of women and children per man declines with increases in the number of men in a household (some multiple-male households contain unmarried men), it might be argued that this difference in family composition as a unit of production, relative to family size as a unit of consumption, somehow influences productivity. But although increases in the number of other persons per man adversely affect the ratio of land to people, such increases do not appear to exercise a strong short-term influence on yields. If the work force quality hypothesis is viable, we would expect yields per acre to increase with increases in the ratio of men to total household size, holding the number of men constant, but the value of this first-order partial correlation is only 0.09.

It would be more plausible to argue that because land holdings per man are higher for the single-man than the multiple-man households, their lands receive less intensive cultivation and therefore yields are lower. Since the ratio of land holdings to household size is almost exactly the same for both groups, the lower yields of the single-male group lead to lower per capita income. This argument is confounded by the data, for while it is true that the lands of the one-man households do receive less intensive cultivation, which probably accounts for their lower yields, this cannot be attributed directly to the ratio of men to land. If that argument were correct, then we would expect to find declines in yields per acre with increases in land holdings within both groups. In fact, there is a very slight positive association between yields and land holdings within both the single-male group and the set of households containing two or more men.

It might also be argued that the group variable used in this analysis is spurious, since the number of men in households is likely to be correlated with the number of women or simply the number of adults in them. That is not the case.

There are nine two-man households containing only one woman; in most the second man is the unmarried son of the *yajaman* and the mother of the house. Yields per acre among these households are extremely high. Indeed, such households are instances of what seems to be a highly productive phase in the domestic cycle, and the proportionally high frequency of them at the time, a demographic feature that distinguished Yaavahalli from some of its neighbors, is one factor accounting for the very large differences between the means of yields and residual income for the one-man and multiple-man households in the sample of forty-eight. There are also three households containing two women but only one man, and these obtained relatively low yields, though there is some association between the number of women and ancillary production. Consequently, yields per acre and residual income do not discriminate very well households with one woman from households with more than one, and such discriminatory power as they do have seems to be largely a spurious reflection of the fact that most households containing more than one woman also contain more than one man. Stated simply, the number of women in a household does not appear to have much effect on agricultural productivity.

There are important efficiencies derived from having more than one woman in a household; one we shall examine presently has to do with livestock and dairy production. Moreover, I strongly suspect that the health and comfort of families containing two or more women was often substantially better than that of families relying on only one, and since I have no measures of such quality-of-life variables, my analysis of the advantages of joint household living is incomplete. But the fact remains that households with more than one man are far more productive than those with only one, and as best I can determine, there is no other demographic factor that might render this association spurious. Let us now try to determine why this is so.

In an earlier, unpublished analysis of these data (cited in Selby 1975), I described the advantage of households having two or more men over those with only one as an economy of scale. That description is not observationally adequate; rather, it is more appropriate to describe the advantage in terms of a technological external economy.

Strictly speaking, an economy of scale occurs when a simultaneous and proportionally equal increase in all factors of production leads to an increase in output that is proportionally greater than the increase in the scale of production. On its face the advantage enjoyed by households of two or more men appears to meet this definition. If two men in a household of ten people own ten acres of land, they are indeed better off staying together than they would be if they divided into two households of one man, five people, and five acres each. But this superficial description masks what is really going on in the organization of work, for factor proportionality in the allocation of labor to land and other resources is distinctly different for the two types of households. Therefore, the definition does not apply to the phenomenon as a whole, though it is relevant in certain special cases.

I have borrowed the term "technological external economy" from Scitovsky (1971), who, quoting Meade (1952), defines it as follows: a technological externality or external economy occurs when the output of one firm depends not only on the factors of production utilized by that firm but on the factor utilization and output of other firms as well. In the case of village households, what happens is that the amount and kind of labor one individual performs (the utilization of his or her time as a factor of production) and the productivity of that labor (his or her output) are both influenced by the allocation of other individuals' time and the productivity of the labor they perform. These criterial conditions of the externality may be empirically realized in several ways, which, taken together, come down to the fact that the members of joint households do more work that is more productively allocated than members of families containing only one man.

Economies of scale. These can be said to occur in the production and use of employment opportunities in at least two ways. A common type is associated with the division and specialization of labor, where a result of increasing the scale of production is the minimization of the amount of labor time required for each unit of production. For example, village women spend a great deal of time on cooking and related tasks. However, the amount of woman-time consumed in food-related activities increases slowly with increases in the number of mouths to be fed because a lot of time is spent in mixing ingredients and pot watching. In a sample of 111 woman-days of labor tabulated from informants' reports of what they did the previous day, I found that women in one-woman families spent a mean of 5.2 hours a day storing and preserving food, fetching fuel and building fires, preparing food, serving it, and cleaning up afterwards. I should note that time estimates for these tasks are approximate at best. Moreover, I do not believe, judging from my observation of domestic work, that women in these households were busy feeding their families for 5.2 hours a day. Some of the time was spent pot watching, which required only the occasional stirring of food or adding of fuel to the fire; some time was also spent playing with young children. Still, the average woman in a joint household containing more than one woman spent only 3.2 hours doing the same things. Although all the women of these households together spent an average of well over six hours a day on food-related tasks, most of this time (4.6 hours) was provided by the mother of the house, freeing the junior woman or women to do other things. The available time freed by the reduced labor cost of food preparation was spent on livestock care. The women of nuclear families also spent an average of over 3.5 hours a day in farm work. Women who have spent over nine hours on housework and farming have little time or energy left for anything else. They spent an average of only forty minutes a day caring for livestock, while the women of joint households spent about 2.6 hours per woman. Since everyone must eat, time spent feeding a family must be treated as an overhead. The economy of scale in cooking for joint families produces woman-time that is spent producing eggs, meat, and dairy products in a community where most diets are protein-deficient. This reallocation of younger women's time in joint families accounts for the fact that such families earned *all* of the Rs. 12,143 derived from sales of livestock and their products during the year.

There are a number of similar cases where the amount of time spent doing something does not increase very much with the size of the task done—selling farm produce in town and watching over silkworms, to take two examples. It is common to see men set off to brokerage houses with bundles of silk cocoons. Regardless of the size of the bundle, it will take the better part of a man-day to sell it, and since joint families produce bigger bundles, each man-day spent selling them is more productive.

Table 6   Economic performance of sixteen households with poorest ratio of land to household size

| Type of household | Yields per acre (Rs.) | Per capita income (Rs.) | Sample family labor used per acre (hr) | Distribution of labor (%) | | | |
				Family lands	*Kuli*	Tenant	Other
One man (N=7)	119.0	160.9	132.8	43.1	52.6	1.9	2.3
More than one man (N=9)	283.8	355.1	192.6	34.8	35.8	25.2	4.2

Cases of this sort, in which the labor costs of production decline with its scale, apply mainly to those with ample land. A second type of economy of scale, wherein employment opportunities per worker increase in number and value with increases in the number of workers, applies mainly to the poor. Consider the data in Table 6, drawn from the sixteen poorest households in terms of per capita land wealth in the sample of forty-eight.

Table 6 shows the proportional division of all family labor from the 100,000-hour sample over four categories of labor recruitment. First, it should be pointed out that while the joint families allocated a substantially smaller proportion of total hours worked to their own lands than the one-man households of this group, they cultivated their lands more intensively nonetheless. Indeed, if the data from the 100,000-hour sample provide an accurate estimate, they invested 45 percent more labor per acre on their own lands than the single-male group. Earlier I said that the land-poor had relatively little trouble in exploiting cultivation opportunities on their own land, but as we see, this statement must be revised somewhat in the case of land-poor one-man families (some of whom do not fall into the poorest quintile of the population). Relatively poor single-male households spent over half their time working as *kulis* but almost no time working as tenants, in spite of the fact that the latter work yields a substantially higher average wage. By contrast, land-poor joint households spent a quarter of their time working as tenants and in doing so consumed well over half the tenancy employment made available during the year in the entire village, much of the remainder going to joint families from adjacent villages.

The reason for this is simple: the presence in a household of two or more men creates employment opportunities in which they may share. Since employers are looking for male workers when they take on tenants, households that can offer two or more men monopolize the market. And because cultivation opportunities on their own land are well exploited by a small proportion of their labor, the availability of this form of employment greatly increases the annual productivity of each man. Average per capita income for joint households in the land-poorest third of the sample of forty-eight is higher than the average for all twenty-one single-male households in the sample. It is important to take note of this fact, for men's work is not only the engine of agriculture; it is also the means of upward mobility.

Contrary to the widespread belief that joint households are less likely to be found among the land-poor because such fathers do not have enough property to bolster their authority, the male heads of relatively land-poor joint families have some of the most obedient sons in the village, precisely because they do not have much land. Bear in mind that as far as men's culture is concerned, a united house is simply one with multiple men, regardless of how they are related to other members. In a number of these nine households, the second or third man is unmarried, and no married son among them has a child over six or seven. The junior men of these households have been told that the only way to a better life lies in delaying marriage until the farm estate can be improved. And since the parents of potential brides are likely to concur in this view, such a boy is obliged to accept his parents' reluctance to arrange his marriage. In addition to pointing out the hard economic facts to his son, the father may justify the burden of celibacy by suggesting that the boy's mother is looking forward to having some growing sister's daughter or other kinswoman return to care for her in her dotage. He is not simply waiting to marry; he is waiting for a particular girl.

Indivisibility problems. These resemble economies of scale in some ways, but here the defining feature is not that more of something is produced or that it may be produced at a lower per unit cost in time when the scale of production is increased, but rather that the scale of production has to reach a certain level in order to acquire a certain good or service at all. You cannot divide people, for example, but only their time. If *kulis* are to be hired to perform a task, it will require the time of one whole person to work with them. The man who has no one to help him will have to choose between that cultivation opportunity and another that calls for his attention. He cannot feasibly turn to his wife to help, because it will take the greater part of her day just to keep the household running. By contrast, the men of a joint household can send one man to supervise the *kulis* while the others do something else.

Indivisibility problems are also encountered in the purchase of such expensive agricultural goods as carts, seed drills, and wells. Because the per capita rate of savings tends to increase when a household contains more than one man, capital will accrue more rapidly towards these investments in any case, but since resources are being pooled, two other things will happen as well. First, a joint household will be able to acquire goods that a nuclear family might have to do without, and second, it will use capital more efficiently. There is no sense in trying to dig a tiny well: unless you have the resources in labor or money to construct one large enough to justify investment in one of the electric pumps now used on most wells, it is scarcely worth the trouble. Likewise, nonessential tools and implements come in fixed sizes. Unless you can afford the price, you can own no cart or seed drill at all. Moreover, since no one needs more than one of either of these, the investment by a one-man family will tend to be underutilized in comparison to the same investment by a joint family.

Interactive decision making and interpersonal comparisons of productivity. These factors constitute the last and perhaps most important sources of the greater productivity of joint households. The advantages of joint households described thus far stem in the main from built-in spatial and physical features of the technology. The most notable exception, the advantage in tenancy employment of men in land-poor joint households, involves a social and economic relation between households, as does the supervision of *kulis*.

Interactive decision making and interpersonal comparisons of productivity, by contrast, are matters of social interaction among members of the same household. If a man is the only man in a household, he makes most of his allocative decisions internally, through discussions with himself. He may acquire information relevant to those decisions in conversations with other people, but it is rare for him to go to someone else, lay out a problem, and solicit advice on a matter of routine farm management. When he makes a decision or goes to work in the fields, there is no one to police his behavior, no one to tell him whether he is working effectively or ineffectively. Much the same applies to his wife (while some of these households contain the mother of one of the spouses, most are nuclear families). Discussions relating to farm management between husband and wife for the most part fall into two categories: they discuss the allocation of her time to work on family lands or *kuli* work, or the husband unloads his troubles onto his wife. In neither case, I gathered, does he discuss with her such things as the details of crop selection or the decision whether to hire *kulis* for some task. Perhaps he does not do this because she is competent and occupied in her own role and will have little to offer on the subject, or perhaps he does not want to appear incompetent or indecisive to her.

In any case, most of the men of these households are relatively young (if only because men who hive off from joint households in middle age often have an adolescent son by the time they do so), and their youth has something to do with their managerial behavior. Viewed one way, young men are foolish not to seek the advice of others, for they are inexperienced managers. But consider the situation in which such a man finds himself. He could turn to his own father or elder brother for advice, but he is likely to get a gratuitous "I told you so" along with practical information from the man who used to run the joint farm enterprise of which he was a member. He could turn to another man like himself, but why seek advice from a person as inexperienced as oneself? Moreover, young householders are fiercely defensive about their status and tend to conduct conversations with one another in which each tries to show that he knows as much as the other.

Yet Yaavahalli is full of experts, *anubhavastaaru*, experienced men noted for their acumen in agricultural matters. They are easily identifiable in the community: they are appraisers who are asked to set fair prices in transactions between households, most typically sales of land, livestock, or the mulberry leaves used in sericulture. The trouble with turning to these acknowledged experts for help is that they are all middle-aged or elderly heads of joint households. On one occasion I was talking to a young householder in the street within earshot of a nearby expert. The young man said that he did not know the answer to a question concerning the properties of a variety of rice, and he turned to this expert and posed my question to him. This was the expert's reply: "It's people like you who leave their fathers and don't get their fields plowed who are the reason we have to get food from his country [America]." A simple request for information was interpreted as an admission of ignorance and used as a warrant for administering a stern scolding. The question had been asked of an expert, but the reply came from a father of two adolescent sons.

Older men label such young householders fools for leaving home and, given the chance, may make fools of them in public. In doing so they make examples of them to their own sons. It is noteworthy that two young men and one adolescent boy who found themselves farm managers through no fault of their own received copious and sympathetic advice from the same men. Note too that the expert not only called the young man foolish for separating from a father who knew the answers to questions like the one I asked, but also called him lazy—a person who does not get his fields plowed. Six adult males were asked to name the households of the village who were hard workers and those who were lazy. Only ten households were identified four or more times as lazy, and nine of them contained only one man. By contrast, the great majority of households called hard workers, *kashta jiivigaLu*, were joint. In a way the statistical data bear these attributions out, for single-male households in fact mobilize much less labor.

The data in Table 7, drawn from the 100,000-hour sample of field

Table 7   Mean hours of labor used per standard acre from the 100,000-hour sample, by recruitment category for single-male and joint households*

	Type of household	
Type of labor	One man	More than one man
Family	104.2	222.5
Kuli	20.0	40.3
Tenant	8.8	57.6
Other[†]	6.4	11.5

*Two rich households using large amounts of hired labor were omitted in the selection of this sample.
[†]Includes reciprocal exchange labor and labor provided by visiting relatives.

labor, show the mean amounts of sample labor per acre (of all age/sex categories) invested in the lands of single-male households to be lower than those of multiple-male households in all categories of labor recruitment. Not only did these families put less than half as much of their own labor time per acre into their lands as the joint households did, but they hired less labor per acre as well. Of particular note is the fact that single-male households hired very little tenant labor, thereby foregoing access to the work of other men who would have a stake in the productivity of the land. Young householders tend to be timid decision makers, and concluding a tenancy arrangement involves telling someone else that you will give him either half or one-third of the net income from the plot he helps you cultivate. As we have seen, there are land-poor young householders who cannot find tenancy employment, and yet there also exist some comparatively land-rich young men who are reluctant to hire them. Labor reciprocally exchanged with other households, which was a significant factor in the work of some families, was also little used by single-male households.

While the yields per acre of the joint households exceeded those of the single-male group by a factor of 1.8 to 1.0, the ratio of their inputs of labor per acre, estimated from these sample data, was 2.4 to 1.0. Clearly joint households receive declining marginal returns for the additional labor they use, but in comparison to the single-male group, they do not, for the most part, appear to be working on very close margins at all. That is, the average revenue product of the additional labor per acre they used, over and above that used by the single-male group, is lower than that obtained by the single-male group, but not so much lower as to suggest that they engaged in useless effort.

Returning home with a bundle of mulberry leaves. Silk cocoon production has become a major source of income from gardens. The voracious worms consume huge quantities of fresh leaves and require frequent cuttings and feedings, work that employs the sexes interchangeably.

What happens is this. Young householders are more prone than experienced managers to make mistakes in crop and seed selection. Moreover, because these families cannot support as many nontraction animals relative to estate size as joint families, there is less manure available for each acre of land. Those among them who have more land than they can prepare carefully themselves are reluctant to hire other men to help them, and thus do a less thorough job at the critical stage of production. Thereafter, the crops they plant grow less abundantly. Since the labor time per acre required to exploit such subsequent cultivation opportunities as transplanting and harvesting is fairly constant, the average physical product associated with each hour spent at these tasks will be lower. Therefore, the young farmer may be working at much closer margins if he hires labor for these tasks than the joint household next door, because his risk of crop failure is greater while the rate he must pay is the same. The lower yields of single-male households mean that there is less income to reinvest, so that the young farmer has less cash to pay wages in any case. Consequently, these men and their wives try to do as much of the essential labor themselves as they can. While the couple is out transplanting or harvesting together, other fields are left untended, resulting in less careful preparation of land, less weeding, and irrigation done at less appropriate intervals.

While young farmers appear to be excessively averse to taking risks in the hiring of labor, they are insufficiently so in other respects. Those who own garden lands are prone to try to redeem themselves with big returns on high-risk crops, and the rate of crop failure among them is somewhat higher than that of multiple-male households. For example, sericulture provides the largest single source of cash income in the village and the most frequent source of windfall returns. Sixteen of the twenty-one single-male households and twenty of the twenty-seven multiple-male households cultivated some garden acreage in bush mulberry, and they devoted similar proportions of garden holdings (averages of 38 and 41 percent respectively) to this crop.

On its face, sericulture is a very attractive enterprise, for the bushes on each garden plot will provide as many as five or six yields of mulberry leaves a year, and there is always a strong market for cocoons. But the attraction is deceptive. The worms must be reared in round basketry trays in a room or building set aside for the purpose, and they must be fed around the clock. People who must do other things find these feedings difficult to manage during the day, and nocturnal feedings result in lost sleep and poorer work performance. Moreover, the worms are extremely sensitive to variations in temperature and humidity, and many die because of this. When mature, the worms are placed in basketry frames called *chandrankies* and put out of doors to spin their cocoons. There they must be carefully watched to ward off marauding crows.

While both women and men participate in sericulture, in joint households it is the specialty of older men. These experts can talk endlessly of the properties of the different "races" or "castes" of silkworms, of the amount of filament each can produce, of the suitability of each to the different seasons of the year, and of how each displays the onset of the different *jeras* or "fevers" that mark the stages of their growth. Because younger members of the household are available for other agricultural tasks, these men have not only the expertise but also the time to manage sericulture carefully. It is chiefly for this reason that the annual income from sericulture per acre of mulberry for joint households is twice as great as that of one-man families. Even though the women of the latter group spent far more time caring for silkworms than those of joint households, it was not enough to prevent the misfortune of a sleepy husband and wife rising in the morning to find trays of dead worms. The statistical data suggest that these households would have been better off if they had pulled up their mulberry bushes and planted the land in food grains.

Poor management, then, is a negative reason for the lower yields and income of single-male households. But there is a positive reason for the better performance of joint families as well. Allocative decisions are made interactively in joint households; that is, the men of a family regularly discuss their affairs with one another. Problems are posed, information is offered or requested, the consequences of alternative strategies are considered, and so together the men decide upon a course of action. For example, I was once invited to eat in the largest household of the village, and there I overheard a conversation involving four of the five adult working men of the family and one of their tenants. A garden plot was to be harvested on the following day and the next crop to be planted had to be selected. Now, the men of this family organized them-selves in an explicitly bureaucratic way. The nominal male head of the household was a man in his eighties whose sole activity in agriculture was the performance of the ritual sacrifice of a chicken to the mother goddess to insure good crops. That act ritually marked him as male head of household, but his eldest son was the real leader among the five men who actually worked. As the most experienced farmer, he oversaw the cultiva-tion of gardens. The second son, who was the best educated, managed family finances; the third son presided over the cultivation of unirrigated land, a task he was assigned, they said, because he was the biggest of the three and had a deft hand with oxen. Their father's deceased younger brother's son handled the family's hiring of labor because he was a popular young man who had a nice way with people. The fifth man, the eldest son's son, had no special job, which may be related to the fact that at one point he had stolen some family jewels and run off to the city.

These roles were an explicit element in the discussion that I will now paraphrase. First, the eldest brother suggested that they plant the garden in *raagi*. The youngest brother then pointed out that *raagi*, being a three-month crop, would come to harvest at about the same time as the *raagi* already planted in the dry lands, thus creating a bottleneck in their demand for labor. The father's brother's son agreed that that would very likely be the case and noted that they would have to provide *kulis* with a meal as well as the customary wage in order to get them during that peak demand season. Therefore, they might have to buy food in order to pay their workers if they had to hire enough for the garden land as well. The second son then said that they would probably have to buy some grain for that purpose in any case. They should not plant *raagi*, however, because the harvest of dry-land *raagi* would create a buyer's market for that commodity. The first brother then suggested that they plant onions, and that was the crop they settled on.

Most households' farm affairs are not so complex as this one's, and a working father would exercise a more decisive hand in the discussion than this elder brother did. General features of this conversation, however, are replicated in many others. An allocation of resources to one opportunity is considered in light of its impact on allocations to others, so that a body of discourse is constructed in which the problem at hand comes to be described in terms of a series of costs, benefits, and constraints that portray it in a more global context. I have no idea of what went on inside the heads of men in single-man households when they were faced with a similar decision, but I can say that people in joint families got talked into and out of courses of action in family discussions. And there is considerable statistical evidence to indicate that they were talked into courses of action leading them to do more work themselves and to hire more workers than one-man families.

Moreover, the statistical evidence conforms to a pattern of interaction that may be observed in conversations between senior and junior men. Older men often tell their juniors that they are worrying about the wrong issues. In the foregoing discussion the second son told his father's brother's son not to fret about buying food for *kulis*, which they were going to have to do anyway; the real issue was avoiding a glutted market.

By far the most common "real issue" older men point to is the importance of conducting affairs in such a way as to be able to exploit every opportunity that comes along for getting wealth out of human energy. The tenant father, for example, notes that the garden plot he and his son are cultivating is a particularly good one, and that its owner appears to have a lot of money just now. He tells his son to suggest to the owner, the next time he comes around, that they plant potatoes after the present crop is harvested. The suggestion should be made now, while the owner has money for the seed potatoes and before their opportunity to continue working that plot is pre-empted by someone else.

Or, a father notes that the gardens have gone unirrigated for some time during the press to get the dry lands plowed, and he decides to hire someone to irrigate them. The son says that it is not necessary to pay someone for such routine work; he will irrigate them himself once his plowing is finished the next day. The father questions the son's assumption that he can finish his other work in time for the irrigation. He decides the son cannot and determines to hire someone rather than leave the gardens dry another day.

As these examples indicate, the chief difference between the decisions of experienced farm managers and those of younger men is that elders seem to know how to keep human energy moving through work into land. They are acute judges of how long it takes to get things done and of how you get people to do what you want them to do. They are emphatic about not putting off decisions because they claim that family fortunes are, for all practical purposes, determined by two things: the land one owns and the amount of useful work one does and uses. Although little can be done about the first of these over the short term, a lot can be done about the second. How much useful work one does, how much of it other people can be gotten to do, and how much of it one can get other people to pay one to do are what, in their view, determine income given a constant estate. Apparently they are right about that.

In reaching decisions interactively, elder men used the eyes and ears and ideas of other family members to formulate bold and informed strategies. Leadership and authority in village families do not stem from control of property or some other form of brute force; they come from being right. An indirect effect of equally partible inheritance is that it goads senior men into a preoccupation with being right. If a man's appraisal of the world is proved empirically wrong enough, often enough, his subordinates will not apply themselves vigorously to the tasks he sets for them. Their conversations with him about farming will turn into conversations with one another in which they quarrel about which course of action is best. Any man can be *yajaman* simply by having a family, but few men are *anubhavastaaru*. Unless, however, a *yajaman* has some of the expert in him, he may not be *yajaman* for very long. Hardship, villagers say, makes people quarrel, and quarrels lead to the division of families. Hardship can come from many quarters, and one of these is being wrong. If a sharp economic reversal can be blamed on a *yajaman*, he may lose the confidence of his brothers or sons, and the family may divide. Expertise, thus, is created through symbolic interaction; it is partly the child of the need to be right in the eyes of others.

The conventional morality of men's *dharma* conforms to the course of *Karma Yoga* described by Lord Krishna in the *Bhagavad Gita*. The wise man of action, the Karma Yogi, concerns himself with doing his duty and ignores pain, fear, and fretting about forces beyond his control. That is what the *anubhavastaaru* are like: when one of them appraises the value of a bullock, he is concerned only with the eyes, teeth, hooves, skin, and muscles of that bullock. For if the bullock is poorer than he states it to be, the man who buys it will say the expert is no expert at all. Thus, senior men of joint families make good decisions in part because they are accountable to others. A social position that depends upon the empirical results of intentional action makes empiricists of those who occupy it. Older men employ a heuristic rhetoric in speaking of farms and families, that is, a code of discourse analysis in which the question of relevance versus irrelevance to the problem at hand is the coordinating opposition for judging anything anyone says. Recall Gangappa's lecture to me:

Look, you have come to this poor village from your big country asking about so many matters concerning our families. If you want to know why we have all of these troubles, it is because in these days no one knows how to behave. All of these families would be so much better off if they stayed together in one house, but the people quarrel and divide into many different houses. I don't know why they quarrel. It is certain that a united house is better; these small houses are not good. Many years ago I quarreled with my father and moved to this place. All of my difficulties started from that time.

According to Gangappa most of the questions I raised were irrelevant to the main determinants of family fortunes. Experience had demonstrated time and again the deleterious consequences of doing what he had done as a young man. So far as he was concerned, any course of inquiry that was not premised on that well-verified proposition was wrong-headed. By staying together, working in unity, and saving, joint households maintain a superior readiness to exploit opportunities for cultivation, employment, and investment. The utilization of that readiness depends upon having a leader who is able to perceive both the immanence and the imminence of opportunities and other members who learn to provide information that is useful.

But if one's status as a male household head depends on being right much of the time, older men have ways of making themselves right. Other things being equal, the harder you get people to work, the better your chances of achieving results that look better than those achieved by other people. The father who noted the need to irrigate the gardens perceived an immanent opportunity his son had ignored. The father who conceived a stratagem for getting income from his patron's capital through a potato crop perceived an opportunity that was about to happen. Either man's success, however, depended largely on the amount of effort each could get out of the people to whom he set tasks. Senior men pursue the goal of getting people to work hard through interpersonal comparisons of productivity.

The father surveys the field his adolescent son has been plowing and says, "Your elder brother would have finished this by now." By setting high standards of work performance, often through invidious comparisons between individuals, older men goad their subordinates into redoubled effort. Unlike the young householder's work, which is not subject to anyone's supervision save his own, the work of joint household members is subject to policing either while it is going on or at the end of the day. Most of the time no negative comment is made on anyone's work, which I suspect to be an indication that most people's work is satisfactory most of the time, suggesting that the informal standards of work performance are reasonable ones. However, a good deal of work policing goes on without anyone's saying anything. When groups of people work separately, each individual performing the same task independently of the others, as when groups of men dig gardens or women transplant grain seedlings, the rate of work may be policed nonverbally. Households who regularly employ numbers of men for digging gardens, for example, often select a young man of the family to lead a group of tenants and *kulis*. Older kinsmen are likely to be notably absent from the work group, avoiding a situation in which a senior man will have difficulty keeping pace with his son or younger brother. The leader of the group will position himself at one end of the line of diggers. If, as they work, he finds that he is getting ahead of someone else in the line, he will stand up and glance toward whoever is furthest behind. As soon as the others see him stand up, they too glance up and down the line to check the progress of their work. When one individual in particular is behind, he will accelerate his work rate for a moment until he catches up. Since the leader of the group has been set a production goal for the day by his father, he has an interest in seeing to it that there are no slackers, and he uses this device to establish his own work rate as the standard for others.

Work policing, which we encountered first in the mustache chant of the Harijan workmen, takes a number of forms, but is most prominent in the performance of heavy work judged to be urgent. Women are not free from it, but the tasks that women commonly perform together typically result in happier, more relaxed scenes than the one just described. When they transplant rice seedlings, they too stand in line, planting seedlings in each row to a breadth of their arm's reach and then stepping into the next row. Here also there is a recognized leader, a woman of the house or the leader of the *gumpu*, or group of women, hired to do the job. On occasion they will sing for a time, and the song may serve to regulate the rate of work to some degree, but the words of the songs do not contain reprimands equivalent to "Yo heave ho, what's the matter with you? Have you no mustache?" Rather, they seem to be a pleasant way of passing time while doing an otherwise boring job. Indeed, it is more common to observe women carrying on a running conversation with whoever is next to them in the line. Perhaps that is why adolescent girls like to stand next to a close friend while doing such work.

Like interactive decision making, critical remarks and admonitory glares thus tend to be elements of work coaching that occur mainly among men, a matter that leads us to the last proposition.

chapter 7

Coming of Age:
The Social Construction
of Patriarchy

In the last chapter we saw that in the great majority of cases, the presence of two or more working men in a household greatly enhances agricultural productivity, apparently irrespective of any other factor. But why should the male-managed family farm be formed through patrilocal residence, and why should males marry later than females? In this chapter I shall argue that these policies for household formation and the other teachings of the elders that follow from them are most fruitfully viewed as cultural devices for the management of adolescent and young adult male behavior. One reason elders might wish to control the behavior of young men lies in the impact their work can have on farm production. But I suspect that beyond this, young males are, given the demands their adult role will place upon them, inherently more difficult for their elders to manage than young females.

> Proposition 6. *Village boys take longer to mature than their sisters; sexual dimorphism in physical strength is a product of mid-adolescence. Boys also have a biologically based tendency to engage in more disruptive behavior than girls. These biological sex differences retard the social and economic development of boys in comparison to the development of girls. Elders mitigate the impact of these factors on the organization of production by marrying boys later than girls and by favoring patrilocal residence, which maintains the continuity of men's authority in the socialization of boys and young men.*

This proposition is supported by studies of psychological development and physical maturation conducted in other populations, by observations of differences in the ways villagers treated girls and boys, and by things they said about their children.

Developmental Sex Differences

The activation of the testes in boys at puberty is coupled with rapid skeletal and muscular development. Puberty does not bring a like development in girls; rather, sexual maturity leads to the slowing and then the stoppage of girls' long bone growth. During the mid-teens the aerobic work capacity and muscular strength of boys undergo rapid exponential growth, creating a sex difference typical of adults that is absent in childhood. This also means that boys reach adult stature substantially later than girls. This is true of American adolescents and is evident in the growth of girls and boys in Yaavahalli too.

In Yaavahalli this sex difference contributes to a difference in the degree of discontinuity girls and boys experience in the course of their socialization. Girls gradually acquire the capacity to perform the activities of women and by their early teens are doing most of the things women do, though years of experience will greatly enhance their skill and judgment. Boys, by contrast, are incapable of even attempting much of men's work until they reach their mid-teens. And since managerial skills tend to be learned through participation in the work force, the economic maturation of boys lags far behind that of their sisters.

The second sex difference of interest is a psychological one that appears to have a physiological basis. In recent years we have witnessed a rapid growth in studies aimed at distinguishing psychological sex differences that are purely the artifacts of particular cultural settings (or purely the stuff of fiction) from those that may be founded on biological sex differences. Maccoby and Jacklin (1974) feel that the evidence indicating greater aggressiveness in males is unequivocal, and that arguments attributing this difference solely to learning are weak, while evidence for a biological basis is strong. The high plasma testosterone level of adult males may be one reason. Testosterone is one of the hormones involved in the physiology of irritability and arousal. Both sexes produce testosterone, but the greater amounts produced by the testes may create in males a greater readiness for aggressive response. However, the sex difference in the frequency of aggressive displays emerges in early childhood, long before this hormonal difference appears, suggesting that some other factor is at work.

A possible explanation for the sex difference in aggressive response among children lies in the prenatal effects of male hormones. The normal male fetus displays high androgen levels; the normal female does not. But when female animals are experimentally treated prenatally with androgens, their behavior after birth is androgenized, so that treated female monkeys, for example, engage in more of the rough play typical of males than their untreated sisters. The same appears to be true of girls who were, for one reason or another, exposed prenatally to similar hormonal environments. Money and Ehrhardt (1972), for instance, found that girls whose mothers were given synthetic progestin to prevent miscarriage displayed decidedly tomboyish behavior. The effects of this androgenization on the girls' external morphology were for the most part minimal, and they adopted female identity without hesitation. But these girls did show a substantially stronger preference for competitive sports and other sorts of vigorous outdoor activity than girls of a carefully matched control group. The proximate biological mechanism responsible for this behavioral difference may lie in the hypothalamus. It appears that the prenatal hormonal environment influences the development of this portion of the brain, so that the hypothalamus takes on a characteristic "set" that influences the individual's threshold of aggressive response after birth. Normally the prenatal hormonal environment is congruent with chromosomal gender, producing characteristic male and female sets and, therefore, thresholds. When the hormonal environment is altered, the result may be relatively boisterous girls or quiet boys, though in other respects these individuals behave like typical members of their gender. They are no more likely than anybody else, for example, to engage in homosexual behavior. The character of the behavioral difference they do display leads us to the next point.

Those who have not reviewed the literature on this subject may be wondering what Maccoby and Jacklin and the many authors they cite mean by "aggression." It turns out that males prove more aggressive than females under a variety of operational definitions. These include "mock aggression," such as the rough and tumble play of boys, which defines aggression as not necessarily hostile.

Maccoby and Jacklin would agree, however, that "aggression" is a very general term. What these authors did was organize experimental studies (along with some ethnographic ones) under general categories of behavior in an effort to bring some order to a chaotic welter of evidence on psychological sex differences. As it happens, sex differences, less reliable than those for variables Maccoby and Jacklin chose to regard as measures of aggression, also appear for a number of other categories of behavior, and these seem to form a pattern. Boys were found to be more active, competitive, and independent than girls in some studies but not in others. Let us suppose that these differences are different guises of a systematic sex difference in the development of the hypothalamus, creating in boys a generally higher level of arousability. This generalized propensity would be subject to a variety of environmental influences that might increase or reduce the influence of the biological sex difference on overt behavior or simply channel it into particular activities. But the generalized propensity would lead us to make one general prediction: when individuals with this propensity interact with one another, we would expect to observe more physical activity and more aggressive displays than we would observe among individuals lacking the propensity. And that is what we see, not only in our own society but in others where the matter has been investigated: boys engage in more rough and tumble play than girls, behavior that boys appear to stimulate in one another.

Lest I be misunderstood, I want to stress that nothing in the foregoing discussion should be taken as indicating an in-dwelling need on the part of boys and men to engage in physical violence or any other form of aggression harmful to others; I am not advocating what is sometimes called the killer-ape theory of human male behavior. Where children are taught that violence is bad, and where the sorts of material conditions that seem to provoke violence are not present, one finds nonviolent males. All I am suggesting, as do Maccoby and Jacklin, is that males display a greater readiness to engage in and to learn patterns of behavior that might be labeled aggressive, competitive, or simply active, depending on the behavior and on the perspective of the observer who labels it. Thus, studies in which authors describe boys as more active or competitive than girls may be ones in which the greater activity or competitiveness of boys involved the same rough-housing play other authors call aggressive.

Because the notion that boys are inclined to be more aggressive than girls is more controversial than the claim that they take longer to grow up, I shall devote some attention to the question of whether village boys are more aggressive than their sisters, and whether this difference might be solely the product of differences in the ways the sexes are socialized. Before we embark on this inquiry, however, it may be useful to prefigure a later portion of my argument by noting that adult villagers' handling of what I suspect is a biologically induced sex difference in their children's behavior has relatively little to do with the prevention of violence. The greater problem is rough and tumble play: boys in groups simply cannot be relied upon to do anything very useful for very long without constant adult supervision. Girls are more reliable. This difference, coupled with the more protracted physical maturation of boys, creates a serious problem in teaching boys how to farm.

The Management of Aggression

Are village boys more aggressive than their sisters? The incidence of physical violence among village children during my stay was so low that in an early version of this study, written before I was familiar with the psychological literature on sex differences, I premised the proposition that boys were more disruptive than girls on the simple observation that they were, for some reason, more physically active and less attentive to and compliant with adult directives than girls. However, in reviewing my field notes for evidence of a sex difference in aggressiveness, I have revised this judgment.

Although physical voilence was rare, those fights that I noted always involved boys. There are, I must admit, some problems with the observations on which this statement is based. The fights I saw pitted schoolboys from different villages against one another. Since boys greatly outnumber girls in the schools, one would expect most violence between schoolchildren to involve boys even if there were no sex differences in aggression. Moreover, since the schools brought together large groups of children, it might be anticipated that a large proportion of fights would occur before or after school, if only because those were the occasions on which a lot of interactions of many kinds occurred. And there may be other reasons to suppose that fights would be more common among schoolchildren. The fact that fights involved boys from different villages could simply be an aspect of intervillage rivalry. Or it could be that adults were much quicker to suppress conflict between children from Yaavahalli, lest fighting cause disputes among neighboring families, than they were to suppress fighting involving children from other villages. Finally, it should be added that I was particularly likely to see fights among schoolchildren. Our house was on the same block as the schools, and the fights I saw occurred almost on our doorstep. Thus, the sex difference I observed in physical violence could be a statistical artifact of the preponderance of boys in the school population, combined with a tendency for schoolchildren to fight and the likelihood that I would see a fight among schoolchildren if it occurred.

Nevertheless, these observations are consistent with other lines of evidence suggesting a sex difference in aggressiveness. One of these has to do with what villagers say about their children. Parents offered two reasons for the practice of sending more boys than girls to school and for keeping boys in school longer. Boys, they said, were more likely than girls to need literacy and mathematical skills as adults. But they added that the schools also exercised a desirable disciplinary influence over boys: the schoolmasters were said to teach boys proper behavior and keep them from fighting. This view stands in ironic contrast to my observations of schoolboys, but it was true that the teachers maintained strict discipline during school hours and scolded boys on those occasions when they did fight.

An apparent presumption of a sex difference in aggressiveness also occurs in villagers' responses to the frame question "What is the *dharma* of ——?" when applied to kin terms. These prescriptions for good behavior among kin specified what persons should and should not do. Senior relatives should give their juniors proper advice and should not give them bad advice. Juniors should heed proper advice and should not show disrespect for their elders. Only in the case of spouses was advice giving reciprocal. The avoidance of quarreling was, by contrast, both a uniform and a reciprocal feature of these responses. All persons should avoid quarreling irrespective of seniority or sex. However, a decided sex difference emerged with respect to the avoidance of physical violence. One informant said that sometimes mothers-in-law and daughters-in-law would have fights in which they would scream at one another and pull one another's hair, a very bad thing to do. With this one exception, potentially violent relationships involved male aggressors and male victims. A good elder brother is one who does not use violence against his younger brothers. A good elder sister advises her younger brother not to fight. A good father does not beat his sons once they reach adolescence. A good mother, among other things, stops her husband from physically punishing teenage sons: "She gives her husband advice in a proper way like this: 'Do not beat my son; he is a man now.'"

Thus, if the avoidance of violence is an explicit part of the *dharma* of males in relation to other males, while females are more often viewed as peacemakers, it seems that villagers presume that familial relations between males hold a greater potential for violence than those involving females.

If so, such a presumption would seem warranted in view of the incidents of violence reported in the life histories I collected. Although there are only half a dozen such incidents mentioned in these texts (and one of these must be regarded as a folktale rather than a narrative describing personal experiences), all the aggressors and victims were male. It should be noted, too, that there were five cases of intrafamilial theft corroborated by two or more informants. In each case an adolescent or young adult male was said to have stolen jewelry, money, or livestock from the household. Several uncorroborated accusations of theft also involved male culprits, though some of them were older men.

The reliability of these reports as measures of the relative frequency of male and female violence is certainly open to question. It could be that female violence occurs just as often but is, for some reason, taken less seriously. Male violence, being the more salient form, is thus recalled more frequently. Even if this is so, we are still left with the question of why male violence would be regarded as the more serious breach of good conduct. But this hypothesis is undermined by the fact that females are reported as quarreling about as often as males. If villagers report female verbal aggression, why would they fail to report female physical aggression, which they would see as a more serious offense?

This leads to the opposite hypothesis: perhaps female violence is regarded as so serious that villagers selectively forget incidents of it or are at least reluctant to mention them in interviews. But if that is the case, one might expect villagers to be concerned with the suppression of female violence, and yet in the kin-term prescriptions mentioned a moment ago, it is males who are cautioned against the use of violence. To support this hypothesis, therefore, one would have to argue that female violence was so heinous that villagers could not bring themselves to contemplate even the possibility that it might occur when they created role generalizations about kin terms. I can find no empirical grounds for believing this.

Thus, it appears that while physical violence is rare in Yaavahalli in comparison to many other communities described in the ethnographic record, when violence does occur it is likely to involve males both as aggressors and as victims. Moreover, villagers note this sex difference implicitly by enjoining males not to use violence against their male kin.

In verbal aggression a similar pattern is evident. I do not know that village boys engage in more acts of verbal aggression, arguing, threatening, name calling, and the like, than girls, but it did seem that most occasions of really harsh or gratuitous verbal abuse involved boys. It is possible that this sex difference is, at least in part, an artifact of another sex difference: boys rather often play in groups, whereas girls tend to focus on one or two close friends, as do their American counterparts. It may be that boys use verbal aggression as a device to rally support from other boys when a dispute arises, or to define themselves as leaders. For instance, when schoolboys from different villages argue, the argument attracts the attention of each party's village mates, who gather around him. Since girls often play in pairs with only the company of younger siblings, there is no constituency to rally should a dispute occur.

But there were also occasions in which verbal aggression among boys seemed completely unprovoked. For instance, one day I asked a group of schoolboys to tell me what villages they came from. When they had told me, I then asked one of them, "And who are your people?" This is the most tactful way of asking a rather tactless question, the name of someone's *jaati*. He said he was a Vokkaliga; the others said they were too: "We are all Vokkaligas," said one. Nearby a younger boy stood wearing over his head a gunny sack which boys wear when herding and which clearly defined him as not a schoolboy. Pointing to him, one of the boys said, "Not him, he's a Beda." ("Beda" is a less respectful name for the Naayk *jaati*.) The other boys quickly joined in a taunting sing-song chant, "Beda, Beda, Beda." Tears welled up in the Naayk boy's eyes, and he ran away. Though caste certainly seemed to be one determinant of girls' close friendships, I never saw girls, or adults, engage in such an act of gratuitous bigotry.

While violence and verbal aggression against other children are uncommon, a third form of aggression, that against animals, occurs daily. It takes two forms: that aimed at preventing crop damage and the abuse of domestic animals, which serves no utilitarian purpose.

Villagers of both sexes drive birds and monkeys from standing crops as the need arises. But most boys and some men cultivate this activity as a sport. With monkeys the object of the sport is to throw rocks that barely miss the animals. Macaques of the region are aggressive animals long accustomed to having rocks thrown at them, and they will stand their ground until a forcefully hurled rock lands close by. At the same time it is bad form to actually hit a monkey, since they are cast in the likeness of Anjaneyasvaami, the monkey god and the village deity. By contrast, it is a display of marksmanship to hit a bird.

As carnivorous scavengers, dogs are among the lowest-ranking animals in the village's ritual bestiary. They are also animals of little utilitarian value that seem to crave human affection. Perhaps for these reasons and because their physical capacity for retaliation lends an aura of risk to the activity, they are the most frequent victims of abuse. They are hit, kicked, and taunted. I cannot say that girls never engaged in such behavior, but I can say that boys did frequently. In fact, dog baiting by boys became so epidemic that my dog-loving wife and I, no longer able to suppress our ethnocentrism, asked the schoolmaster to put a stop to it. He told the boys that henceforth dogs were not to be beaten in front of our house. Pilappa, the Holeya shaman who liked to play the avuncular sage with children, added that "colored people," like us, loved dogs and that it was against the code of our *jaati* to mistreat them. This seemed to be a cogent explanation to children taught from early childhood to respect the ritual peculiarities of other groups, and dog baiting largely ceased.

But by far the most common form of aggressive display among village children is not hostile. It is simply physically active, often rough, competitive play. Sometimes the play seems rule-governed. Some of the boys played a folk version of field hockey, for example, and wrestling matches, with a clear selection of opponents, occurred from time to time. But much of this play consisted of apparently random chasing and wrestling. And village boys did far more of this sort of thing than village girls. As a matter of fact, the other forms of aggressive display in which boys engaged were often outgrowths of this rough and tumble play. Tempers might flare in the course of casual play, giving rise to threats. Or mock attacks by boys against one another might, at the suggestion of one participant, give way to organized attacks on monkeys.

Assuming that the sex difference in aggression I believe I observed would have been confirmed by more rigorous study, let us go on to the next question: could differences in the way the sexes were reared be solely responsible for the difference in aggression? This is a conundrum I cannot possibly resolve, but I can offer several observations casting doubt on any explanation relying only on social learning.

For one thing, violence is severely punished. Indeed, the only routinely legitimized form of physical violence is the paternal spanking boys receive for fighting, dishonesty, and other major breaches of good conduct. This may well prompt further aggression in some boys who indirectly retaliate against the punishing father by attacking a peer, but it is the boy, not the father, who generally starts the cycle of violence. And otherwise children are presented with both verbal and observational models for behavior that uniformly emphasize cooperativeness and nonviolence. Verbal aggression, quarreling, is also punished; to engage in disruptive arguing is regarded as an offense in itself, for both adults and children, irrespective of the substance of the case leading to an argument. Occasionally the informal village *panchayat* of elders settled a dispute by fining both parties, simply because their argument broke the peace. Thus, boys receive no overt encouragement to display hostility.

Men do provide a model for boys' attacks on monkeys and birds, but I can find no reason to believe that girls are discouraged from this activity. Girls do engage in it sometimes, and since it serves a practical purpose, one would imagine that adults at least tacitly approve their doing so. But only boys cultivate skill in throwing and slinging rocks as a sport, and the fact that some men do this too is just as plausibly viewed as a continuation of a childhood interest as it is as a model for boys' behavior.

It may be true that girls would be regarded as immodest if they engaged in rough and tumble play like boys, but this does not explain the sex difference in behavior. If different socialization practices explained the more frequent rough play of boys, we would expect to find that the sexes displayed similar frequencies of the behavior at early ages. Then, as time passed, the frequency of such play would decline sharply among girls while among boys it increased, remained constant, or declined less sharply. I do not believe this occurred in Yaavahalli. Moreover, we might expect that girls would be scolded for rough and tumble play—that they would be told it was unladylike or something of the sort. As it happens, Yaavahalli had one definite tomboy, the daughter of Pilappa, the man I just mentioned. Not only did she engage in rough play, but she engaged in it with boys. To my knowledge she was never scolded for this; at any event she continued to engage in it. But regardless of the adult view of girls who play like boys, the great majority of girls to all appearances never engaged in as much rough and tumble play as boys from the outset of their lives.

Nor did adults explicitly encourage rough and tumble play among boys. They did not, for example, organize games for them. Wrestling and weight lifting are both folk sports among men in South India. But perhaps because the men of the village had little time for such activities, I never saw them in Yaavahalli. Thus, the wrestling of boys can scarcely be regarded as an imitation of men's behavior. Rough and tumble play is initiated by boys themselves, and adults simply allow them to do it, provided it does not interrupt the activity or rest of other people. When it does, boys are scolded or told to go somewhere else.

Presently we shall see that young girls engage in a good deal more useful work around the house than boys. Hence, it could be argued that girls engage in less rough play because they have less free time in which to do so. The trouble with this argument is that the work girls do is an outgrowth of their play. They start by playing with infants and playing at cooking, and later attach themselves to older girls and women as they begin to take part in useful domestic activities. Villagers seem to regard this progression by girls as a natural expression of the feminine *dharma*, and while we may regard the phenomenon as cultural, the imitation of same-sex adult behavior, it is nonetheless the case that the play of girls left more or less to their own devices is compatible with learning the useful tasks they will be asked to do later. With boys, as we shall see, this is not so; adults must actively intervene in their play to turn boys' attention to useful pursuits.

But perhaps the effects of differential socialization on the behavior of boys and girls are more subtle than I have thus far supposed. It could be that girls receive messages not readily observed by an ethnographer that lead them to be less aggressive and more compliant with the wishes of their elders than boys. Among some groups of northern India, girls are regarded as a bane on their families and are told that they are. Indeed, in some areas women of a neighborhood engage in public ritual wailing on hearing of the birth of a girl; by contrast, the birth of a boy is an occasion for joy. Hence, girls spend their childhoods making up for the offense of being female with modest, dutiful behavior, whereas boys, treated like little princes, sometimes bully their sisters in the arrogant belief that they are the more valued sex.

Might this phenomenon occur in Yaavahalli? Earlier I noted the absence of any conspicuous doctrine of female inferiority in Yaavahalli, and I can find no evidence indicating that village parents preferred boys to girls in general. Though it was recurrently evident that sonlessness was regarded as a misfortune, it was also unfortunate to have too many sons, since the arrival of each son reduced the estate that each would inherit. Thus, it seems that most girls came into the world with no stigma attached to their gender. Moreover, I would not expect to find girls disfavored as a sex in Yaavahalli. The populations in which girls are regarded as a burden are usually ones where women make little contribution to farming or other income-producing work and where each girl requires a dowry to marry. In Yaavahalli women make a major contribution to farming, and a bride price is paid. Girls are generally not burdens to their families and so are not viewed as such.

Finally, if one examines the kinds of play for which adults provide resources, it seems unlikely that parents prompt aggressive behavior in boys while deliberately retarding it in girls. I noted two forms of play that adults encouraged by giving children something to play with, sometimes offering verbal instructions as to the use of the resources. The first of those is what we might call work/play. Children often engage in play that rehearses the work of their elders, and occasionally they are provided with tools or other objects to use. For example, I once observed the children of a group of well-diggers mimic the adult practice in which men fill and lift baskets of dirt to the heads of women so that they can be carried away to the back fill. The boys picked up lumps of laterite scattered around the area and placed them on the girls' heads; the girls then dumped them on the pile of back fill. The girls' mothers had given them the thick fabric pads women use to cushion headloads, and my photograph of the incident shows little girls chasing about with small clods balanced on disproportionately large pads, a sight that seemed to amuse the adults present.

In this and other examples of work/play in which adults implicitly endorse an activity by providing material resources for it, parents legitimate and instruct children in the sexual division of labor; by giving the girls their pads, the mothers approved their task. But they do not encourage children of either sex to engage in rough and tumble play or any other aggressive display. Rather, they encourage the cooperative imitation of useful work by both sexes. I suspect, however, that a difference in the way girls and boys seek objects to play with could have an indirect influence on the incidence of rough play. Toddlers of both sexes are occasionally given broken pots and other containers, which they fill with earth and empty after the fashion of American toddlers playing in a sandbox. Girls soon organize their play into imitations of food preparation, often under the tutelage of older girls, while boys tend to abandon it by age five or six. Thus, because girls are exposed to a same-sex role model for a relatively sedentary activity, cooking, they are less likely to engage in active play than boys.

Food sharing is the second form of play to which adults routinely donate resources. Groups of children, often of both sexes and various ages, are given snacks. The play behavior derives from the fact that the oldest child present is given the food with the usually tacit understanding that she or he will share it with the other children, an understanding that becomes explicit in the scolding the child will receive if food is not shared. As in other Hindu communities, feasting and fasting are a part of every major ritual, food handling and preparation are subject to elaborate ritual constraints, and food sharing is a mark of ritual intimacy; ordinarily reciprocal exchanges of cooked food occur only between persons of the same *jaati*. Food giving is also clearly associated with love and virtue. Hence, a man who wished to illustrate that his wife was a virtuous woman said, "She feeds my mother well." It is scarcely surprising, then, that children sometimes turn snack sharing into a little ritual in which the oldest child will distribute the food, provided the younger children do what he or she tells them to do, such as seat themselves in a circle.

Though girls may share food more often than boys because they are more often put in charge of younger siblings, children of both sexes do receive food to distribute and are subject to the same requirement that they share it. In doing so children imitate patterns of family behavior observed in adults; the older child plays nurturing parent to the younger children in an even-handed allocation of resources in which all are expected to be cooperative and calm.

I should close this section with two points. The first is a disclaimer: I do not regard my suggestion that village boys are more disposed towards aggressive displays than girls, and that this difference is not solely explained by village child-rearing practices, as anything more than an informed opinion. A systematic study of village children's behavior might have led to different conclusions. Second, I do not mean to make too much of the difference. Village boys are hardly hooligans; though there are some boys who engage in repeated episodes of fighting, the average village boy is, by American standards, unusually nonviolent. All I mean to indicate is that the average boy is more likely than his average sister to hit the dog, to race about and wrestle noisily with his friends, to argue with them and convert his arguments into threats, and to run away with them, who knows where, to throw rocks at monkeys. He is, in short, harder to manage, if what one wants from children is calm, cooperative behavior focused on useful work or the care of younger children.

Moreover, adults do seem to favor calm, cooperative behavior that is not disruptive of purposeful activity in that the models of behavior adults present to children endorse and demonstrate such behavior, and so it seems unlikely that the sex difference in behavior is produced solely by differences in socialization practices. Adults do handle girls and boys differently, but differences in socialization practices are to be viewed in part as responses to differences in the behavioral patterns with which children present adults. Finally, it should be noted, before we begin our examination of the socialization process and the ways in which village institutions mitigate the problems of becoming a competent adult male, that socialization does not end with the conclusion of childhood or even the beginning of adult married life. Socialization is a continuing process in which women and men tend to become, in temperamental terms, increasingly alike. Women become more assertive, and men become more circumspect, until, by middle age, most individuals display the public self associated with elderhood, the decisive yet diplomatic pragmatist capable of guiding the activity of younger people through an unrelenting regimen of manual labor, in spite of the frustrations and disappointments presented by the agricultural landscape and the political economy of the larger society.

Village Childhood

Apart from the rejoicing that accompanies the birth of a first son, there seemed to be little difference in the ways girls and boys are treated in the first year or two of life. As a matter of fact, infants and toddlers are treated as rather androgynous beings. Some parents who can afford to do so have toddlers photographed dressed in both male and female garb in order, as one informant put it, "to see what the baby would have looked like if it had been a boy or a girl instead." Certainly there appeared to be no marked difference in the age at which girls and boys are weaned (which never occurs before age two) or in the way they are toilet-trained, which is succinctly described as permissive. Infants are nursed on demand, unless the mother happens to be at work in the fields, and they are carried and played with a great deal. Often the principal baby-carriers are older girls, who imitate the behavior of mothers as they show off and compare their young charges. On other occasions aunts or grandmothers are mother-surrogates. Thus, many children, a clear majority I would guess, form attachments to two or more female caretakers, though the mother is set apart by the fact that she nurses the child. And while the amount of time a small child spends in contact with women and girls is far greater than the amount spent with older males, village men frequently play with young children. Indeed, it was nothing odd to see a grandfather playing with a toddler while carrying on a sober conversation with his friends.

So it would seem that, apart from language acquisition, the village child's major intellectual task is to figure out who his relatives are and his place among them. And since females provide the bulk of child care, it would also appear that from the child's perspective the core of his social world is composed of females to whom the males are attached in various ways that become evident to him as he grows older.

I recall writing in a letter that village children seemed to talk earlier than our own and to walk later. Whether or not that is so, the almost constant holding and carrying village infants receive during their waking hours discourages exploration and the development of physical independence. Likewise, there is no doubt that village toddlers are talked to a great deal, by a variety of people, and with grammatically adult speech. Adults commonly address questions to young children; the child is asked if he wants something, or if he shows discomfort, what is the matter. Surrounded as he is by physically controlling but nurturant and inquisitive elders, the child by age three or four is more likely than many of his American counterparts to use language rather than independent action to get what he wants. This predilection obliges the child to construe himself as a dependent junior to his relatives and creates many situations in which he is susceptible to the verbal instructions of elders. To get what he wants from a doting adult or older sister, the child must be willing to listen to the elder's view of the world. But while both girls and boys tend to display this verbally managed dependence, girls are in a far better position to use it as a device for the acquisition of adult patterns of behavior.

Girlhood

The village household is an open classroom for learning to be a woman. A girl is constantly exposed to adult female role models, and by age seven or so she will have begun to practice the skills of womanhood. By this age there is likely to be a younger child in the family, and she will be called upon to become one of its caretakers, an activity girls mostly treated as a privilege rather than an onus. Later, girls are drawn into food preparation, housecleaning, animal care, and the fetching of water and fuel. From time to time young girls also accompany women to the fields and take part in the less demanding tasks such as weeding. By age twelve or so, two things will have happened: other family members will have come to rely on a girl as a routine contributor to household welfare, and the girl will be basically competent at most things women do. She will be able to bathe and feed an infant, cook a simple meal, milk cows, irrigate or transplant in gardens, keep a house clean and tidy, and so on.

But there are several other features of girls' socialization that are at least as important as the rapid acquisition of mechanical competence. The position of girls is like that of an ethnographer who is able to be a constant participant in and observer of her informants' lives. Girls do not merely learn manual skills; from early on they are exposed to the routines and strategies of women. Girls learn women's roles holistically; they learn how child care, food preparation, animal care, farm work, and housecleaning may be effectively coordinated. The twelve-year-old girl has learned to be a manager as well as a worker.

Girls are also exposed to a feminine esthetic, activities cultivated for their own sake beyond the utilitarian purposes they serve. The bathing and dressing of babies is one of these. Bathing and fresh clothes make a baby clean and comfortable, and cosmetics are used for ritual protection from supernatural harm, but these measures also make a baby beautiful. The cultivation of cuisine as an art in Yaavahalli turns chiefly on the combination of many herbs and spices to produce a variety of *masalas*, powders, which are used to spice food and to prepare the chutneys and pickles served as condiments. Every family has, or at least claims to have, its own recipes, so that in teaching a girl to cook the notion is also conveyed that she is being made privy to esoteric knowledge. Another distinctly feminine art is the painting of designs in red and white paste on cow-dung floors and courtyards. In learning this craft girls learn not only the designs of intricate patterns and the order in which different elements of a design are to be added, but the fluid, dancelike movements that characterize a stylish painter at her work as well.

Finally, in the holistic learning of the female role and in developing a taste for the artistic facets of women's activities, a girl of twelve will also cultivate a series of relationships with women and other girls that approximate the relations she will be called upon to develop when she marries. The fact that others rely on her services indicates that a role has been constructed for her among the women and children of the household. But beyond that, most girls develop close friendships that focus on the sharing of useful activities. One day Lakshamma will go to Nagamma's house to grind spices; the next day the two girls will do the same thing at Lakshamma's house. A sociogram in which I asked villagers to name their friends revealed that cross-caste friendships are fairly common among adults of both sexes. But close girlfriends are invariably members of the same *jaati*, perhaps because girls spend so much time in one another's homes and because of caste restrictions on the preparation and sharing of food: a Naayk girl could not help a Vokkaliga girl cook or even enter the cooking area of a Vokkaliga house.

The fact that girlfriends are caste mates typically means that they are relatives as well, since the lineages of each *jaati* are divided into moieties for purposes of marital exchange. Thus, girlfriends are either classificatory sisters or sisters-in-law, and the terminology used to describe the relationship will label one girl as senior to the other. In most relationships the junior girl tends to defer to the leadership of the senior even though she may be only slightly younger. Thus, in the course of growing up girls acquire practice at establishing relationships that are rather like those they will have to establish with sisters-in-law and other young women when they marry.

At about the age of twelve, a change begins to take place in a girl's relationship with her mother, a change prompted by the presumption that girls will marry at the age of fifteen or so and that they will, in most cases, reside patrilocally. The mother becomes guru and the daughter disciple in a period of accelerated training that refines the basic competence the girl has already developed. Explicit technical instruction is given in food budgeting and cooking. Girls take pleasure in this, for it is at this time that they learn special family recipes for more complicated dishes and condiments. They also receive what amounts to sexual education: how to deal with menstruation and, shortly before they marry, at least a rudimentary notion of how to deal with a young husband.

Less pleasing for the girl is the greater manual work load expected of her during the early adolescent years. At age eight or nine, a girl would rarely spend more than three or four hours a week working in the fields. By eleven or twelve, eight to fifteen hours might be expected, while twenty or more hours per week would be common among girls during the last years before marriage, though the amount of farm work girls do varies a great deal, depending on the season and a family's wealth. Among poorer families adolescent girls are hired out as full-time *kulis* during seasons of peak demand for labor. The amount of animal care asked of adolescent girls also increases substantially.

The early adolescent years are usually poignant ones for mother and daughter, years that presage marriage and the separation of the girl from her family. But dread is buffered by the knowledge that a girl will most likely marry within walking distance of her natal village and she will have many occasions to visit her home, notably at the birth of her first child. Moreover, the fifteen-year-old girl is fundamentally competent to be a woman. She has probably been caring for young children for half of her life. For the last five or six years she has been a regular participant in the organization of women's work. And for several years she has been called upon to perform all the farm tasks women do, and to put in at least as much time doing them as married women at her household's level of wealth. A fifteen-year-old boy is, by contrast, a neophyte.

Boyhood

At the age at which girls begin to be incorporated into the activities of their mothers, boys find themselves increasingly at loose ends. Though they continue to receive concern and affection from their female relatives, six-year-old boys cannot be carried around and pampered. Nor do they seem to want such treatment. Left to his own devices, the young boy finds other boys who have been left to theirs, and they form a play group whose structure and activities are negotiated by the boys themselves. Only when play becomes disruptive, when a dispute occurs, or when play interferes with some useful activity, do adults intervene.

Within a year or two of the time a boy begins to make a place for himself in a peer group, adults begin to place some restrictions on his time. The amount of farm work a boy does depends on whether or not he is sent to school, since schooling consumes the better part of the day for much of the year. When they return home, schoolgirls, often without any explicit instructions, begin to take part in the domestic work of the household. Boys are often given a particular task, such as feeding livestock, that may leave them some free time to play. Boys who do not go to school are taken to the fields fairly routinely, from age eight onwards, whenever there is some task, such as breaking clods of earth in newly plowed gardens, in which they can help. Indeed, the standard unit of labor for operating the bullock-drawn *kapile* (a leather bucket irrigation device) still used in some gardens is a man with a boy to help him in a task that familiarizes boys with the handling of bullocks.

On the average, boys under twelve spend about twice as much time in the fields as girls of the same age, a difference that reflects the sexual division of farm labor in other age groups. This is the average for the village as a whole; poor girls spend about as much time in the fields as most boys, just as poor women do as much farm work as most men. Girls from *sovkaar* families spend almost no time in the fields.

But though boys under twelve spend more time in the fields than girls, they still are not spending a very great proportion of their time there. Between the ages of eight and twelve, a boy of a middle-income family will spend increasing periods of time in the fields with an average over the period of ten to twelve hours per week, or roughly 10 percent of his waking hours. When boys are at work in the fields, however, they are under direct adult supervision. And whereas girls often go to the fields to weed with a close friend, sometimes in the company of a woman, sometimes not, boys seldom do; they are separated from their friends, although brothers do go to the fields with their father.

Some boys also serve as shepherds, and of these some, indentured servants to *sovkaar* families, spend most of every day engaged in this activity. The herding of sheep and goats takes a boy some distance from the village and thus isolates him from other people, but shepherds are told not to fraternize with other children lest they lose track of a valuable animal. Consequently, boys who are indentured as shepherds grow up as social isolates. The *patel* employed a man who had grown up in this fashion and remained a social isolate: he never married, he ate alone in a corner of the house where he slept, and, unless spoken to, he scarcely ever said anything.

The lives of village boys, as a group, vary somewhat more than the lives of girls. More boys than girls attend school; indeed, by the time of my stay only a few boys of school age had received no schooling. But boys drop out of school at various stages depending on birth order (oldest sons tend to receive less education), family finances, and academic performance. By contrast, schoolgirls generally come from wealthier families, so that financial considerations and the need for their labor in the fields do not figure in plans for their education. Nor were girls I knew withdrawn from school because of poor performance. The regimen of the schools, which emphasize rote learning, is extremely strict by American standards; some boys have difficulty in adjusting to this and are withdrawn. Thus, the education of a girl tends to proceed according to a long-range plan: it has been decided that she will complete primary school, middle school, or (in the case of the *patel*'s daughter) high school, and she does. The education of boys, which is pursued at all but the lowest levels of the economic order, is subject to a series of contingencies that may lead to the termination of schooling in the middle of an academic program.

It is perhaps for this reason, and because education is a mark of prestige among men, that schooling was a salient element in the life histories of many of them. Not only did they note the level of education they received, but they often described the circumstances under which they left school and sometimes implied that the degree of concern their elders showed for their education was an indication of the degree to which they were loved. Boys' lives are also more varied in another respect: the poorest boys, who are indentured, have virtually no childhood after the age of eight.

But beneath this variation lie some persistent patterns in the socialization of boys that are strikingly different from the experience of girls. As we have just noted, boys are separated from their friends when they work in the fields, and they work under the supervision of older workers, whereas girls often work with close friends and are sometimes unsupervised. The only task boys regularly perform without supervision is herding, and this they do alone.

Why is the work of boys managed in this fashion? Recall that in the

studies cited by Maccoby and Jacklin, boys tend, when presented with
male peers, to engage in rough and tumble play, which some researchers
call "mock aggression" and others simply describe as a "high activity
level." In other contexts girls are often just as active as boys, but they are
less prone to this form of play. This does not mean that the behavior of
boys in groups cannot be controlled; the village schoolmasters control it
every day. But adults are likely to have to resort to one of two measures
to control boys in groups: either they can impose stricter discipline than
they would find necessary to secure compliance from girls, or they can
channel the activity of boys into a game in which the adult simply
imposes rules on rough play.

Neither of these measures is very effective if one's aim is to teach
boys farm work while managing to get some useful work done oneself.
The problem with strict discipline is that it absorbs too much of an
adult's attention. If an adult is trying to break clods of soil, or weed, or
dig onions in one section of a field while children are doing the same
thing elsewhere, he will be repeatedly diverted from his work as the
children's work degenerates into active play. Moreover, the instructional
purpose of the work will be subverted. Earlier I noted that the productivity of children's work was so low as to be unmeasurable, and while
adults regard children's work as helpful, they view its main purpose as
educational. By taking children to the fields, they teach them good work
habits from an early age. Good work habits amount to doing the same
thing over and over in spite of the physical discomfort involved and the
lack of varied stimulation that accompanies a repetitive task.

That is the trouble with the second measure: it is difficult to make
repetitive work into a game that compares favorably, in terms of varied
stimulation and freedom of movement, with the games children play on
their own. Even if one could concoct such a game, it would not induce
good work habits. Adults often work alone in the fields, and though they
sometimes sing to pace their work, adults are often silent when they
work together. When they do talk, they chat about matters other than
the work at hand, which, one might conclude, is not very interesting. If
we can infer the internal conversations farm workers have with themselves from those they have with one another, it would seem that the
worker's object is to divert his attention from the physical sensation of
the work he is doing and thus from the discomfort it imposes. He lets his
mind wander while keeping his hands and feet moving at a steady pace.
Hence, converting routine farm work into a game in which, for example,
one sees who can gather the most weeds is counterproductive. It encour-
ages the child to work at a pace he cannot sustain, and it undermines one
of the objects of having children work in the first place: learning good
farm work habits is largely a matter of becoming desensitized to drud-

gery. Occasionally groups of men employ competition in their work; we saw this earlier in the chant of the Holeya workers and the use of the gaze to regulate work pace among diggers in gardens. But such reliance on external controls occurs only in the performance of very arduous labor and only among experienced workers. The child who comes to depend upon the external control of competition with peers or constant adult supervision will not readily learn to use daydreaming and idle conversation as devices to get him successfully through a work day.

By separating boys from their peers when they work, adults substantially mitigate the problem of policing their behavior. A boy's work will not degenerate into mock fights with clods of dirt or episodes of monkey chasing if there is no male peer to stimulate this behavior. There is only a supervising adult, who will coach his attention back towards the task at hand if it is diverted to something that interrupts his work.

This way of managing boys' behavior is one aspect of a basic difference between male and female childhoods. Earlier I described the household as an open classroom for the holistic learning of women's work. When girls go to the fields, they are given specific tasks just as boys are. But before they go and when they return, they are engaged in other tasks, so that they learn not only how to do particular tasks, but also how various activities may be fitted together in a congruent process. They learn, for instance, not only how to cook, but how long a pot may be left while one does something else. In the course of this learning, a place for each girl is interactively created in the organization for work of women and girls, even if the organization consists only of the girl and her mother in a nuclear family household. No strict distinction is drawn between work and play for girls. Play that rehearses adult female behavior is simply converted, as the girl matures, into practice of that behavior. The girl who plays with an infant at age five is left in charge of the toddler at age seven. Play at cooking is turned to actual food preparation as the girl is taught to perform simple tasks. Then, the distinction between work and play is further blurred when girlfriends care for young children and perform domestic tasks together.

For a boy the distinction between work and play is categorical. Work is what happens when you are separated from your friends and set to a task that is utterly unlike play with peers. Whenever a boy is not needed to work in the fields, he is, for the most part, free to play with his friends when he is not in school. Boys are asked to do chores around the house from time to time and, after a fashion, provide care for their younger brothers: boys' play groups often consist of a group of older brothers followed by a group of tag-along younger brothers. But boys are not set to child care or housework on a regular basis as girls are, and to the extent that they have much more time for free play, adults are more permissive with boys than with girls.

In others ways they are much stricter. That boys do about twice as much farm work as girls of the same age occurs mainly because boys are called to the fields more often, not because they work longer at a stretch, since adults seem to regard it as unreasonable to ask any young child to perform the same repetitive task for more than an hour or two. This means that while many boys spend only a small portion of their waking hours at farm work, they will find their play activity interrupted by requests for work rather often.

Thus, if village boys do have a greater proclivity to rough and tumble play than their sisters, the difference is culturally amplified in village child-rearing practices. If girls are not as prone to bursts of potentially disruptive physical energy as boys, their behavioral style is compatible with the same-sex role models the community provides them. They turn readily to child care and housekeeping tasks as activities in which they can cultivate close friendships while they rehearse the behavior of women. The boys' tendency to engage in rough play when presented with male peers is incompatible with the care of young children and the performance of housekeeping tasks. And since boys will not be expected to run households when they mature, adults have little reason to channel their behavior in this direction. Moreover, given the reluctance of adults to ask boys in groups to do anything useful, boys will not develop peer relationships unless they are given play time in which to do it.

This creates a situation in which adults are obliged later on to intervene in boys' play in order to teach them farm work. By age twelve most boys will be asked to make a rather substantial contribution to farm work, and for some individuals this will prove a persistent problem. Preadolescent boys are rather often scolded for disappearing with their friends when their parents need them and for laziness, which appears to be a passive-aggressive response to demands for work. Part of the problem may derive from the fact that boys do not yet do men's work. This leads us to the cultural amplification of the sex difference in biological maturation.

By age twelve, as we have seen, girls can do most of the things women do and by their mid-teens are social adults in the sense that they may marry. At age twelve a boy will have performed mostly tasks that persons of both sexes and various ages perform. He will not have performed *kashta kelsa*, the work that distinguishes men from women, because he will not be physically able to perform it until the burst of muscular and skeletal growth thats occurs in adolescence equips him for it. Boys do play at men's work; in a common game an older boy takes the

Adolescent boys digging a garden with *gudalis*. These boys had been working for many hours when this picture was taken at dusk, requiring the large aperture and slow shutter speed that account for its poor quality. But it does show the range of motion entailed in the task: the boy in the background is starting a swing; the boy in the foreground is completing one. The foreground individual's technique is less well coordinated than that of more experienced workers.

role of plowman and chases around after a younger one who plays the bullock. But unlike the girls who do women's work, boys have no opportunity to practice many of the skills their adult role will entail. And because they participate in agriculture in a piecemeal fashion, they have only limited opportunities to gain experiential knowledge of farm management. Thus, if boys are a somewhat disaffected group, it may be because they are asked to work while they wait to be men, whereas girls can act like little women.

By their mid-teens boys spend more time in the fields than any other cohort of the population. And as they begin to participate in heavy manual labor, a situation is created for them comparable to that created for girls at a much younger age: their daily routine becomes an open classroom for the holistic learning of their adult role. Not only do they learn all phases of farm work, but they are increasingly exposed to deliberations in which alternative farming strategies are considered and to rationales underlying choices among strategies.

Adolescence is a period of discontinuity for both sexes, but the changes that take place in the lives of boys and girls differ. Discontinuity in a girl's life occurs when she is married. Her life may change after marriage to the extent that she will perhaps do more agricultural labor, more food-related work, and less livestock care in her conjugal household than she did in her natal one. But these are merely proportional changes in a set of activities in which she is competent; the major discontinuity is expressed in where and with whom she does them. Asking a girl to leave her home and establish a place for herself as a married woman in a new setting is asking a lot, and girls approach marriage with a mixture of excitement and dread. Perhaps Hindu mothers-in-law have come in for a good deal of implied criticism in the ethnographic literature because many of us are unaccustomed to seeing women in positions of genuine authority that are explicitly feminine, and are therefore inclined to view the role as particularly authoritarian. But in Yaavahalli the anxiety of girls towards marriage is largely a dread of the unknown. Mothers-in-law are rarely ogres, and most young brides are reasonably successful in their adjustment to marriage, both in the eyes of their elders and in their own estimations of themselves. Bear in mind that some marry within their natal village, and few marry into one far from home. Moreover, the culture provides recourses for girls who do have difficulty in adjusting to married life. They may visit their parents' home frequently, especially when pregnant, and young women who face serious physical and emotional adjustment problems have a special recourse. Serious or protracted cases of *sustu* or periods of depression are likely to be diagnosed by the girl's in-laws as symptoms of spirit possession. That ailment is treated by a period of rest in the girl's natal home, where a shaman is brought in to perform *mantras* to exorcise the offending spirit. So, when a girl fails to adjust, it is not regarded as her fault. The spirit is in her, as the force behind her behavior, but it is not of her.

By contrast, a boy's difficulties in adjusting to the male role in work, or for that matter in school, are likely to be attributed to laziness or weakness, and there are reasons for this. The social controls men impose on boys are more severe than those women impose on anybody. As we shall see presently, men view their own lives as a struggle to master their weaknesses, and they regard the imposition of this somber view of life on their sons as a simple matter of telling them the truth. Thus, if a father employs rather Draconian measures to change a truculent boy's behavior, he is convinced that he does so for his son's good. Moreover, a boy's adjustment to a man's role occurs in public. His ineptitude in handling bullocks and heavy implements is visible to any passer-by, whereas the mistakes a girl makes in learning domestic work are largely hidden behind the walls of her home. And since adolescence is the period in which a boy establishes his reputation as a worker, the inevitable negative comparisons between his work and more competent performances are likely to be taken to heart by his male elders. Hence, their public criticism of his work may in part be a response to their fear of embarrassment.

Men's dourness and their fear of a son's embarrassing the family, however, are but aspects of two more fundamental reasons for the comparatively severe socialization of boys. First, elders have a vital interest in speeding the economic socialization of boys; second, adolescent boys are difficult people to police. By their late teens boys are becoming the strongest members of the community. The period in which a household contains one or more young unmarried males is often a time of rapid economic growth fueled by the energy young men can generate. It is therefore important for a boy to make an adequate psychological adjustment to the demands of men's work so that his physical ability can be fully exploited as it matures, and this is all the more vital in that his labor may be used to enhance the productivity of household resources in order to mitigate the further crowding of those resources that will be occasioned by his marriage. This may be done by employing him to improve existing irrigation wells or work on new ones or to increase yields in order to increase savings that may be used to defray the cost of more land or the construction of new wells. The economic maturation of boys is a race against time.

The problem is that boys are not entirely willing participants in the race. This problem has two notable facets: first, the awakening of their interest in girls by the same physical maturation that makes them capable of men's work, and, second, the persistence of the male peer group, operating independently of and increasingly in contradiction to adult dictates.

In the management of their own behavior, adolescent boys tend to try to find new ways to extend the freedom of childhood into adult life. If you ask them what they like to do, they will tell you that they like to sing *bajana* (religious songs) in the temple at night; they like to take part in dramas; they like to attend the cinema with their friends. They would rather do such things than pursue their studies or work in the fields because they are more interesting. If you ask girls about what they like to do, they will say they prefer cooking, child care, and other domestic tasks to working in the fields, although they too like to go to town on market day or to see the cinema.

In short, if you ask older boys and young men what they like to do, they rarely describe something that is materially productive, whereas girls and young women commonly describe themselves as wanting to do things that have to get done. There is a marked contrast, moreover, between the ways older men talk about themselves as social beings and the ways young men talk about themselves. Singing *bajana* and participating in dramas are well and good, say older men, but they are trivial matters in comparison to the serious business of farming. There is no such contrast in the ways that older and younger women talk about their lives. Regardless of age, women like and dislike the same aspects of what they have to do. The only difference is that when you are quite young or relatively old, you get to do more of what you like than in the years in between. Therefore, with boys, elders face the problem of getting them to be interested in matters to which they must attend if they are to be successful adults.

Adolescent boys, then, tend to talk about themselves as persons who have friends who do interesting things together, such as putting on plays. They do not talk about themselves as farmers trying to get the most they can out of the resources at their disposal. Consider the following response to the general question: "Who are your friends and what do you do together?"

> See, this group of four friends [they have just been named] like to make some mischief together. What that means is that we like to go to the cinema together. One time Narayanaswamy will give the money for the cinema and tiffin and the next time another friend will give it. . . . Now one time when I joined this group, you see, Kempanna was saying he wanted to marry the daughter of H. C. . . . See, H. C. had three girls, two of whom were married, but no sons. So we suggested to Kempanna, let's see if we can find a way to celebrate the marriage. . . . See, Narayanaswamy was all the time working in H. C.'s house as a tenant, and so he kept joking with H. C., "Look, Kempanna is a good man and a good worker, so why don't you

marry your daughter to him?" [There follows an account of how the marriage could not be arranged because of Kempanna's parents' objections.] Narayanaswamy talked to H. C.'s daughter and advised her that Kempanna wanted to marry her. She said that she wanted to marry Kempanna also. So we said to Kempanna, "Look, you make friends with Pilamma [the girl] and enjoy [have sexual relations with] her, and we will support you."

The narrative goes on to describe how, after many tribulations, the lovers were finally married. At one point in the account Kempanna begged Narayanaswamy to help him, promising in return to help Narayanaswamy arrange a marriage with Kempanna's own younger sister. The two had a falling out when Kempanna could not make good his promise.

In this narrative we see a group of young men trying covertly to pursue a sexual interest against the interests of some elders. While H. C. was willing to accept Kempanna, he turned to a different prospective groom in another village when arrangements with Kempanna's family hit a snag and he and his wife realized that they had delayed their daughter's marriage too long already. Because most girls are married shortly after reaching sexual maturity, but boys are not married until they are considerably older, a dynamic is established in which parents who permit a girl to remain unmarried for very long after puberty are vulnerable to the sexual conspiracies of young men. In a society where young men cannot get regular sexual access to women except through marriage, they have a strong incentive to help one another out in arranging love matches. Narayanaswamy could use the fact that he was Pilamma's classificatory brother, and thus safe, to act as an intermediary for Kempanna if the latter would reciprocate the service.

One way to maximize the productivity of young men is to make several years of hard work a precondition for marriage. Parents of girls foster their interests by supporting this precondition. In the end, the purpose of hard work is prosperity, but in this context hard work is directed at a different goal. A girl's parents will not marry her to a man who does not have an established reputation as a worker, because they are concerned for her future. Reciprocally, the parents of sons tell them that they must prove themselves as workers in order to get a wife. Note that Narayanaswamy trades on Kempanna's good reputation as a worker in his conversation with H. C. Thus, for Kempanna, hard work is directed at the acquisition of an attractive wife, not at prosperity—wives in effect become an incentive stimulating the rapid economic socialization of young men.

Whether they are the parents of boys or girls or both, elders have an interest in restricting the sexual access of young men to young women.

By marrying their girls very young, they insure that there are simply not very many unmarried sexually mature girls around. Then, by demanding distance and modesty in the interaction of potential spouses, they make it very difficult for any sexual relationship to be established without recourse to a marriage system that is managed by the elders. Thanks to this system, parents of girls get good workers for their daughters and those of boys get a lot of work done. Moreover, the practice of marrying girls out young and marrying sons when they are an average of five years older often creates an added bonus, a period of economic growth that occurs in households that contain one or more unmarried young men but in which older daughters have already begun to marry out of the family.

This period in which people invest in farming rather than in wives and the children they will bear cannot be achieved unless there is a substantial difference in age at marriage for boys and girls, enabling elders to use a boy's interest in girls to develop his interest in farming.

The Construction of Patriarchy

The later marriage of males (and the biocultural conditions favoring it) creates a set of circumstances favoring patrilocal residence. This policy, as far as villagers are concerned, goes hand in hand with their preference for equipartible patrilineal inheritance.

These two policies constitute the outwardly visible institutional form of a process whereby a special social relation, patriarchy, is constructed to define and legitimate relations between fathers and sons and between elder and younger brothers. It is this process that establishes the basis for agriculturally effective male-managed joint family farms.

Let us begin with a review of some of the circumstances favoring patrilocality. Imagine a family containing both girls and boys. Assuming that same-sex siblings marry in birth order, consider what will happen if a policy of matrilocal residence is followed. Having invested one's efforts in getting the eldest son to be a good worker, one will be shipping him off to his in-laws just as the investment is beginning to pay off. Perhaps that will not matter if he can be replaced quickly with an in-marrying groom who is just as good, but should the first married child be a son, the family will be deprived of a male worker until the first daughter marries. What certainly cannot be accomplished under a system of matrilocal residence is a period in which the household contains young unmarried males working hard in order to improve the family estate so that they can marry. Because the daughters will remain at home, the male labor force will simply shift from one composed of their brothers to one composed of their husbands.

But as we have seen, there is already a sharp discontinuity in a boy's life, brought about by the rapid change in the work expected of him. A change of residence brings on a further discontinuity, facing elders with the question whether they can really get the same performance out of grooms that they got out of sons. Avunculocal residence would create the same problem, even though it would make it possible to acquire unmarried male workers. As it happens, avunculocal residence, combined with matrilateral cross-cousin marriage, is the marital strategy of choice for couples who have daughters but no sons. A man's sister's son is a desirable groom for the same reason that her daughter is a desirable bride: one has come to know the child from the routine visits of his mother, who, as a kinswoman, is a trusted figure. Still, the attempt to substitute avuncular for paternal authority is regarded as a risky venture unless the boy's natal household is much poorer than the one into which he marries.

Now, I would not argue that only one set of institutions is appropriate to the material conditions of this community. Some of them work as well as they do only because self-fulfilling prophecies support them. Other ways of forming households might work as well. Patrilocal residence, however, turns out to be a simple and effective social invention under these conditions, and it is not only the standard residential policy of the village and region, but an institution that is amplified and elaborated in a variety of ways.

Patrilocal residence insures that the relationship between father and son will continue as an economic relationship into the son's adulthood and the father's old age. Elders mistrust young men as being too involved in petty concerns with sex and entertainment. Having reared a son and thus established a continuity of authority and socialization, elders would prefer to keep their own young men rather than take a chance on someone else's. Continuity of socialization is achieved by keeping a boy in the household where he was reared. Continuity of authority is achieved by assuring him that the estate he works to improve now will be his in the future. Bear in mind that among avunculocal horticulturalists, boys who work for their father before living with their uncle generally are not called upon to invest in a complex technology containing many capital instruments that may be acquired through hard work, the case we find in Yaavahalli.

Viewed one way, continuity of authority and socialization is a practical matter that appears on the surface of social interaction. Ordinarily, no one seriously considers any alternatives to patrilocal residence, except when a household has no young man to inherit its farm enterprise. When this circumstance does arise, the family trying to recruit a young man is regarded as being in a vulnerable position, as is any young man it might recruit. As one informant put it, "Look, there is a kind of grudge between *maava* (wife's father) and *aLiya* (daughter's husband). Mostly they do not talk to one another directly; they talk through their wives when they want to say something." In this society, where aggression even of the verbal sort is rare, people are afraid of covert aggression in any irregular social relationship. It is irregular for one man to move into a household containing another man with whom he has not been reared. The content of the fear varies with the nature of the relationship. In the case of *maava* and *aLiya*, *aLiya* is afraid of being overworked, excluded from decisions, and consequently pitied by his friends as someone lacking the nerve to stand up to his father-in-law. *Maava* is afraid that *aLiya* will not accord him the respect that a son would; still worse, he might demand a share of his estate to establish an independent household shortly after joining the family; worse yet, he might steal from him. Thus, on the surface, people simply regard patrilocal residence as the normal development of paternal and fraternal relationships. How that development comes to be regarded as normal in the first place, then, is the interesting issue.

My life history materials contain a number of cases in which young men are described as engaging in acts regarded as criminal (such as stealing) or "crazy" (that is, so certain to bring misfortune on the actor as to be beyond rational understanding). From my outsider's point of view, it seems plausible to view this behavior in terms of conflicts young men experience in facing up to their lot as village farmers. Because they are sexual and, in some ways, social adults (they can go to the cinema with friends) before they are economic adults (capable of managing their own behavior in light of life's harsh realities), they are likely to engage in more reckless behavior than their wives and sisters. From the elder's perspective, the problem is one of managing young men's behavior, and they approach the problem with moral talk aimed at explaining the karmic consequences of reckless acts. Whose sermons are likely to be the most effective? This question leads us to a more detailed interpretation of the continuity in authority and socialization fostered by patrilocal residence.

In growing up, every boy hears his male elders talk about their own experiences and those of their ancestors. I will present two stories, one by an elderly man, Marappa, the other by his middle-aged son, Kenchanna. Although these were told in response to my request for a life history, both men assured me that this is the sort of thing one also tells one's son.

THE STORY OF GOLDEN GRAIN

The elder's account can be summarized as follows. The family originated in a village near Bangalore. There were seven brothers living together, with their wives and children, farming thirty acres of land. A famous astrologer came to the village and told the villagers that if they planted paddy at a certain time, the plants would bear golden grains. He would tell them the proper time, but they must agree to give him half of the gold they reaped. Everyone planted their paddy at the appointed time except the seven brothers, who arrived late but planted their fields anyway.

The other fields grew healthy plants, but they bore only ordinary rice. Only straw grew on the fields of the seven brothers, and the brothers went to cut the straw for fodder. When they did so they found golden grains hidden in the stem of each plant. Quickly, they took the straw to a hill near the village so they could thresh the grain in secret.

The astrologer, however, knew what had happened, and so with the village guard he went to the hill to ask for his share. The brothers refused, set upon the astrologer and guard, killed them, and buried them under the granary where the grains were stored. Discovering the men's disappearance, the villagers sent for police, and the brothers fled in seven directions. Their lands were given to the families of the murdered men. "I do not know what happened to the others, but our grandfather moved to Mellur, where he had to work as a *kuli*."

THE STORY OF KENCHANNA

Kenchanna, the elderly man's son, had his own story, which I give in abbreviated form.

Our forefathers came from Mellur [the village to which his great-grandfather fled]. As a young man our father had to work as a *kuli*, but he saved and bought lands, eventually thirty acres. My father sent my elder brother and me to school. But I would not listen to my father and formed the habit of talking loudly and hitting the other boys. My father reprimanded me, but I continued my bad ways. Then he chained a log to my leg, and I had to walk to school carrying that log. I began to play hooky, so my father chained a log to my other leg. Finally, my father gave up and withdrew me from school.

After that I had to work in the fields, but I didn't like to work, so I began spending a lot of time with my friends. I began taking money to spend on my friends as well. That was the time of the Independence Movement to free our motherland from the foreigner. And so my friends and I formed a party of fourteen to take part as *satyagrahis*. [He goes on to describe how he spent the better part of five years away from home as a nonviolent demonstrator and was jailed at least twice by the British.] . . . I was married by this time. I had ruined the greater part of my portion of our estate because of my political activities. Also, I had a falling out with my elder brother, so I sold what remained and took up lands in this village.

Because I did not listen to my father, I am not an educated man. My father worked as a *kuli* so that we might have land, but I ruined my inheritance, so I too had to work as a *kuli*. But I learned the teachings of the fathers of our country, Gandhi, Nehru, and Bose, and I am suggesting their teachings to my sons. Others do not follow those teachings. Those who have seats in the group *panchayat* suck the blood of the poor people. I tell my sons not to listen to the words of the despoilers.

The samples I have selected are atypical. Kenchanna is one of only two villagers to take part in the Independence Movement, the other being a man from a community adjacent to Kenchanna's native village for whom the movement also provided a haven from family problems. The story of the golden grain is the only case of murder I ever heard about, and most fathers do not have such difficult problems with their sons as Kenchanna's did or use such harsh measures to correct the problems they do encounter. On the contrary, most young men never do anything that is seriously disruptive of household harmony in the process of sowing wild oats. But, as best I can determine, all boys hear "mistakes of the fathers" lectures from the older men of the family. These are not "sins of the fathers" lectures, because the speaker rarely attributes malevolence to himself when he talks about his youth; he simply portrays himself as misunderstanding social reality. He did not recognize the consequences of his acts, or as villagers say, he did not know how to behave. Most life histories of men from middle age onward are marked by a dramaturgy of remorse followed by redemption.

The most common error of informants was to do things that led to the partition of a patrilocal joint household. That is, as we have seen, regarded as a terrible mistake. But had I chosen a more typical story and told the reader that the elder who related it also extolled the virtues of hard work, moderate habits, and proper conduct generally to sons who usually behaved well (as had the speaker in his youth, except for separating from his father), then the role of this talk as a dramatic resource fostering household patrilocality would be lost. It is precisely because the talk does not always work, because young men sometimes do things that are much worse than demanding their share of the estate, that the talk is important.

Regardless of the specific nature of the mistakes a man said that he or some ancestor made in the past, they always involved a contravention of the teachings of the elders, and they always led to a decline in prosperity. This feature of the stories not only attributes legitimacy to those teachings, but establishes the dramatic basis for a dialectic of redemption as well. From an outsider's point of view, life historical narratives in which the speaker describes the errors of his youth and goes on to tell of his efforts to settle down, work hard, and make something of himself are simply descriptions of typical features of the male life cycle. As constructions of social reality for participants in the situation, they are something more. Each story may be regarded as a special realization of a representative anecdote, to borrow a term from Kenneth Burke (1969), a culturally standardized drama of the father/son relationship. In that it talks about events that people observe to happen, it is a representation of reality: "My father worked as a *kuli*." To the extent that it selects certain events and not others, it is a reduction of reality; each story provides particular dramatis personae, events, and circumstances for the following dialectical scheme:

Thesis: A family is living in prosperity.
Antithesis: Junior members rebel against their elders.
Synthesis: Junior members establish new households at lower levels of prosperity.

New thesis: Junior members live in remorse and poverty.
Antithesis: They work hard to recoup their losses for their own children.
Synthesis: They are now the elders of a family that is more prosperous than before.

As a son, the speaker will say, he failed to follow the teachings of his elders and suffered the consequences. Through hard work, he redeemed himself as father for his own children. In acknowledging the truth of the elders' teachings, he construes them as *credenda*, things to be believed. By locating his own redemption in efforts on behalf of his children, just as his own father labored on his behalf, he portrays the teachings as *miranda*, something to be admired. Fathers may be incorrect in their construction of the social world, but how can their motives be questioned when they are legitimized by years of labor?

The practical impact of this ideology on the behavior of young men cannot be directly measured, but recourse to the patriarchal anecdote, the story of how a man eventually internalizes his father's wisdom as he works for his own children's welfare, is effectively available only to the man who has reared the adolescent or young man to whom he is speaking. Continuity of socialization is maintained as the speaker takes the role of father in retrospectively examining himself as a son, to his son. In effect, he says that the advice I am giving you now is advice I would have given to myself; indeed, it is the advice I was given. The continuity of authority is maintained as, down the generations, fathers are portrayed as legitimizing their advice by the redemption of their labor. In the full text of his narrative, Kenchanna says that when he left school, "I destroyed the plans my father had made for me."

When a young man is asked to join a household other than the one in which he was reared, he is being offered inheritance rights in a farm, but it is not a farm that was created specifically for him. The offer, therefore, does not contain the moral force of paternal investment found in a father's assurances to his sons. Sons can trust their father to take their interests to heart in the future because he has pursued their interests in the past.

Thus, because patrilocal residence has been the usual practice in the past, perhaps out of a practical preference for wanting to keep one's physically mature, but socially and economically immature, young men around rather than hazard someone else's, an ideology has developed that further amplifies the strength of the practice. This ideology does much more than simply say one ought to live patrilocally: it offers an explanatory scheme to justify the practice, one that is experientially palpable to speaker and listener alike.

The man who portrays himself as economic father, a man who is usually biological father as well, is father indeed. The interests of father and son are made consubstantial in the father's management of the farm: I built this place for you, it is ours, and now I am asking you to donate your labor to it. A boy grows up hearing about his father's love through his mother's continual attribution of paternal concern as the motive behind the father's work. While fathers talk to their sons about their own lives, the person who usually explains the father's behavior in terms of paternal investment is the mother. She offers an experientially convincing explanation: the father continually works and voices concern for the material welfare of his family, so there is no counterevidence to what the mother says. Moreover, the reliability of the source of this information is based on the still more fundamental social knowledge of the mother's devotion. Father, along with everyone else, extolls the virtues of motherhood: he tells the son that his mother is absolutely trustworthy, and she tells the son to obey his father.

Thus, in order to understand the cultural significance of patrilocal residence—and its consequence, equipartible patrilineal inheritance—one must go beyond the fact that they are devices for allocating people to households and allocating land to people, and recognize them as contexts for symbolic interaction that are created through symbolic interaction. The practice of keeping sons at home and bequeathing them the family estate is regarded as an appropriate development of paternal and fraternal relationships, that is, of prior patterns of interaction among males. At the same time, the practice creates a context in which effective joint family farm management can continue. Patriarchy, the symbolic legitimization of paternal authority over sons in the material context of prevailing residential and inheritance patterns, constitutes a device for managing male behavior. There may be other ways of successfully managing male work in similar technologies, but this one persists because it creates conditions conducive to its own repetition. In middle age a man looks back and sees that the joint household of his youth was more efficient than the nuclear family he or his neighbors established after household partition, and accordingly he sets out to establish a similar joint household with his wife, using their son or sons as its raw material.

Hypergamy and Consanguineous Marriage

Once the circumstances favoring the later marriage of males, patrilocal residence and equipartible patrilineal inheritance, have been established, the last two teachings of the elders fall plausibly into line, provided we assume that the policies of village elders are aimed at the evenhanded enhancement of their children's welfare. We have already been implicitly working under this assumption in the matter of inheritance, which assures each son of sharing equally in the estate established by his parents.

This leaves elders with the problem of providing for their daughters. They do this by marrying girls up the economic order if they can and by trying to avoid sending girls to households significantly poorer than their own. The parents want to see each girl equally well settled. Kempanna was one of two sons who together stood to inherit land equivalent to a good deal less than one-third of H. C.'s estate. H. C. and his wife proposed that they make up the difference by transferring land to Kempanna and his prospective bride, which when combined with Kempanna's patrimony would create an estate equal to that their other two daughters would inherit. Kempanna's parents demanded a full third of H. C.'s holdings. Eventually public pressure (and the lovers' sexual liaison) obliged Kempanna's parents to recognize the equity of H. C.'s proposal. The result was a curious arrangement in which the young couple lived at Kempanna's house but divided their labor between the two joint family households and contributed a portion of the income of H. C.'s land to the maintenance of Kempanna's household.

This case illustrates the strictness with which village elders try to provide equitably for all of their children. The practice of seeking cross-cousins or cross-uncles as grooms for their daughters is likewise premised upon a girl's best interests: she is not simply marrying a husband but marrying into a family, and so the question arises as to who can be best trusted to treat the girl well. The culturally standard answer is families who are related to one's own through prior marital alliance.

Hypergamy and old-relationship marriage also serve the interests of households as bride receivers. Earlier I noted that older village women tend to view themselves as managing the circulation of young women through marriage among male-managed family farms. In one sense or another, I suspect that this is common in societies of plow agriculturalists in which the male-managed family farm has proven to be an ecologically successful domestic unit. Women have to make the best of the situation because no alternative is readily available, and one way they make the best of it is to see their daughters suitably married. Another is to try to acquire daughters-in-law to their liking.

But there is a fundamental difference between the status of women in Yaavahalli and that of women in agricultural communities in which women make only a small contribution to farm work. In those villages of North India, for example, where women contribute, say, a fifth of the farm labor force and much of that at harvest time, disputes among the women of a joint family can be avoided by division of the domestic establishment while the male farm corporation is left intact. Each woman can have her own apartment, or at least her own hearth, where she tends her own children and cooks her own food, because women's labor time is an underutilized farm resource. The men of the family, who continue to farm together, need the women in the fields seldom enough to leave each woman adequate time to do her own separate domestic work.

In Yaavahalli, where the average woman is a half-time farm worker in a labor intensive technology, such an arrangement will not work very well. It is not simply that the women will have to get along in the fields even if they cannot get along at home. The effective utilization of women's time in farm and livestock production requires both centralization in the organization of domestic work and the establishment of procedures for the equitable division of labor among women. In short, the women too need to constitute a corporation.

As we have seen, the amount of labor invested per woman per day in domestic work, notably in food-related tasks, which consume a good deal of time, declines sharply when joint family households are compared to nuclear family units. The bulk of the additional woman-time joint households acquire by centralizing domestic services under the direction of the mother of the house is used to care for additional livestock, which increases both a family's cash income and the amount of protein in the diet. While this means that the women of joint households do not systematically provide more field labor per woman than other women, I suspect that the women of joint households do all sorts of work more proficiently than women who have no one, save perhaps a young daughter, to help them out. For one thing, joint households provide pregnant, lactating, and menstruating women with some release time from field labor, which the women involved certainly welcome and which may improve their health and thus their long-term productivity.

But more than that, women in joint households probably waste less time. Women of nuclear families often seemed to me to be rather harried, pulled as they were by simultaneous demands of domestic work, livestock care, field labor, and their children. Indeed, one of the problems we had in assessing the allocation of their labor was the fact that they were often doing more than one thing at a time. The frequent interruptions to which they were subject meant that a larger fraction of their time was spent in turning from one task to the next. In an effort to splice field labor into their busy domestic schedules, these women would sometimes go to and from the fields three or four times a day. The time they spent just tidying up after a domestic task, making sure the children were accounted for, walking to the fields, getting a farm task under way, and walking home afterwards might, when repeated several times over, easily come to as much as forty-five minutes a day.

Women in joint family households were much more likely to spend half-days or full days in the fields, and, free from distractions and interruptions, they may well have worked more proficiently as a result.

An examination of daily reports of field labor shows a clear pattern of turn taking among the women of joint family households containing two or more relatively young women or adolescent girls; the woman who worked in the fields one day was usually replaced by someone else the next. And with the exception of periods of peak demand for farm labor, a woman who spent a full day in the fields was usually assigned only light and highly preferred duties, such as cooking and child care, on the following day. Even in stem families consisting of an older couple and a young nuclear family, there is ample evidence of efforts to maintain equity in the division of labor between the women. Though the younger woman did far more field labor than the older because she was fitter for it, the older woman compensated for days on which heavy physical demands were placed on the younger one by taking on the more onerous tasks around the house. She fetched the water and tended the livestock while the young woman rested. Thus, there is not the slightest indication in the data that mothers-in-law treated their daughters-in-law as drudges to be exploited.

Earlier I noted that it is regarded as bad form for the men of a joint household to interfere in the affairs of the women. The man who does so subverts the authority of the mother of the house to work out arrangements for the division of women's labor that are both equitable and efficient.

The problem is that the twin goals of equity and efficiency are not always compatible. Sometimes someone has to be asked to do more farm work than someone else, and more than she would like to do. Not only must allowances be made for the pregnant or menstruating woman who needs extra rest or for the lactating woman who requires time to nurse her infant, but also the demands for farm labor are sufficiently variable that short-term equity in the division of farm labor among women cannot always be sustained. If the farm work of a household containing two young women calls for the labor of one on one day and the labor of both the next, the woman who works both days will have to accept the situation gracefully if household harmony is to be maintained.

That is why hypergamy and consanguineous marriage are such salient aspects of marital choice for households as bride receivers. Recall that the amount of farm work women do declines sharply with increases in per capita land wealth. This means that a family that chooses a girl from a poorer household can ask her to do more farm work than the daughters of the house have been accustomed to without asking her to do any more than she has been accustomed to herself. This, coupled with the fact that she will be pleased with the diet, clothing, and housing she receives in her conjugal household, makes such a girl a desirable choice. A girl from a wealthier household, by contrast, will be asked to adjust to more farm work than she is used to and to accept a lower standard of living into the bargain.

Likewise, a girl who is linked to a family by a prior marital connection will be better known to them than most girls who are not. Understandably, both families tend to put the best face on matters during marriage arrangements. A girl will always be on her best behavior when she meets prospective in-laws, which means that it is hard for the prospective in-laws to know if the nice, accomplished girl with whom they are presented will continue to be so nice and accomplished a year after she marries. By marrying in an old relationship, parents secure a girl whose behavior they have been able to observe throughout her childhood and who is therefore more predictable. Perhaps this means they would tactfully reject out of hand some girls because they had displayed unsuitable temperaments, but it is frequently the case, as we have seen, that children are reared with the possibility of certain consanguineous matings in mind. Thus, the desirability of such marriages, founded on the anticipation that they will foster harmony in a household, tends to be a self-fulfilling prophecy. People assume that consanguineous marriages are good, and in managing their relationships with kin in suitable households, they take measures aimed at promoting their chances of getting the match they want, measures that enhance the likelihood that the marriage will display the virtues attributed to it. In managing the circulation of women through marriage among male-managed family farms, then, women are not merely managing the formation of husband/wife pairs; they are also managing relations among women in response to the demands made on those relationships by the substantial participation of women in farm production.

Summary

This concludes the synchronic portion of my argument. The teachings of the elders of Yaavahalli make admirable sense from the perspective of parents whose aim is to foster the welfare of all of their children as village farmers. It is well to marry sons later than daughters because boys are not prepared to be men as soon as girls are prepared to be women. It is well to keep sons at home under paternal authority and therefore well to provide for each son by assuring him of an equal portion of the parental estate. This means that parents of sons who also have daughters must settle their daughters through marriage elsewhere. And, when possible, parents try to marry their girls into households wealthier than their own and into households of trusted kin. Likewise, for the sake of harmony in the patrilocal joint family household, they also endeavor to select brides from families of trusted kin and from households poorer than their own.

To say that the teachings of the elders make sense from the perspective of parents who wish to foster their children's welfare is to attribute a motive. What could people possibly hope to achieve by doing what they tell themselves and one another to do? The people of Yaavahalli gave us a clue about where to look for an answer to this question. Joint family households are to be favored because they confer greater prosperity on those who form them. Since this policy is clearly founded on the community's agricultural adaptation, it seems warranted too to ask if the other policies concerning household formation are also aimed at fostering a successful agricultural adaptation. The empirical investigation of these questions required an examination of the material conditions under which villagers live and farm. These material conditions include the biological properties of their bodies, and since the teachings of the elders all turn on the distinction between male and female, the material conditions we examined included biological sex differences. The reproductive role of women, the greater strength of men, and the slower and in some ways more difficult maturation of boys are all biological facets of life that are culturally amplified in the organization of villagers' labor and further amplified in their policies for household formation. The more rapid maturation and less disruptive behavior of girls is a resource villagers can utilize; the reproductive function of women, when amplified into cultural motherhood, places constraints on women's lives that must be mitigated if women are to be materially productive. Mitigation is achieved in part by assigning women the tasks that are most compatible with child care and, further, by centralizing domestic services in joint households to enhance the contribution of women to primary production.

The greater physical strength of men is a resource that is intensively exploited in farm production. And in the act of exploiting male strength, circumstances are created that favor male management of farming. But the slower maturation of boys coupled with their greater proclivity to behavior disruptive of routine farm work, creates a problem that is mitigated by their later marriage, patrilocal residence, and the equipartible patrilineal inheritance that follows from these practices.

Thus, given the technological and environmental conditions under which villagers live and the biological properties of males and females, the sexual division of labor and the domestic policies through which the sexual division of labor is organized provide a cultural means for achieving a relatively proficient agricultural adaptation.

It might be argued that achieving a proficient agricultural adaptation should make sense to anyone, but I have suggested that the teachings of the elders make sense from the perspective of parents for several reasons. Village children do not know how to succeed as farmers; they learn how from their elders. Left to their own devices, the young, especially the boys, will not do what must be done. More self-evidently, it is, after all, the elders—that is, the parents of grown and near-grown children—who espouse the teachings of the elders, a fact which might lead one to suppose that these doctrines serve their interests. And since the empirical consequence of obeying the teachings of the elders appears to be the fostering of the welfare of a couple's children, it would seem warranted to regard this as the motive, the underlying presumption, on which the teachings are premised, a motive that is in any case evident in villagers' portrayals of their own affairs.

It might also be argued that these interests are selfish—parents want agriculturally successful households to support them in their declining years—and that the enhancement of the welfare of coming generations is a secondary consideration. But while I would certainly presume that villagers prefer to spend their old age in a prosperous household, I do not think that this is the primary interest served by the teachings of the elders. For one thing, it is inconsistent with some of the policies. For instance, when a girl marries up the economic order, the chief beneficiary is the girl, not her parents. But more important is the fact that children are the focus of interest in social situations in which the teachings are employed as guides for behavior.

In a sense the teachings of the elders are an emergent property of village social structure; people use them in making social arrangements for their children. Though they learn these doctrines from their parents, it is not until villagers are parents themselves that they have occasion to use them in making real decisions. Moreover, villagers repeatedly stated that they did not really understand the wisdom of their elders until they were grown and attempting to manage a family. This suggests that the meaning of the doctrines emerges from the experience of being a parent. As a young person one learns the teachings of the elders; as an adult one experiences them as true.

That is why the teachings of the elders are to be viewed as a child-centered doctrine. The village child is a social fact for his parents; his needs, demands, mistakes, and successes constantly impinge on their awareness. Over years of bonding and responding to the child, parents become habituated to looking out for his interests, and when arrangements are to be made that will influence the course of his adult life, they are made against this background: the past affection and investment of interest in the child prompt continued interest. Parents view the child as their creation and try to see that the finished person is as well provided for as possible.

Parental interest in a child's material welfare is not as paramount a concern in some societies as it is in Yaavahalli. There are certainly societies, for instance, in which men use their daughters to foster their own political ambitions through material alliances. Herein lies another notable aspect of parental investment in Yaavahalli. In societies in which men use their daughters as political pawns, it may well be that mothers do not share their husband's aspirations. In Yaavahalli parents rarely disagree in such matters; both parents want the same things for the same children and invest tremendous amounts of time and energy in pursuing them. In the next two chapters we shall inquire into how this state of affairs may have evolved.

chapter 8

The Development of
Agricultural Intensification

> Whichever way the eye turned dead bodies were to be
> seen. During August the average number of dead picked
> up in the streets of Bangalore was twenty. From September
> 1 to 10 the number had increased to forty-one. . . . People
> argued, not unnaturally, that if such things occurred at
> headquarters, most terrible scenes were necessarily to be
> witnessed in the interior.
>
> —Digby, *The Famine Campaign in Southern India* (1878)

This chapter begins an inquiry into how the agricultural adaptation of
the people of Yaavahalli may have evolved. It will of necessity be more
speculative than the synchronic portion of my argument, which was
certainly speculative enough, because data on many points are either
scanty or unavailable.

The terrible drought that greeted me upon my arrival in India imposed great hardships on the people of the *taluk*, and yet they came
through the drought better than I, many government officials, and the
people themselves feared they would. They did so because the rural
population was fairly well prepared for the catastrophe before it happened. The most obvious evidence of this cultural fitness was the scores
of irrigation wells that dotted the landscape and the gardens they irrigated; these meant that the people could, for a time, farm without rain.

At the time I took this self-evident fitness for granted; it was not
until long after that I realized that the creation of the agricultural landscape I observed was the most important phenomenon I had to study.
Those wells represented countless cubic meters of moved earth, and the
moved earth represented countless hours of human labor. The remaining
question is obvious: what prompted all of that labor? Its answer de-

pended on the recognition that all of that labor was cultural behavior; it was organized and managed through the manipulation of symbols. This recognition leads to a rephrasing of the question: how did the people of the *taluk* talk themselves and one another into all of that work?

My choice of Yaavahalli as the village in which to pursue this inquiry was serendipitous. When I arrived in the area, I told the block development officer that I wanted to study village agriculture. He sent me to Yaavahalli because that village had many wells and therefore a lot of ongoing agriculture for me to study in spite of the drought. What this meant, though I did not realize it at the time, was that I was sent to a village that was culturally fitter than most to deal with the current crisis and was thus an ideal place in which to study the evolution of the adaptation I observed. All I had to do was discover the cultural characteristics that set this community apart from the average one and then try to determine whether and how these differences fostered the community's greater agricultural capacity. That is why this evolutionary inquiry must be made despite the hazards of speculation about certain facts: the data the people of Yaavahalli provided offered an opportunity that should not be ignored.

Two basic questions are entailed in this inquiry: what happened in the course of the region's agricultural development, and why did it happen that way? The descriptive question is the subject of the present chapter; the theoretical question concerning the evolutionary mechanisms responsible for stimulating agricultural growth in the region is the subject of the next chapter. Each of these chapters relies on a work by the Danish economist Ester Boserup. In the first of these, *The Conditions of Agricultural Growth* (1965), Boserup suggests that the labor intensification of agriculture, hereafter spoken of as "agricultural intensification" or simply "intensification," occurs as a response, substantially initiated by farm people themselves, to increased population density. Did this happen in Yaavahalli? If our descriptive account of the region's agricultural growth suggests that it did, how and why did villagers' behavior conform to Boserup's predictions? Her second book, which deals with the role of women in economic development, provides the key. In it she notes that increased population growth and the agricultural intensification that goes with it are often accompanied by changes in mating patterns and the sexual division of labor. Among sparse populations practicing simple horticulture, women often do most of the farm work. This "female farming" tends to be associated with rather widespread polygyny. Plow agriculture, which is generally found with much denser populations, is usually "male farming." However, when farming becomes extremely labor intensive, as it has in Yaavahalli, women may re-enter the farm work force as the only available stock of the additional labor required. Monogamy prevails under plow agriculture. I accord key status to these observations because they call attention to an important fact. Farming in traditional societies occurs under what Sahlins (1972) aptly calls the domestic mode of production, in which people work in and for families. Boserup's general observations concerning relations between demography, intensification, mating patterns, and sexual divisions of labor suggest that the organization of farming is highly responsive to the costs of reproduction. Thus, for example, men will work harder and have fewer wives when the labor costs of rearing children increase on a crowded landscape. I believe she is right. I also suspect that the intensification response to increased population density occurs in part because farm people recurrently define reproductive fitness in terms of productive proficiency and in the course of doing so produce mechanisms of cultural evolution that mimic those of natural selection. More on this later; let us now turn to the descriptive task.

Boserup's Hypothesis Revised

Briefly, Boserup's hypothesis about intensification goes like this. If farm people can respond to increased population density by migrating to less crowded areas, they may well do so, because the alternatives, getting poorer or working harder, are costly. If migration is not feasible, the only alternative to getting poorer is working harder to get more out of available resources. Because farmers are increasing labor inputs while other factors, such as land, are held constant, the marginal product of their labor declines, and the average product of all work done declines in its wake. Nevertheless, farm people do the necessary work and thereby protect their incomes from decline, averting the Malthusian cataclysm.

While this hypothesis has been the basis of much fruitful work in anthropology, which has generally confirmed Boserup's predictions, her formulation of the hypothesis has been subjected to criticism, notably by Bronson (1972), and must be revised. First, her hypothesis should not be regarded as a unilinear theory of agricultural evolution, which is clearly a multivariate process that occurred in different ways in different places. Rather, one should ask whether she has isolated an important variable in agricultural change. I believe she has, provided we modify the empirical definition of intensification.

Boserup presumed that intensification meant increased labor inputs per unit of land and that it could be measured in terms of fallowing periods; the shorter the period, the more labor intensive the farming. We shall not make these assumptions. Instead, intensification will be defined in terms of energetic output per worker per unit of time. Much more often than not this leads to increased labor per unit of land, but not always. For instance, Bronson notes that in Meso-America annually cropped, and by Boserup's definition intensively cultivated, infields produce more per unit of labor than long-fallowed swiddens called *milpa*. By my definition it is the *milpa*, not the infield, that represents the labor-intensive portion of the system. I would predict the amount of *milpa* a family cultivates per capita to be an inverse function of the amount of infield it owns per capita. People walk long distances to these fields and do a lot of relatively unproductive work on them because they cannot get more infield to feed more mouths.

Revised in this way, Boserup's hypothesis becomes a corollary of Chayanov's rule, which holds that the amount of work farm people do depends on the number of mouths they must feed. I have added the notion that the amount of work they do also depends on the per capita or per worker availability of other resources, so that as they are crowded farmers will attempt either to substitute labor for other factors of production or to acquire new resources, such as more *milpa*, more irrigation wells, or more wage work, to expand their cultivation and employment opportunities to feed more people. They will do this even if it means a decline in the de facto wage they receive for their labor. How people do this depends on a host of environmental, economic, and cultural factors. Thus, one should not take existing taxonomies of farm systems too literally in making predictions about specific cases, because local conditions are highly variable.

In the *taluk* the local fact of life one must bear in mind is that in the past large numbers of people died in famines that were the result of poor rainfall, which is a recurrent problem due to the monsoon weather system upon which the region depends. As a result, the aspect of intensification that is most important in this setting is that directed at increasing cultivation opportunities in droughts so as to maximize the minimum food production of bad years. The solution to this problem was tied to another local environmental factor, the hard, porous, lateritic soil, which allowed the construction of open pit wells, but only at the expenditure of huge amounts of human effort.

Intensification in Yaavahalli

The purpose of this chapter is to answer three straightforward questions. First, did intensification through well digging occur in response to population growth? If one looks at the short-term development of households, it appears that more often than not the reverse is true: efforts to increase productivity precede the population growth that results as young married couples begin to have children, who in turn must be provided with the means to make a living once they reach adulthood. In the next chapter considerable importance will be attached to this tendency of households to provide for population growth in advance of need.

But, if one takes a longer view of village economic history and examines the population as a whole, it does appear that the period of agricultural intensification dating from the 1920s occurred, in part, in response to population growth. In the early twenties two events occurred: rural population density returned to the level prevailing at the time of the great famine of the late 1870s, and there was a drought. This drought was far less severe than that preceding the great famine, but it caused considerable hardship and it seems to have frightened rural people. At any event, the sustained development of the labor intensive garden cultivation I observed appears to have begun at that time and to have gathered momentum in the years following Indian Independence when population was growing rapidly too.

Second, there is the question of whether farm people took the initiative in spurring this development themselves. Beyond doubt, government actions and the development of a market infrastructure, which made it easier and more profitable for villagers to sell their crops and easier and relatively cheaper for them to buy more advanced agricultural technology, also played roles in the intensification process. Thus, the question is whether farm people were tugged into a new age by economic forces beyond their control or whether their initiatives contributed to the creation of these forces.

Although I can offer no conclusive answer to this question, one telling point can be made: by the time of my stay, at least, villagers' demands for agricultural improvement loans and improved technology in the form of irrigation equipment, better seed, chemical fertilizer, and so on far exceeded the government's financial and physical ability to provide them. Moreover, the most powerful and prestigious members of rural communities, the *sovkaars*, had become entrepreneurs who provided the leadership for agricultural development. These individuals, of whom Yaavahalli's *patel* was one, organized the construction of roads, irrigation tanks, and such public facilities as the veterinary dispensary, all of which promoted agricultural growth. They also took the lead in organizing various cooperative societies that strengthened the average villager's hand in dealing with the larger economy. In the course of doing these things, these entrepreneurs constantly dunned the government for a greater share of resources that were demanded elsewhere as well.

Certainly personal gain was a result, and one may presume a motive, of the *sovkaars'* entrepreneurial activities. But there is little question that they represented a groundswell of popular demand for agricultural development, for not only was public entrepreneurship the basis for success in local electoral politics, but ordinary villagers were grudgingly willing to accept a certain amount of graft on the part of their leaders in order to get the personal loans and public facilities they wanted. Thus, the rise of this rural bourgeoisie was simply a practical, albeit, from the perspective of the poor, inequitable, device by which ordinary people pursued their private interest in agricultural intensification. Farmers were not tugged into intensification; they pushed for it.

The third question has to do with the consequences of agricultural intensification for farm incomes. As we shall see, during years of more or less average rainfall the development of labor intensive garden cultivation has allowed villagers to maintain roughly constant per capita incomes, over the long term, in spite of increases in rural population density. There have, however, been some changes in the form income takes. Over the years villagers' consumption of manufactured goods has doubtless increased; their consumption of animal protein has probably declined. But the most fundamental change in farm income has occurred in years of poor rainfall: the digging of wells, which drought-proofed farming to some degree, famine-proofed the population to the same degree. Therefore, the ability to increase minimum per capita income—the income attained in years of drought—made it possible to forestall a disaster similar to the great famine even though the population had grown.

These three questions are most easily discussed through an account of the region's demographic and economic history, much of it based on oral history from villagers.

Survivors of the Great Famine

Our inquiry into the relationship between intensification and population growth begins with the founding of the village. Yaavahalli was founded sometime during the first third of the nineteenth century. I am sorry I cannot be more exact about the date; its determination depends upon the birth, marriage, and death dates of various village ancestors, which are impossible to determine precisely. But the date of the founding is less important than the circumstances that brought the founders to Yaavahalli and the conditions they encountered when they came.

The founding of Yaavahalli was almost surely an indirect consequence of the Mysore Wars, which concluded at the end of the eighteenth century with the defeat of the Muslim warrior Tippu Sultan at the hands of British-led armies. These wars, coupled with periods of less than favorable weather for agriculture, caused considerable dislocation and mortality in rural populations.

In recalling the oral history of the village they heard as children, elders of the *patel*'s lineage (the founding one) were agreed on two points. First, the founders came to Yaavahalli because they did not have enough land to go around in their natal village. This is also a common feature in the stories of lineages whose local founders came to the village later. Second, the area around the village was uninhabited at the time of settlement: "You can say this place was a no man's land when the brothers came here" (that is, the brothers of the *patel*'s lineage who, with a Naayk family, established the village). Thus, a migration to an area of sparse population was undertaken in response to relative crowding at home. It is hardly surprising that the area was sparsely populated, since Yaavahalli lies close to Tippu Sultan's military bastion in the Nandi Hills, a factor that had scarcely made the place attractive to Hindu farmers.

In any case, the sparseness of the population had a major influence on farming practices: "In those days there was so much land that they could feed their cattle simply by allowing them to graze. And they could get all of the food they needed by just plowing once and scattering the seed."

Thus, though there were surely irrigation tanks already in the region, agriculture was by modern standards extensive: a relatively small amount of labor was spread over a relatively large amount of land. And provided rainfall was adequate, the average product of their labor was, in nutritional terms, high by modern standards. Villagers of the time had solved the problem of crowding by the simple expedient of moving to an uncrowded place.

The system of land tenure prevailing at the village's founding is not clear. If the elders' oral history is to be believed, their ancestors simply walked in and began farming a no man's land. But sometime after its founding Yaavahalli came under the *joodidar* system, which the newly established Wodeyar dynasty of Brahmin Rajas of Mysore sometimes used to establish a reliable revenue settlement. According to legend, the Raja, who was then touring the countryside, came to visit an adjacent village, where he was entertained by the Brahmin priest of a large temple. The Raja was so taken by the beauty and demeanor of the priest's daughter, who placed a garland of flowers around his neck, that he made her father *joodidar* of ten villages on the spot.

In principle the *joodidars* were tax collectors; in practice they were landlords whose demands placed considerable stress on villagers, who describe themselves as having been "slaves" under this regime. We do not know how villagers responded to these demands, but judging from the circumstances, we can guess that they did not dig wells to increase farm production, since all but two of Yaavahalli's irrigation wells date from the 1920s. They did not have to dig wells to maintain their incomes at prior levels; they just had to work harder with the existing technology. This they might have done in two ways: they could have increased the areas under cultivation, or they could have intensified cultivation practices by increasing the number of plowings and by using other preparatory measures to increase yields.

If they started by expanding the area cultivated, which would have meant that the ample pasturage that greeted the founders would have begun to disappear, they could not have continued to do so for long, because the population was increasing rapidly. By 1871 the population density of the *taluk* as a whole, including the town, had reached 236 persons per square mile. We have seen that by the 1960s, when population was much denser, the people of Yaavahalli acquired the bulk of their income from gardens. It seems to me that in order to maintain dietary standards modern villagers would regard as reasonable, the region's 1871 population would have had to cultivate an area of unirrigated land about equal to the combined areas of the dry lands and gardens I observed, leaving little room for expansion.

Thus, it is likely that by the middle of the nineteenth century, a process of agricultural labor intensification was under way in response to population growth as well as to the demands of the *joodidars*. As the number of plowmen and pairs of bullocks increased, each acre of dry land received increasing amounts of preparatory labor that increased yields per acre. But the amount of work performed by each man and animal could not have increased after a certain point, since the amount of preparatory labor an individual can perform is restricted by the seasonal window during which this work must be done. Somewhat greater opportunities for expanding the amount of work done by each individual may have been achieved on tank-irrigated paddy land, whose cultivation was not subject to such severe constraints. But by all accounts, this land was usually cropped only once a year, and the highly labor intensive transplantation technique was not widely used for rice cultivation until this century. Seed was simply sown on plowed fields. This means that women's contribution to farming, limited as it was chiefly to weeding and harvesting, was smaller, both absolutely and proportionally, than that I observed. And while the lives of men would have contained periods of intense effort, the character of the prevailing technology would have left periods of little farm activity as well. It was in the nature of the tank-irrigation system that all fields served by a tank had to be planted at about the same time, since it was difficult to flood one field without flooding adjacent areas as well. This meant that the practice of carving out many small plots and maintaining them at different stages of cultivation was not feasible. Therefore, the creation of many small cultivation opportunities permitting villagers to do more work over the year was not feasible either. Villagers required a more manageable irrigation system using wells to do this.

But few irrigation wells were dug. For the most part villagers and *joodidars* alike were getting by without them, and there seem to have been institutional factors impeding well construction. The farmer who dug a well on his own could increase his yields, but the share of the crop he owed the *joodidar* would increase as well. One presumes that the *joodidar* would have welcomed this unearned increment to his income, but the farmer, in addition to paying the *joodidar* for his own work, faced a further disincentive. Like the nineteenth-century Irish farmer, the villager acquired no equity in his agricultural improvements. He could use the well he dug, but he could not sell it or borrow money against it, since it became part of the *joodidar*'s estate. Nor were *joodidars* much interested in funding the digging of wells, in spite of the benefits they might achieve. Indeed, for a time, about the only thing the *joodidars* appear to have done to stimulate growth in farm production was to allow the immigration of more villagers.

The *joodidars* seem to have viewed their position as that of aristocrats who received a more or less fixed agricultural income from the state in return for their priestly and administrative services. They concerned themselves hardly at all with the business of farming, a calling beneath their station in any case. Disaster was immanent in the circumstances of this growing but technologically stagnant population; all it took was protracted drought to prove this true.

I described the impact of the famine of 1877–78 in the first chapter. Recall that upwards of four million people died in all of South India. When the *taluk* was censused in 1871, some fifty-nine thousand persons were counted; when the census-takers returned in 1881, they found about eighteen thousand fewer people. Adjacent areas suffered similar reductions in population, so that death, not migration, must be the explanation for this severe decline. And since population probably continued to grow from 1871 until the famine and since there surely were births between the famine and the 1881 census, it is a conservative estimate to say that one-third of the *taluk*'s population died.

If anything is painfully evident in contemporary written accounts of the famine of 1877–78, it is that government botched efforts at famine relief. There were a number of reasons for this.

When the rains failed in 1876, it was evident that serious hardship would result, but plans to mitigate the hardship did not anticipate that the rains would fail again in 1877. Consequently, the government made no administrative provision for a calamity of the magnitude that occurred. A commission was hurriedly established to deal with the problem, but it proved notably ineffective.

Yet even if the administrative apparatus for famine relief had been more realistically planned, both stocks of food and transportation were inadequate. In Mysore, where Yaavahalli lay, famine relief was further complicated by the fact that it required coordination between the largely Indian government of the princely state and that of the British Raj, on which the Mysore government was bound to depend for assistance.

Behind all of these circumstantial problems lay an ideological one. Some of the leading Englishmen who served on the commission displayed a suspicion, common to Englishmen of their class at the time, that poverty was largely the fault of the poor. To prevent lassitude and dependence on government, they felt that government must never give the poor anything for nothing. For them this meant that the proper way to relieve a famine was to provide public works projects for the indigent. But because of deficient forward planning, administrative inefficiency, and indecision, as well as the insufficiency of the resources available, the works programs that were implemented were not available until millions of people were too debilitated to work, even though work loads were later reduced for many in recognition of their condition. Contemporary descriptions of some of these projects reminds one of nothing so much as concentration camps.

In Mysore, relief officials experienced what might be called a bad case of cognitive dissonance. The British displayed a pronounced tendency to judge Indian peoples by their own cultural standards. As I noted earlier, Buchannan, a Scot, perceived a resonance of his own ethnicity in the farmers of Mysore; other observers also characterized Mysoreans as industrious and frugal. In contrasting them with the people of Madras, Digby (1878) said of Mysoreans that they were "of a better class," that they possessed "more force of character and independence of conduct." He then quoted one Colonel Pearse, an officer of great experience in the region, as saying that, "The people are very tenacious of their holdings. . . . They are, moreover, very thrifty." Given this image of Mysoreans, one would suppose that officials went out to villages anticipating ready acceptance of the relief work they offered.

In the event they were astonished when villagers told them that they were too weak to work, for time and again relief officers simply refused to believe them. In one case recounted by Digby, the officer demanded that the men of a village strip to the waist and, having examined them, pronounced them fit. Most relief funds were intended for irrigation works, and in another case an officer found that villagers were afraid to work in wells. Now this may have been one reason more wells were not sunk earlier, for the work can indeed be dangerous, and Voddas of the time, a *jaati* for whom earthworks are the traditional occupation, did in fact accept relief work on wells early in the famine. I suspect, however, from my own experience in studying the matter, that officers simply did not understand the effects of the rapid dietary decline on work performance. While famine causes the body to consume its own muscle tissue rather quickly, the effects of malnutrition on work performance will be felt in a miasma of lassitude and dizziness long before they are visible. In 1965 poor villagers consumed sweet coffee on foodless days as an antidote to these invisible symptoms. Ravages on livestock became severe early in the great famine, so that villagers' diets must have been virtually devoid of animal protein for a good while before relief officers came, and they reported to the officers that for some time they had been living on wild roots mixed with what remained of their dwindling grain stocks. Thus, while the people officers encountered may not have looked too badly off, it could still be the case that they would have found hard work on the surface of the ground extremely difficult, and the business of climbing on ropes up and down well shafts impossible.

Eventually it was realized that if lives were to be saved, food had to be given away with no expectation of work in return. But it was too late; for thousands the camps became little more than central places for dying. And many thousands of others never made it to the camps because they were physically unable to walk the distance to them. By 15 March 1877 Digby reports that only 4,200 persons in Kolar District were receiving free food, and meals were meager. In the administrative postmortem that followed the famine, it was recommended that in future crises greater effort be made to bring both relief works and gratuitous aid closer to the people.

But for four million people this belated understanding of the rapidity with which a major famine could reduce people to a state in which they could barely walk, much less work, hardly mattered. Feckless planning coupled with the prejudicial view of some that free food would destroy the work ethic compounded a disaster that would have been serious enough, given the severity of the drought and the limitations on the material resources available to the government.

One is inclined to suspect that this response by government to the famine did not inspire villagers to place much faith in officials to deal any better with future crisis. As a matter of fact, in Yaavahalli and surrounding villages the behavior of the most apparent representatives of government, the *joodidars*, inspired in villagers what may best be described as an intense class hatred, which endured until my stay.

One modest relief measure employed by government in various places in South India during the famine was the forgiveness of taxes. This was a modest measure indeed in view of the fact that the government had little hope of collecting normal revenues under prevailing conditions. But according to the oral history of Yaavahalli, the local *joodidars* continued to demand their shares of whatever crops could be harvested, in spite of the hardship this imposed.

At the time of my fieldwork, one could still find a number of bellshaped pits in the fields that villagers said had been used in times past to conceal from the *joodidars* food harvested at night. Villagers dared not store it in their homes, where it might fall prey to the prying eyes of the *joodidars'* agents. Thus, villagers would steal into the fields at night, remove the earth covering a pit, and take only so much grain as they intended to cook at one time. This implacable resistance to the *joodidars*, who "sucked the blood of poor people," is perhaps the most salient feature of the famine when it is described by village elders as an event experienced by villages as communities. The ancestors of many of the people I knew in Yaavahalli lived in other villages at the time of the famine, and apparently community response was much the same everywhere in the area. Villagers, by and large, refrained from stealing from one another and presented the *joodidars*, who were after all agents of the same government that claimed to offer famine relief, with a united front. When their agents came to a village, everyone told them that no one had anything to give.

But most recollections of the great famine in the oral history of villagers focus not on the response of the government or of villages to the crisis; rather, they focus on the personal experience of families. As best I could determine, there were no survivors of the famine still living at the time of my fieldwork. Such individuals would have been in their late eighties at the least, and the famine is bound to have taken a great toll of infants and young children. There were, however, a number of elderly persons who were the children and, in some cases, the younger siblings of survivors, and it is from these people that I, and younger villagers, heard accounts of the disaster. "At that time there was a great famine in our country, and many people were dying for lack of food. First my grandfather died and then my grandmother. Then my sister also. After that my father and mother moved to this place and took up lands here."

This example illustrates two common consequences of the famine. First, it altered the age composition of the population: the old and the very young were the most likely victims; relatively young adults and older children were the most likely survivors. Not only did some survivors lose their parents, and with them the stabilizing leadership of joint family households, but some young couples were also faced with starting new families to replace the children they had lost. Other individuals lost spouses as well. This disruption in domestic relations may be related to a second factor: a good deal of intervillage migration followed the famine. People may be more inclined to leave a place of grief in which they have lost, in human terms, much of what tied them to it.

At any event Yaavahalli was one of the places to which people migrated, and, apparently, no one left. The immigration did not mean that newcomers crowded onto the lands of the village's existing population. To explain why not, a distinction should be drawn between a revenue village and a village settlement. A revenue village is a parcel of land that is treated as a survey unit on tax rolls. Doubtless, when surveys were originally made, names of actual settlements were used to label parcels of land predominantly cultivated by their residents. But by the time of my stay, the people of Yaavahalli, which was not a revenue village, cultivated surrounding lands in a number of revenue villages, two of which had entirely disappeared as living communities.

What happened was that the *patel* of Yaavahalli interceded with the *joodidars* living in two adjacent villages to secure lands for the new immigrants. Thus, while the population of the village expanded during the generation following the famine, the area of land cultivated by the villagers expanded as well. The newcomers cultivated land that had been cultivated by residents of other communities. And according to oral history, there appears to have been a deliberate selection of these immigrants by the leadership of the village. The immigrants did not approach the *joodidars* directly, but entreated the *patel* to make an appeal on their behalf. Of the seven lineages whose founders came to Yaavahalli during this second wave of migration, five were Vokkaligas, one was Naayk, and one was Holeya. All the immigrating Vokkaliga lineages included men who either had already married women of the *patel*'s lineage or married women of that lineage sometime after arriving in the village. This solidified the authority of the *patel*'s lineage, since the new arrivals owed it the double obligation of being both bride receivers and land receivers. How many individuals, if any, were rejected by the *patel* and his kin as new immigrants we do not know. In the next chapter we shall see that criteria of marital selection among alternative grooms seem to have been at least indirectly employed in recruiting most newcomers. Either the new men had already been selected as fit to marry the lineage's women and simply came to the village in search of better prospects, or, after a period of settling in, it was decided that they would make fit grooms. And in choosing grooms or in presenting individuals to *joodidars* as prospective tenants, a major criterion was whether or not the individual was a strong and industrious worker.

This influx of immigrants meant, for a time, that relatively young adults, the cohort of the best farm workers, constituted a larger proportion of the village population than before. And the fact that these persons were chosen from a pool of potential immigrants, all of whom were survivors of a dreadful famine, may indicate that they were relatively robust individuals. But in spite of the rather high quality of this labor force, the farm technology of the village and the region does not appear to have become markedly more labor intensive during the years following the great famine.

The sharp decline in population may have been one reason for this. While population density may not have been pushed back to that of the days of ample pasturage, it certainly was pushed back. And although population growth must have been for a time more rapid in Yaavahalli than in most other villages, because of immigration, surely the village did lose people to the famine. Thus, given the expansion of the area the people of Yaavahalli cultivated, the effective population density of the village (the ratio of population to land cultivated) was probably lower than it had been prior to the famine. In years of at least moderate rainfall, therefore, this population could feed itself fairly comfortably without digging the irrigation wells that provided the best locally known means for increasing the productivity of land.

Moreover, the old conflict between the *joodidars* and the farmers— the fact that *joodidars* were generally unwilling to invest money in well construction while villagers were reluctant to invest large amounts of their unpaid labor in it—may have been exacerbated by the villagers' bitter resentment of the *joodidars'* insensitivity to their plight during the famine. There followed then a substantial period in which little was done to solve the region's basic ecological problem, the catastrophic impact of a major drought on farm production.

The traditional unirrigated staples of the region were probably subject to selection for drought resistance over a long period. The people who survived a drought planted seeds from the plants that survived. But even so, rainfed crops fail to the extent that the rains fail, and in severe droughts such as that of 1965, yields fall to a small fraction of normal. A major difference between a serious drought and years of moderate drought is that in the former the tanks tend to dry up to the point of being useless. These broad shallow lakes depend chiefly on current rainfall for their water and are subject to extremely rapid evaporative loss. When one considers the fact that the tanks themselves cover a lot of ground, and that it is difficult to distribute water evenly over fields using the system of floodgates and canals with which they are provided, the inefficiency of the antique tank system is all the more apparent. In a persistent drought, the available irrigation water recedes until, eventually, it falls below the level of the floodgate; when this happens, farmers may try to grow a quick crop of gram around the remaining puddle before it too dries up, but the paddy crop is lost completely. That is what happened in the terrible drought of the 1870s, and again in 1965.

The failure of villagers to dig wells as a solution to this problem was certainly not due to a lack of knowledge concerning well construction or the cultivation of gardens, for villagers dug their own drinking water wells, and there were a number of irrigation wells in the region used in cultivating gardens. Wealthy people, notably *joodidars*, had bordered gardens constructed chiefly for the cultivation of areca and coconut palms, betel leaf, and bananas. These are ingredients in ceremonial prestations used in religious rituals and feasts, especially those given in conjunction with life-cycle rituals, so that the ownership of a garden in which to grow one's private supply was, and is, a mark of prestige. The ritual status of these crops also conveyed a ritual status to these gardens. They were sacred places that would be defiled if, for instance, one did not shed one's sandals before entering. Thus, although some produce from them was doubtless sold, they were tended after the manner of botanical gardens, places of contemplation cultivated as an avocation. Still, some villagers did cultivate mulberry for sericulture and some vegetables were grown, and so the fact that the gardens of *joodidars* were not beehives of commercial activity cannot be taken as indicating that it had occurred to no one that wells could be used to cultivate gardens as a routine farm enterprise.

Nor should too much be made of the institutional problems dividing *joodidar* and farmer as impediments to well construction, for in this century the expansion of garden cultivation was moving briskly along even on some *joodidar* lands. The villagers' oral historical account of their failure to dig wells is therefore not entirely satisfactory. Their hatred for the *joodidars* cannot be discounted as a factor, but one suspects that some other factor (or factors) was at work as well. Fortunately, we have rather concrete data concerning a likely factor, the relative costs of well and irrigation-tank construction.

During the dry season of 1966, the village headman had a fairly large well dug by a gang of "mud" Voddas, a caste that specializes in constructing earthworks. Some sixty adults, evenly divided between the sexes, were observed to spend 9,422 hours digging a well thirty-five feet in diameter and forty feet deep. How much land this well would irrigate depends upon the season and crop, but it would be no more than about three acres. After completing the well, this gang moved several miles down the road to construct the first completely new irrigation tank to be built in the area in many years. Conceived in part as a reclamation project, the tank consisted of an earth-filled dam across a severely eroded horseshoe valley. The *taluk* engineer estimated that the tank would, when completely filled, irrigate forty to sixty acres of previously unirrigated land. The people who had worked in Yaavahalli were joined by twenty of their caste mates, and this group of eighty remained at the site for about six weeks before completing the dam. For this latter project I do not have labor input data based on direct day-to-day observation.

This is unfortunate because, in the construction of the well, for which we do have such detailed records, it was found that the hours of work accomplished varied substantially from day to day: the highest day comprised 262 man-hours and 219 woman-hours, and the lowest 56 man-hours and 49 woman-hours. Most of this variation was due to interruptions caused by rain, although a labor dispute between the Voddas and the *patel* was responsible for the shortest work day. Thus, simply knowing the number of days the Voddas were present on the tank site does not provide a basis for an accurate estimate of the total hours consumed in the tank's construction. If they worked 42 eight-hour days without interruption, the total would come to about 27,000 hours; if their work days averaged around five hours, as they did on the well, the total would be around 17,000 hours.

Imprecise as these estimates are, they leave little question that in terms of the initial earth-moving labor involved, well irrigation is far more expensive than tank irrigation. Using similar pools of skilled labor, it cost over 3,000 hours of labor per acre irrigated for the well (or about a man-year per acre), in contrast to something between 300 and 700 hours of work per acre irrigated for the tank. Nor were modern machinery or engineering techniques that might have reduced labor costs used in the construction of this tank. While construction was nominally under the supervision of the *taluk* engineer, this young man, who had never designed an earth-filled dam, deferred, wisely I suspect, to the folk engineer, the Vodda headman, who spent the better part of one afternoon explaining to him how the tank would be constructed. Hence, there is good reason to believe that design and construction techniques were traditional ones similar to those employed in the construction of earlier tanks.

Before rural electrification (a relatively new development at the time of my fieldwork), which allowed the use of electric irrigation pumps, the irrigation of gardens was a laborious process as well. Garden irrigation required the use of a leather bucket lift or *kapile*, which consumed many hours of work by men and bullocks to supply water to the fields. A tank required only the service of one man to operate the floodgate to supply water to a large area. Thus, it cost huge amounts of labor to gain access to the subsoil water that would provide continuous and relatively drought-proof cultivation opportunities. Tank irrigation, rather inefficient and unreliable in other ways, was at least comparatively cheap in terms of effort.

The population of the *taluk* regained 1871 levels in the following way. Between 1881 and 1891 population grew by almost a quarter; between 1891 and 1901 it grew by about a tenth. The end of the next decade showed no growth at all because of outbreaks of plague and influenza that took many lives. However, population had almost reached 1871 levels by 1901, and it took an increase of fewer than 2,000 persons between 1911 and 1921 to complete the demographic recovery from the great famine.

There were also droughts in the interval between 1881 and 1921: though none was nearly so severe as that of the late 1870s, droughts occurred in 1891, 1904, 1905, 1908, and (a mild one) 1914. Mortality due to epidemics may have been another factor in the failure of the population to respond to droughts by digging irrigation wells. A number of elderly villagers reported losing family members to disease when they were young children, and this may have had a demoralizing and disorganizing effect on the work of village households (Hayavadana Rao 1930).

At any event, after 1921 population and garden cultivation both grew steadily. And for some reason a drought, which according to rain-fall tables must have occurred in 1923, was a critical event in this pro-cess. Villagers remember droughts—indeed, they are one of the historical markers one may use to determine the ages of villagers—but the people of Yaavahalli remember that drought in particular. Somehow it was the last straw, the rude awakening that made people realize that they had to dig wells if they were to protect themselves from the recurrent famines that had plagued their ancestors.

Was the sustained period of agricultural intensification that followed a response to population growth? In answering this question we must recognize other economic and political factors that must have played a part in intensification.

The decline and final abolition of the *joodidar* land tenure system was one of these. While final abolition did not occur until after Mysore became part of independent India, *joodidars* began to dispose of some of their holdings prior to that time, partly to fund a way of life that came to include college education for sons and partly, perhaps, in anticipation that their privileged position would not last forever. And although a number of wells were dug by villagers in land the *joodidars* held, they were more likely to be dug in newly acquired private land. Later, the final abolition of remaining *joodidar* holdings was followed by a period of rapid growth in garden cultivation. Thus, intensification may also be viewed, at least in part, as a response to a change in land tenure.

Transportation and markets were also improving. A narrow-gauge railway and, later, paved roads made it easier for villagers to transport farm commodities to market. The establishment of silk spinning and weaving mills, of brokerage houses for silk cocoons, and of grainages to supply silkworm eggs made cocoon production highly rewarding. World War II strengthened the silk market by creating a demand for parachutes and provided growing markets for other farm produce in the city of

Bangalore as well. The development of the market economy was, however, complicated by the imposition of government price controls, which made black-marketeering a way of life in Yaavahalli and surrounding villages for some time.

The introduction of rural development programs was another major factor stimulating growth in garden production in the last years prior to my stay. For the first time the government offered really substantial amounts of credit for the construction of wells and the purchase of irrigation pumps. And new varieties of seed, improved silkworm strains, and the availability of modest amounts of chemical fertilizer greatly enhanced the productivity of agriculture.

But in spite of the contribution of these factors, I believe that the agricultural intensification that occurred was a response to population growth. This view relies in part on a particular interpretation of the word "response." Intensification may be said to occur in response to population growth in at least two senses, one sequential, the other symbolic. In the sequential sense, a period of intensification follows a period of population growth. Thus, an archeologist might note that the construction of large irrigation works in a region came after a period during which settlements grew in size or number and conclude that the irrigation was a response to the demographic change.

If one looks at the history of Yaavahalli and the *taluk* in terms of eras, much the same relationship emerges. The great famine showed that the population of the 1870s could not be reliably maintained without further labor intensification of agriculture. Hence, when the population again attained the 1871 level, an era of intensification followed. But if one looks at the relationship between population growth and agricultural intensification since the 1920s for the population of the region as a whole, no clear pattern emerges from which a causal inference could be made: population density and intensification grew together. One could just as well say that intensification stimulated further population growth as the other way around. If, however, one examines the performance of individual households, a solution to this puzzle seems to emerge. Most wells were dug by households at one of two stages of their development. Many were dug by families before or shortly after the marriage of grown sons. Some others were dug by nuclear families who were struggling to meet the needs of growing children. Thus, well digging often occurred in anticipation of further growth in households: the children were growing in number and growing up, and eventually the sons would marry and have children.

That is why I believe we must use the term "response" in a symbolic sense, rather than a sequential one, if the relationship between population growth and agricultural intensification is to be understood as

Vodda boys and women at a well construction site during a work stoppage. The older men are away discussing a problem with the contractor. As a *quid pro quo* for observing their work, I lent these people my 100-foot tape to check their progress. At no point did the diameter of this well deviate from 35 feet by more than 6 inches, a measure of the workers' skill. A nearly perfectly vertical face like this prevents erosion and the slumping of soil into the well.

a form of cultural behavior in Yaavahalli. Intensification is symbolically managed behavior; in Yaavahalli people plan to dig or improve wells and plan to exploit the gardens they construct. To ask whether this occurs in response to population growth is to ask whether population growth serves as the justification for the planned behavior. In Yaavahalli it does; people intensify their agriculture in anticipation of family growth. They respond to population growth as an idea, an event they expect to happen. What they do not seem to do, at least not very often, is dig a well for some other stipulated reason and then decide to have more children than they had previously planned to have. Prosperous households may grow faster than poor ones, but that seems to occur because they lose fewer infants and small children as a result of poor nutrition and poor medical care rather than because they plan a larger number of pregnancies.

The question of how this situation arises, how continued population growth comes to mean that one must labor-intensify agricultural practices, is the subject of the next chapter. But the notion that villagers do make this connection is associated with the second of the three issues to be addressed in this chapter. If villagers engage in agricultural intensification in order to meet the demands of anticipated as well as current growth in the size of families, one would expect that, as Boserup suggests, they take the initiative in seeking out the means to do so.

As I have noted, the growth in the region's agricultural economy was stimulated by a change in land tenure, by government development programs, and by expansion in other sectors of the economy. These developments provided new opportunities that served as incentives to agricultural growth. However, the behavior of villagers in responding to the changing economic order indicates that, far from being the passive recipients of new opportunities, they often took the lead in creating them.

Recent Intensification Programs

Although the goverment has provided loan programs and other resources to assist in agricultural development in recent years, these programs do nothing unless villagers avail themselves of them. Availing oneself of this aid can be a complicated matter: some farmers, for example, made dozens of trips to town in an effort to secure government loans for well construction. Once secured, the programs entail work for the beneficiaries of them, for their main impact on farming lies in the greater number and variety of cultivation and employment opportunities they provide for farm people. In short, they are sought on the presumption that the human labor necessary to make the most of the new resources will be forthcoming. What is more, a government development program is regarded less as something the government gives than as something local political entrepreneurs demand and get for their communities. People say of such notables as Yaavahalli's headman that they obtained a road or the marketing cooperative or well-construction loans for their constituents. This picture of rural development as a process whereby village leaders undertake initiatives with the government aimed at acquiring resources that villagers already regard as valuable may or may not be adequate to describe particular events. It is perfectly possible, I suppose, that a government official might tell a village headman. "We're going to put a veterinary dispensary in your village," whereupon the headman might go home and tell his followers, "Well, I got a veterinary dispensary." But this issue is less important than the fact that villagers describe themselves as active agents of economic change and judge their leaders according to their entrepreneurial ability to acquire public resources for the purpose of initiating change.

That villagers uniformly so describe the development process is important for two reasons. The first is that villagers mean what they say. There seems to be little question that village-level politicians win or lose elections on their ability to deliver public goods to their constituents. That, at least, is what everybody says, and since election results in particular cases seemed to bear them out, it is reasonable to suspect that village politicians take this sort of talk seriously and do in fact undertake initiatives with the government.

Second, this pattern of discourse is exactly the sort one would expect to find in communities where intensification efforts using local resources were already common. By this I mean to suggest more than the notion that once people have spent their own wealth on something, they will see the merits of spending someone else's for the same purposes. Rather, I believe there is some evidence to suggest that the importance of government development programs was amplified by the fact that further agricultural intensification in the region had begun to be limited by constraints on the local labor force. As we have seen, Yaavahalli is a prosperous village that imports a good deal of farm labor and exports virtually none. Those who come to work in Yaavahalli are, in effect, intensifying someone else's agriculture. Similar terms of trade have begun to prevail between Yaavahalli's region and certain areas lying to the east. The initial phases of the period of well construction appear to have been accomplished chiefly with household labor. Later, increasing amounts of local hired labor were used. At the time of my stay, many thousands of hours of labor were used to enlarge and renovate old wells, most of it some combination of household and local hired labor. The more land a household had under irrigation, the less family labor they were able or willing to mobilize for well renovation and the more they hired for that purpose. People with substantial amounts of garden land chose to spend their time working in the gardens rather than deepening the well. In the same way, as more local labor was devoted to the cultivation of established irrigated land, it became more difficult to hire local labor for the construction of new irrigation facilities.

During the dry season of 1966, the remedy for this problem could be seen in the gangs of workers walking from the east to work on well and tank construction. The homes of these people lay in areas of scantier rainfall and lower population density where the topography made irrigation more difficult than in the region around Yaavahalli. These migrations were made possible, to a considerable extent, by government loans for well construction. The fact that a farmer received a lump sum sufficient to pay for the digging of a well allowed him to hire a gang to

complete the work quickly, instead of having to dig the well a bit at a
time as money became available from current revenues. Indeed, the
government's requirement that he show the *taluk* engineer a finished well
by a specified date virtually obliged him to hire a gang of workers.

But while the government substantially funded these migrations, it
was village folk who organized them. Workers came, as I have noted,
from the east, where annual rainfall is considerably lower than that prevailing in the areas to which they migrate in search of work. One might
wonder whether their time would be better spent in constructing irrigation facilities for themselves instead of for others. But their native landscape is not only drier but also much hillier, and the water table lies
considerably further below the surface than it does towards the west. In
traveling through their region, one sees tiny hamlets nestled in level
areas, surrounded by rocky hills. The few wells in evidence are usually
close to settlements, and there are hardly any tanks of any size. Often
these hamlets were dominated by two or three large houses, sometimes
by only one. This architectural feature mirrors an economic fact: most of
the best land is owned by few people.

Thus, when I asked migrant workers why they came to dig in
Yaavahalli instead of digging at home, I was hardly surprised to hear
them say that to stay home would be fruitless. There was no point in
attempting to increase the area under irrigation in such adverse conditions, and so they came to intensify someone else's agriculture because
they could not intensify their own. They were, at the same time, intensifying the utilization of their own *labor;* they were simply doing so at *kuli*
(which is to say low) wages. This migratory work pattern would appear
to be a variant of, not an exception to, the intensification process Boserup describes.

Sometimes migrants would simply stop at a village to inquire if
work was available. Workers said they had done this for some years. But
over time, stable social relations were constructed out of this random
door-to-door selling of labor. Local entrepreneurs would discover that
certain headmen of migrant groups were able to deliver, on order, large
gangs of well-disciplined laborers. Migrant headmen, in turn, discovered
that certain entrepreneurs, local to the villages they frequented, had the
political connections necessary to acquire government contracts for a
variety of projects in which large gangs might be employed. Moreover,
though I am not sure the migrants knew this, these same entrepreneurs
were also instrumental in aiding (or hindering) their neighbors' acquisition of government loans. Help in obtaining a loan had a price: either a
direct kickback, which was risky, or a promise that the entrepreneur
could "build" the well for the recipient. To "build" the well meant that
the entrepreneur would hire the migrant labor for the well digging. He

would, of course, exact a fee for this, just as he would for government contracts. This practice, by which *sovkaars* became hydraulic potentates in miniature, was one factor in the blossoming of class consciousness among other villagers. They could not do without such notables if they wished to prosper, but they loathed paying the price for them. The ballot box was a recourse in these matters if the entrepreneur aspired to or (more likely) held office. Typically the incumbent would point with pride (or with *jumba*, "arrogance," in the view of his rivals) to the many developments he had fostered, ignoring the side payments he had demanded along the way. The reform opponent would, with the recurrent metaphor of *sovkaar* as vampire, vow to end the "sucking of the blood of the poor." If he was successful, often as not, villagers would find either that he could not deliver the goods so well as his predecessor or that he, too, took his pound of flesh.

Those who administer development programs in India regard graft as no less unfortunate a matter than we do in our own society. But its very existence is, I would suggest, an indication of the initiative ordinary villagers display in developing their agriculture.

Unfortunately I know of only a few transactions between entrepreneurs and clients in which the financial details are specified, and these are merely reports that may have been embellished through the anger of villagers who viewed themselves as victims. But if these cases are in fact typical of prevalent practices, the following picture emerges: villagers who financed intensification through the entrepreneurial system paid net interest rates ranging from 10 to over 25 percent per annum when the fee or kickback to local notables was added to the interest charged by the government.

Generally, the poorer the household the higher the net interest. In part, this variation may be explained by social distance. The entrepreneur might have to spend some portion of the income he received for the facilitation of a loan on bribes to officials. Moreover, a few words might not be sufficient to turn the ear of officialdom favorably towards his client: repeated entreaties and negotiations, and hence a number of trips to town, might be needed. Thus, in transactions near the 10 percent net interest rate, a notable might be peddling his influence for a rather low (though undetermined) hourly fee. He might be willing to do this for a close relative or for someone who might be able to return a useful favor in the future. In either case, the favored party would probably be someone of above average wealth. However, we must also look at the matter from the client's perspective and ask not what he would have to accept by way of interest rate, but what he would be willing to accept; for poorer clients do accept loans at rather high rates, which is a measure of the value ascribed to the opportunity to intensify cultivation.

The holders of private notes were notorious for foreclosure on land held as collateral; the government, as creditor, was not. Interest charged by private moneylenders started at about 18 percent (though I often found that private loans were clouded by a variety of vague contingencies that made precise determination of net annual interest all but impossible). Thus, the entrepreneurial system provided safer, and probably cheaper, credit, even at its highest rate, than private sources. Poorer villagers regarded as foolish the borrowing of money from moneylenders for well construction, not only because the interest was high, but also because they believed that the lender's real goal was not the interest but foreclosure on the debtor's land. A safe loan, by contrast, even at 25 percent interest, was an economically attractive proposition, given the almost fivefold increase in village product per acre brought about by well irrigation.

In buying a well a poorer family was purchasing the chance to work less for others and much more for itself for a higher hourly return. The benefits of this were so great that such people were quite willing to contribute several hundred hours of their own labor to construct the well in order to work out the fee they had paid the *sovkaar* to get the loan. What villagers objected to was the injustice they perceived in such arrangements. Like everyone else, the entrepreneurs espoused the Gandhian social gospel of mutual self-help, but in demanding money for help, they failed to live up to this moral standard.

I hope the reader will not draw the conclusion that the sort of graft I have just described is somehow a reflection of a trait of political culture peculiar to this region. On the contrary, similar graft is a common occurrence around the world wherever the demand for public goods greatly exceeds the government's physical capacity to supply them and wherever the government's administrative capacity to allocate those goods according to predetermined criteria of deservingness is limited. Indeed, given the practical difficulties of administering rural development programs in the *taluk*, it is perhaps a wonder that there was not more graft. The rural population's appetite for improved farm technology was so voracious compared to the resources available to meet these demands, and the administrative capacity of the government to police the allocation of these scarce resources at the local level was so limited, that a gray market was almost bound to develop. Nor was it the case that graft was entirely the idea of those who received it. This may be illustrated by an incident that arose from the fact that people from neighboring villages who did not know me were unaware that I could understand Kannada.

One morning as I was talking with the *patel*, a middle-aged man came to visit him. He apologized for interrupting us but explained that his business was quite urgent. It seems that the man had applied for a loan to dig a well some months before but had been unable to get any action on his case. The matter had become critical because the well was a stipulation of a marriage arrangement. His son was to be married soon, and he had promised the bride's parents that a new well would be dug and would become part of the groom's patrimony. What could he tell his *biigaaru*? Unless the well was at least begun by the time of the wedding, the whole arrangement might collapse.

He had come to the *patel* for advice and assistance. As a father the *patel* could understand the gravity of the problem, and as a man of influence he could help to solve it. Perhaps the *patel* could put in a word for him with the appropriate officials, and perhaps he could repay the *patel* for his assistance with a gift of perhaps several hundred rupees.

The *patel* upbraided the man for suggesting that his services could be bought. He added that he was not a government official and thus had no control over the disposition of particular cases, but if the man would present him with the details of his case at a later time, he would certainly consider putting in a word on his behalf.

This man's request and the *patel*'s response clearly describe the dynamics of the gray market. The officers who administered the Land Mortgage Bank were constantly harried by farmers demanding that a particular case be given priority treatment. Most loan applications were legitimate and deserving under the stipulations of the loan program, which meant that most of the time officers had no formal basis for giving one application priority over others, apart from taking them in order of the date of application. This was certainly one criterion they employed. But apparently the availability of funding was so erratic that while a few applications could be acted upon rather quickly, others might sit in the files for many months before action was taken.

This situation frustrated many applicants and, since a few got prompt action, gave them the impression that favoritism was involved. It was. It was widely believed that people like the *patel* could deliver blocks of votes at election time, and this influence could be translated into influence over bureaucrats. Though it is by no means clear that the intercession of a notable always made much difference in the treatment an application received, it certainly did sometimes. Given a choice between two applications of similar merit, the bureaucrat might choose the one advocated by a notable, or the one favored by the more powerful of two notables, or the one supported by a notable for whom he had not done a favor for some time.

At the other end of the system, village farmers were busy mobilizing ties of village, kin, and caste and bidding up the price they would pay for loans in order to secure the services of useful notables, who were reputed to pass on a portion of the fee they received to the loan officers who helped them out.

Graft was apparent in the allocation of some other farm resources too. Which farmers would receive the first or largest allotments of a new variety of seed? Often it was the village notables, their kin, and their supporters. Chemical fertilizer was in short supply at the time, and the officers of the cooperative societies that distributed it were reputed to sell 90-kilogram bags for the 100-kilogram price, having removed 10 kilograms from each quintal bag to use in filling other bags that they would use or sell for themselves.

Thus, in a number of ways villagers filled the gap between the village and governmental agencies with a gray market infrastructure of their own making. And while we may conceive of more efficient or just ways of allocating development resources, villagers had little choice, given the political economy in which they lived. In principle, the government tried to provide competent and well-supervised officers at the local level to assist in the extension of new technology to farmers. These were the village-level workers of the rural development program. I have said nothing about these individuals until now because, around Yaavahalli, they exercised little influence in determining who got what. Although they did provide useful technical information, they were mostly young; many were strangers to the areas they served; and there were few of them. Anyone who relied on a village-level worker's patronage was not likely to get very far, for the village notables, who were largely the products of the unequal distribution of land over families, would have already exercised their stronger influence. And while influence peddling was an open secret, the fact was that from the perspective of higher-level officials, rural development programs were, by and large, doing what they were supposed to do: loans, seed, and fertilizer were being distributed to farmers who were using these resources for their intended purposes.

Had reluctant village farmers been dragged into a new technological era, this gray market would not have existed. Rather, one would have expected to see skeptical villagers subjected to glowing but, in the end, ineffective lectures on the benefits of new technology by earnest village-level workers, while the local notables sat at home and grumbled about the replacement of tried and true ways with new and unproven ones. But this did not happen. Instead, almost every time an innovation was made available there was an avalanche of demand for it, whether it was sperm from superior bulls, or insecticide, or a new variety of silkworms. This was true even though some innovations proved disappointing. It should be noted that government technical experts did not always feel that villagers used new technology effectively. Sometimes, as in the cultivation of maize, a new crop in the region, the problem was a lack of information. Once villagers learned about maize cultivation from the

example of a well-informed neighbor, they immediately began to cultivate it much as the agricultural experts wanted them to. But in other
cases the introduction of an innovation did not take adequate account of
the conditions of village farming. Villagers might not, for example, obtain yields from a new crop as high as those promised by the technical
experts because they could not obtain the amount of fertilizer the experts
used on government farms. But despite disappointments, villagers
proved eager to try each new innovation that came along.

We have thus far seen that agricultural intensification became the
fashionable thing to do once the rural population passed prefamine density. Exactly how the fashion spread will be the subject of the next
chapter. But we have already noted that the pattern of villagers' investment in wells and other agricultural improvements suggested a recognition on their part that a growing family with an estate of constant size
was not necessarily condemned to declining fortunes, provided people
were willing both to work more to get more from the land they had and
to engage in political efforts to avail themselves of new technology that
would enhance the productivity of their manual labor.

One question remains: if, as Boserup suggests, intensification is
undertaken to protect real per capita income from decline, what were its
effects on rural incomes in this case? A precise answer to this question is
not possible because the available statistical data at the local level are, for
the time in question, neither reliable nor complete. What is more, the
question is actually not so simple a one as: did per capita income rise,
fall, or remain constant? We must ask whose income—for the effects
were not uniform—and specify the period and method of computation.
My own best guess, again based more on the oral history of my informants than on anything else, is that intensification amplified the inequality of rural incomes, in part because big peasants follow Ricardian principles even when economists do not. The standard sharecrop rent for
unirrigated land in the area is one-half of net production; for irrigated
land it is two-thirds. Needless to say, the increase has relatively little to
do with amortizing the landowner's increased investment, and it is assur-
edly not a risk premium. As more land was irrigated, the discrepancies
between landowners' and tenants' incomes increased accordingly. As for
kuli labor, there is little doubt that intensification had vastly increased
opportunities for this sort of employment, but there is also little doubt
that wage increases had not kept pace with inflation in food prices.

An ancillary effect of these increases in the variance of household
incomes is that the size of transfer payments from rich to poor households in hard years had probably increased as well. These are often called
loans by the parties to them, but in fact they are better regarded as notes
of indenture, for many remain unpaid indefinitely. Thus, when a client's

debt to his patron increases from Rs. 1,000 to Rs. 2,000, the real change that takes place is in how long, hard, and loyally the client will work as the patron's tenant. In such cases the social relations of production between households have become more traditional in the sense of becoming more a matter of status and less a matter of contract, even though a contract is alledged to exist. Scarlett Epstein (1962) noted similar phenomena in a village whose agriculture had received water from a new irrigation project.

There is also little doubt that agricultural development has been coupled with an increase in the incidence of landlessness, not in Yaavahalli, but in nearby villages. Some rich families have refused to act as traditional patrons to their poorer tenants; that is, they would not make unsecured loans to be repaid from the proceeds of future tenancy cultivation. Rather, they would offer to buy a poor family's land outright, offer a short-term note secured by land (on which they might well foreclose), or offer a *boogya* loan. In this last arrangement, the creditor takes the use of a parcel of land in lieu of interest until the note is fully repaid, a practice often tantamount to a purchase of the land. The ruthlessness of certain well-to-do families in these affairs was a further element in the atmosphere of bitter class consciousness among poorer villagers.

It is important to note this increase in economic inequality because it is a factor in several issues to be discussed later. However, the majority of villagers, in Yaavahalli in particular, are freeholding middle peasants. If one compares their current incomes to those they recall from earlier times, the following image emerges. Their consumption of manufactured goods has undergone a sharp increase. These goods were either simply unavailable or were more expensive (relative to farm commodities) in years past, when villagers had less cash income anyway. A village household's propensity to buy manufactured goods is closely tied to variations in farm yields: in poor years they buy hardly any; in average years most people spend all but a small portion of their income (above that reinvested in farming) on food; and in good years expenditures on manufactured goods, while still modest in absolute terms, may exceed those of average years by 100 percent or more.

Middle-aged and elderly villagers tended to claim that dietary income in average years had declined somewhat. Male heads of households were asked to rank periods of their life (in five-year intervals) in terms of general well-being. If certain important cyclical factors, notably household partition, are taken into account, the secular trend reflected in their responses is downward. I do not set too much store by these data for two reasons. First, as ranked data they tell us nothing about the absolute size of declines in material well-being. Second, I asked a worthwhile question of the wrong people; I should have asked the senior women, who are the dietary budgeters of households. Still, I can see no reason to believe that dietary incomes have generally improved. Narrative interviews with informants suggest that most people eat less meat than they used to because they produce less. Men are especially likely to complain about not having meat—meat eating is a feature of their particular variant of masculinity—so that this may have influenced their responses. Per capita consumption of dairy products may also have declined because many households cannot resist selling a large portion of their milk for the high prices offered by the dairying cooperative. Incidentally, a preference for curds is typical of women, and so it is not surprising that a portion of the cash earned from dairying is spent on women's clothes, bangles, and cosmetics. On the other hand, villagers probably eat more fruits and vegetables because they grow more than in the past.

As for the consumption of grains, which provide the bulk of people's caloric intake, and of the various pulses from which they acquire their vegetable protein, I can see no reason to believe that there was any great secular change from the 1920s to the 1960s because the ratio of population to staple production in the region as a whole did not change very much, according to government statistics. What may well have declined a bit is villagers' *net* dietary income in *average* years: they are eating as much as they used to or more, but they are also burning more calories.

But villagers' *minimum* per capita food income in years of poor rainfall has almost certainly increased. As I noted in the first chapter, there were no deaths in Yaavahalli during my stay that could be directly attributed to malnutrition, in spite of the fact that the village experienced a drought of the century, only twelve inches of rain, in 1965.

This fact should not blind us to the hardships many villagers experienced. I regularly asked random samples of village households to report the food they had eaten on the previous day, and while these reports were not exact enough to allow a precise estimation of calorie intake, it was clear that many families faced recurrent periods of moderate to severe hunger, and for some these persisted until the harvest of the dry lands in the fall of 1966. On some days some families went without solid food altogether, and on many days a number of families reported diets that could not have amounted to more than 1,000 calories for the men and somewhat less for the women and children. American dieters who have subsisted on like amounts should bear in mind that villagers' diets were deficient in vitamins and all but empty of animal protein on these occasions, and that they were routinely engaging in manual labor all the while.

It took me a couple of months to understand the degree of dietary stress that some of my neighbors were undergoing because they made so little fuss about their predicament. I suspect that a population with little or no historical experience of food shortage might have displayed panic in similar circumstances, but in Yaavahalli there was none. On the contrary, villagers employed careful famine-management strategies, which, they assured me, they had learned from their elders in the course of growing up. A few of these measures were undertaken by the village as a whole. Certain ceremonies marking major Hindu holidays were canceled both to avoid the costs they entailed and to prevent arguments that might have occurred over who was to contribute to them and how much. Indeed, the *patel* and several other village elders told me that quarrels were especially likely to erupt due to the nervousness and exhaustion to which hungry people were subject, and that they were making special efforts to prevent these.

Within poor households several steps were taken. First, everyone was told to stay indoors when not working, preferably lying down. This avoided needless waste of energy and reduced the headaches and dizziness malnourished people are vulnerable to, especially when they are exposed to bright sunlight. Second, family members were enjoined to abstain from discussing any subject that might lead to an argument. This concern for the prevention of social disruption was a prominent feature of their famine-management strategies. Other measures had to do with the budgeting of money and food. Poor households would try to estimate their potential earnings from tenancy and *kuli* labor for some time in the future and allocate their resources accordingly. As stocks began to run low, poor villagers would try to supplement their diets with wild plants and, on a few occasions, with rats they killed. Once I found people digging in the fields for caches of grain stored by rats.

As days approached on which there would be no food at all, families would explain their plight to a wealthier neighbor in hopes of getting *kuli* work or a free gift of food. Usually they got one or both. But the women invariably set aside a few *paise* against such days. This money would be used to purchase coffee and perhaps sugar, though sugar, along with milk, might be begged from another household. Then, on the morning of a foodless day, the mother of the house would make coffee with as much sugar and milk as she could get and dole it out to family members. The caffeine may have stimulated hunger, but together with the sugar it also gave people the burst of energy they needed to get through a working day that would produce the wage to purchase *uta*, "real food."

Thus, the privations of their ancestors had inculcated in poor villagers the cultural means, the grace, courage, and practical knowledge to get through periods of hardship. But these same cultural means had been available to the ancestors as well, and in droughts past some of them died. During my stay no one did, because the gardens were able to produce enough to keep everyone alive. That is the truest measure of the villagers' efforts to labor-intensify their agriculture: they had created sufficient cultivation opportunities, in spite of their increased population, to tide them over weather conditions that had killed their ancestors.

In summary then, to what extent does the economic history of Yaavahalli and environs conform to Boserup's argument in *The Conditions of Agricultural Growth?*

Intensification does seem to have occurred in response to increased population density. In times past villagers often appear to have responded, when they could, to increased crowding of their resources by migrating to less crowded places. That is what led the village founders to come to Yaavahalli, and the descendants of subsequent immigrants often reported that their ancestors came to Yaavahalli because there was not enough land to go around at home. The likelihood that this was true is strengthened by the fact that the villages of origin of these migrants were uniformly old and large settlements. But when opportunities to immigrate were unavailable, intensification appears to have occurred. When the founders first came, there was ample pasturage for livestock, and fields were often plowed only once. As population increased, pasturage was probably converted to farm land and preparatory labor per acre was increased.

Although these measures may have been sufficient to protect villagers' incomes from declining during average years, they did nothing to protect the population from the ravages of a severe drought. When, in the 1870s, a protracted drought did occur, the result was devastating famine.

Agricultural practices did not change very much in the decades following the famine, despite the fact that there were several droughts in these years, though none so severe as that leading to the famine. Initially this may have been due to the reduction of the rural population and perhaps the disorganization caused by the great famine. The disincentives built into the *joodidar* land tenure system may have been a factor as well.

Population grew by fits and starts until, by 1921, it once again attained prefamine levels. Shortly after this happened another drought occurred, and from that time forward villagers began to steadily increase the intensity of their cultivation, chiefly through the digging of irrigation wells, as the rural population continued to grow. Examined on a household-by-household basis, it appears as often as not, that well digging occurred prior to an increase in household size. This might seem to support the reverse of Boserup's hypothesis, but if one considers the view villagers took of well digging at the time of my stay and assumes that villagers took a similar view in previous years, a modification of her hypothesis is sustained: intensification was a response to population growth in the sense that villagers recognized the probability of growth and turned to well digging in advance of need.

This strong tendency to provide growing families with improved agricultural resources gave rise to a phenomenon that supports a second element in Boserup's argument: villagers did indeed take the initiative in intensifying their own agricultural practices. Certainly a number of factors helped them to do this. Improved markets and transportation and a change in land tenure stimulated agricultural growth, as did the introduction of rural development schemes later on. But the enterprise villagers showed in taking advantage of these opportunities was quite striking. In contrast to the stereotype of traditional farmers who must be prodded into trying new technology, the people of Yaavahalli and many surrounding communities swamped government agencies with demands for agricultural assistance. It should be borne in mind too that much of the well digging that took place over the years prior to my stay was done with family labor, and that regardless of how a family got a well, more work had to be done to derive substantial benefits from it.

As villagers provided themselves and one another with more and more cultivation opportunities, the third prediction of Boserup's argument came true. Though population continued to grow, median per capita income did not decline much in average years, though inequality in income probably increased. A few *sovkaar* families got rich by local standards, while the poorest families probably had to struggle harder than ever. The composition of income doubtless changed too: more manufactured goods were consumed; animal protein in most people's diets probably declined. But the most dramatic effect of intensification on income occurred during years of poor rainfall. This famine-stressed population had, through their efforts, taken a major step towards drought-proofing their agriculture.

Agricultural intensification had become the fashionable thing to do. Good farm people, those respected and emulated by their neighbors, were those who strove constantly to enhance their productivity, not only to increase their current income but to provide more adequate farm resources for their children as well. By contrast, those who seemed lazy by comparison, or who mismanaged their lives by allowing a joint household to divide or by trying to marry a son before sufficient effort to improve the farm estate had been made, were scorned.

To villagers it seemed perfectly natural to judge people in this way. They were well aware that they would be judged too, and that these judgments could be quite salient at certain times, notably during the arrangement of marriages. One question remains and then my argument is finished: how did agricultural intensification become the fashionable response to population growth?

chapter 9

The Evolution of Intensification Fitness

Intensification became fashionable in Yaavahalli at least in part because villagers made decisions about their own and one another's behavior using the teachings of the elders as guides. These traditional domestic customs, in other words, far from impeding agricultural growth in the region, actually stimulated it.

To suggest that people make decisions about behavior, deciding that one course of conduct is superior to another under particular circumstances, is to say that people select among behaviors. And villagers forcefully select for behavior on those occasions when brides and grooms are chosen and, less commonly, those when migrants are accepted or rejected as residents in the community. On these and other occasions, the teachings of the elders provide criteria for making decisions that enhance the population's intensification fitness, its capacity to respond to population growth with agricultural intensification. In decisions that lead to population growth through migration or marriage, the basis for continued reproduction, villagers employ standards of wealth and productivity.

There are two substantive tasks before us: one is to describe the cultural mechanisms that may have prompted intensification in the region generally; the other is to account for the concentration of agricultural growth in Yaavahalli. The latter task is problematic. On the one hand, cultivation in Yaavahalli is more intensive, on the average, than in nearby communities because a substantially larger proportion of land has been brought under well irrigation there than in the *taluk* as a whole; on the other hand, per capita land holdings are higher in Yaavahalli than elsewhere. This would seem to contradict the notion that intensification occurs in response to population growth, for if it does, one would suppose that cultivation in Yaavahalli would be less intensive than elsewhere. The resolution of this apparent contradiction, to which I shall return, is based on the idea that intensification occurs through symbolic interaction. Farming behavior occurs in response to the farming behavior of one's neighbors as well as in response to the forces of nature and one's stomach. Thus, one's farming practices depend in part on the sorts of neighbors one has, so that the question becomes one of how the people of Yaavahalli recruited or created industrious fellow villagers who in turn influenced the behavior of those who recruited or created them. The answer to this may lie in the fact that Yaavahalli is a young village built by immigrants, many of them refugees from famine and crowded conditions back home.

Staying on Track

We shall turn presently to the substantive role of villagers' domestic customs in stimulating agricultural intensification, but before doing so it may be useful to place the microevolution of village farming in a broader evolutionary context.

Like many anthropologists, Durham (1978) and Harris (1979) to name two, I have been struck by the extent to which cultural evolution mimics biological evolution. It is easy to overstate and oversimplify these analogies, but at the same time it is important that we explore them because they bear on two related and fundamental features of our species. First, at some time in the Paleolithic a basic biogram or biological template of modern humanity was established; subsequently, genetic drift and natural selection differentiated breeding populations mainly in biological details. Further biological speciation in the human line substantially ceased because cultural speciation became the chief mechanism of human adaptive radiation. Second, for this to occur, as Durham points out, it was necessary for cultural evolution to stay "on track" with natural selection. That is, cultural practices must have been selectively rejected or retained, to a considerable extent, on the basis of their adaptive advantage for the survival and reproductive success of individuals. Were that the case, natural selection in populations could be retarded as individuals with varied genotypes adopted similarly adaptive cultural phenotypes.

The power of cultural adaptation to "short-circuit" natural selection could not, however, rely on human cleverness alone. The capacity for language, culture, and tool use would have to be guided by biologically based predispositions that would prompt reproductively successful behavior. Harris suggests four of these. We get hungry and prefer sweets and meats, foods rich in readily usable calories and high-quality protein. The physiology of taste may also lead us to reject many toxic substances, to like salt, and much else. Second, the physiology of exhaustion coupled with experientially based recognition of the consequences of our actions prompts us to seek least-effort strategies in the performance of tasks. Third, we are hypersexual. The suppression of estrus in women has been coupled with the capacity for more or less continual sexual activity, and most people display a strong to exclusive preference for the heterosexual kind. This capacity has a profound influence on relations between the sexes and often serves as the basis of strong sexual bonds. Critics of this notion point to a host of examples—post-partum sex taboos, high divorce rates, and so on—to deny importance to sexual bonding. They miss the point. No one to my knowledge is arguing that our sexuality of itself drives women and men into loving companionship; Harris merely suggests that it predisposes us to judge events in terms of sexual costs and benefits. I would add that our sexuality seems to convey a high trainability for sexual intimacy and interdependence, which is a basis for the durable matings that in fact are highly typical of our species. This is related to the last of Harris's four predispositions, our craving for the affection and approval of others. Though we do not as yet fully understand the biological basis for human affect, there is ample evidence from a welter of sources, ranging from work on infant social response to studies of the psychological impact of social isolation, for supposing there is one.

Harris suggests, in effect, that cultural evolution stays on track with biological evolution by producing adaptations suitable to prevailing environmental and demographic conditions because humans respond to these biologically based standards for judging the costs and benefits of behavior. I suspect, however, that Harris would readily admit modifications to his list, provided there were theoretical and empirical grounds for them. In this connection I would note that Durham, Harris, and I adopt a generalist position concerning human biology; what interests us about it is the variety of ways it may convey to humans the facultative capacity to achieve a wide spectrum of cultural adaptations. This position contrasts with the rather more particularist views of many who have attempted human applications of sociobiology, that branch of the theory of evolutionary ecology that seeks to explain the evolution of behavior in terms of natural selection. Such applications have sometimes postulated genetic programming for rather particular and often complex patterns of human behavior. Seldom do they specify the proximate biological causes, the features of anatomy and physiology that are programmed by genes, underlying the behavior. Proponents of these arguments object to the request for proximate causes on the grounds that the fruitfulness of a theory should not be judged according to the rapidity with which its details are empirically confirmed. They demand a chance to pursue their inquiries. They have one. Perhaps, for instance, a genetic basis for incest

avoidance can be demonstrated. What I really object to is wildly speculative genes-for-this, genes-for-that arguments that draw attention away
from the distinctive attribute of our species, its capacity to achieve cultural adaptations. I am also dismayed by the fact that some sociobiological arguments tend to portray particular social status quos, notably sexual ones, as "natural," embroiling the study of the relationship between
human biology and behavior in rancorous and often fatuous public con-
troversy. Thus, I object not to a human sociobiology, for indeed I am, in
a way, employed in constructing one, but to the particularist sociobiologies that have been offered thus far.

Harris does too; he does not want his list cluttered with a lot of
empirically baseless genetic predilections, the postulation of which
merely serves to obscure the workings of cultural change. Therefore I
will leave Harris's list as it is and go on to observe that all societies are in
the end built and sustained by men and women who mate and who rear
children, generally, though not always, with their mates. It is because
humans do these things, and because they judge behavior in terms of
nutritional, energetic, sexual, and affective costs and benefits in doing
them, that cultural evolution often mimics biological evolution, not only
in the sense that cultural evolution has tended to stay on track with
natural selection, but in the sense that some specific mechanisms of
cultural selection closely resemble mechanisms of natural selection. To
see how this may be so, we must return to the view of human sexual
biology adopted earlier.

Biology as Circumstance

My entire argument is premised on the notion that the *dharmas* of the
sexes constitute cultural amplifications of biological sex differences. Note
again that the relationship between biology and behavior is not a deterministic one; biology is not destiny but circumstance. The biological
circumstances of being male or female that we have discussed may be
either directly observed or readily inferred from observations of behavior. Biological sex differences are also palpably experienced by those who
bear them, and these experiences become subjects in female and male
culture. Women talk to other women, not to men, about pregnancy and
nursing because men, in an experiential sense, do not know what they
are talking about: it would be rather like describing colors to someone
who is color-blind.

Thus, people can and do attribute meanings to biological sex differences, but while biological sex differences are much the same from one
population to the next, the meanings vary. Why do they vary? As we

shall see, while sex roles and sexual divisions of labor differ, they differ in rather systematic and predictable ways; varied sex roles are, to a considerable extent, simply different ways of talking about the biological circumstances of being male and female, and these vary in response to the material circumstances in which people live.

The *dharmas* of the sexes in Yaavahalli are the basis of the family. If a person takes the *dharma* of his or her gender as the premise of his or her behavior, that person will mate with someone who assumes the other *dharma* and create a family. Mating and related domestic matters entail decisions concerning who will marry whom, where they will live, and so on, for which the teachings of the elders are guides. All along we have been dealing with the question of why these domestic policies rather than others persist in the population, and we have answered it by constructing a rudimentary model of villagers' models for behavior that stipulates biological and environmental circumstances under which the teachings of the elders might yield the benefits claimed for them. Our present task is to address, if only in a highly speculative way, a different but related question: how might these same domestic policies stimulate agricultural intensification in response to—indeed, in anticipation of—population growth? Answers to both questions have to do with the way in which the management of reproductive behavior (and that is what the *dharmas* of the sexes and the teachings of the elders manage) is implicated in the management of farm production.

To observe that the management of families and the management of production are to a considerable extent aspects of the same process is to define Yaavahalli, to a considerable extent, as a community in the domestic mode of production. While there are a few people, such as the *patel*, who run what might be called profit-making businesses with hired labor, and while villagers do participate in a market economy, for the most part units of production and consumption are the same: households. Most people, including those who hire labor and those who sell it, are simply farming to rear families who will be farmers; the management of farms and that of families are elements of social reproduction: they produce new villagers.

To say that villagers undertake productive activities for reproductive ends is to imply that they pursue reproductive interests. By "interest" I mean symbolically managed attention. Reproductive interests include such matters as mating and the rearing and provisioning of children. These are material interests; attention is purposefully focused on phenomena regarded as costs and benefits in order to influence courses of events. This distinction between interests in general and material interests in particular, then, is the same as that of ordinary language. When we say we are interested in something, we mean we attend to it. When we say something serves our interests, we mean it serves the purposes to which we attend.

Cultural Selection

Reproductive interests are perhaps the most intently pursued of all interests because strong ones are favored by cultural selection. Others have attributed other meanings to this term, but I am using it to speak of alternative behaviors selectively rejected or retained, notably, for our purposes, according to their influence on success in social reproduction. The basic standard of cultural selection is defined by a question: to what extent does a pattern of behavior create conditions conducive to its own repetition?

Cultural behavior fosters or impedes its own repetition in various ways; for example, cultural selection favors behavior that controls the symbolic environment in which children develop and live. Those who take a strong interest in children and their development exert a strong influence in their socialization. And those who keep children nearby when they grow up or send them to live with culturally similar groups enhance the likelihood that the children will perpetuate the cultural behavior of those who reared them. Therefore, in some measure at least, cultural selection tends to favor ethnocentrism.

Likewise, behavior that enhances the mating success, the fertility, or the survivorship of an individual or group is favored by cultural selection, since such behavior creates biological circumstances favorable to maintaining or increasing the frequency with which it may be repeated by future generations. In contrast to natural selection, however, which favors genes that enhance these same biological phenomena, cultural selection is a Lamarckian process that does not require reproductive failure in biological terms to produce adaptive success (Boehm 1978); we can mend our ways if not our genes. Often successful behavior is simply copied by previously less successful individuals. Nevertheless, all human populations culturally regulate reproductive behavior and access to the resources on which reproduction depends and in so doing produce mechanisms of cultural selection that often mimic those of natural selection: they bring about changes in learned behavior in ways that resemble those by which natural selection alters gene frequencies.

How Cultural Selection Imitates Natural Selection

Processes of cultural selection resemble those of natural selection in a number of ways and for a number of reasons. One of these has to do with the fact that people regulate sexual reproduction and impose standards of marital selection—that is, conditions for marriage—on one another. Marital selection follows from the incest taboo. Because one must marry out of the family in which one was reared, one is obliged to bear the costs of standards imposed by others, who may turn to an alternative mate if one fails to meet them. Thus, marital selection is a cultural analogue of sexual selection, the process whereby gene frequencies are altered by variations in the mating success of individuals.

But whereas sexual selection requires that some individuals be more successful in mating than others in biological terms, marital selection does not. Almost everyone in a population may eventually marry and have children without altering the fact that their behavior in the process of finding and keeping a spouse has been influenced by marital criteria imposed by other people, for often the issue in marital selection is less one of whether someone will marry than how well or when. Hence, the qualities of those who get the best spouses (or the most spouses) tend to be perpetuated as others attempt to display them.

The observation that marital selection influences individual behavior brings to mind another similarity between cultural selection and natural selection. A basic standard for both processes is reproductive success, success in perpetuating genes through offspring in one case, success in perpetuating culture through children in the other. And both work at the individual and group levels. An individual enhances his inclusive genetic fitness with behavior that improves the mating success, fertility, or survivorship of relatives who share his genes, so long as this behavior does not entail reproductive costs greater than the reproductive benefits for the individual. Group selection, here more specifically kin selection, then, is responsible for the cooperative, sometimes self-sacrificing, behavior observed in animal societies.

The supportive behavior people exhibit in the complex kin groups and networks they form has its genetic consequences; protecting a relative's child does protect the survivorship of some of one's genes. However, the resemblance between kin selection in nature and nepotism in culture appears to be largely an artifact of the close tie between biological and social reproduction. Women generally rear the children they bear, and men who are their mates or their kin attach themselves to these children in various ways. Hence, while people certainly support their kin, the patterns of that support may not always correspond very well with the coefficients of genetic similarity between individuals, though they often do.

Rather, cultural group selection seems to turn on joint reproductive interests. People may come to share interests in mating or rearing children in a variety of ways. In some cases a common position in society may be the basis. For example, the male elders of a society in which polygyny is widespread may coalesce to impose on younger men standards of marital selection that delay the age at which they marry, thus making widespread polygyny demographically feasible. Having endured this period of enforced bachelorhood (imposed through an age-set system, perhaps, or simply by high bride prices), such men serve their own interest in reaping its benefits by imposing it on the next generation.

Rather often group selection favors a particular sort of settlement or domestic group, such as a joint family, because those who form such groups reciprocally enhance the welfare of their children, perhaps by allowing more proficient utilization of resources. The size and composition of these groups appear to be responsive to technological and environmental circumstances, a tendency that points to another way in which cultural selection resembles natural selection.

In achieving adaptive radiation through cultural selection, variations in the structure of human societies came to resemble in some ways structural variations in animal societies, in part because human and animal societies were responsive to the same sorts of environmental pressures, and in part because cultural selection amplifies reproductive functions and secondary sex differences, which are similar to ones found in many other species, to produce marriage patterns, sex roles, and sexual divisions of labor that convey reproductive advantages to those who employ them.

This is particularly evident in the evolution of marriage practices and sexual divisions of labor in farming societies. Recall that Boserup notes in her book on the role of women in development (1970) that female farming tends to be found in societies with low population densities; these are also societies in which polygyny is rather common. Male farming, by which she means plow agriculture (though men do most farm work in many horticultural societies too), is found with much higher population densities. In these polygyny either tends to be restricted to the wealthy or is banned altogether.

Now, if we regard farm work as a cultural version of parental investment, the care and protection adults of other species provide for their offspring, it is immediately evident that variations in male behavior across farming populations mimic variations in male behavior across other species and sometimes between populations of the same species in different environmental conditions.

Among higher vertebrates maternal investment is almost invariably high; paternal investment is variable. When it is low, one often finds harem keeping or widespread promiscuity among males. When paternal investment is high, one more often finds monogamous matings. The greater variability of paternal behavior is due to the differential way in which sexual selection influences the morphology and behavior of the sexes. The reproductive success of a female is a function of the number of offspring she bears; that of a male is a function of the number of impregnations he achieves; the reproductive success of both sexes is a function of the survivorship of offspring. Thus, so long as maternal investment alone is sufficient to insure a fairly high survival rate, a male enhances his reproductive success by forming a harem or by mating with every female he can but attaching himself to none. In such cases one observes a good deal of direct competition among males for mates; any biological trait that aids an individual in driving off rivals is said to be favored by intrasexual selection. Intrasexual selection is responsible for much sexual dimorphism because traits that aid a male in competition with others might prove deleterious to his female offspring—increased body size increases the length of maturation, for example, which would delay breeding in females to no compensating reproductive advantage. This may be true in humans, for the same factors that contribute to the greater aggressiveness and athletic ability of the male seem also to lengthen his childhood and shorten his life. Sexual selection also favors traits that improve a male's ability to attract females; this process, epigamic selection, is related to the fact that males, on the whole, are the courting sex.

But suppose that maternal investment alone is not sufficient to secure a high level of survival, as is the case with most species of birds. When this occurs, a male will increase his reproductive success by attaching himself to a single mate and aiding her in the rearing of their young, though he may enhance his reproductive success by copulating with the mates of other males. Perhaps that is why males of such species are extremely jealous and often abuse an adulterous mate in addition to driving off potential rivals. Likewise, any biological trait that contributes to strong sexual bonding in such species will be favored by natural selection.

In other species, then, the rate of polygyny is a function of its reproductive cost for males. The same is true of farm people. Polygyny is common where men can rely on the women to do the farm work; it is low where men must work hard to support their children on a more densely settled landscape.

A full accounting of this phenomenon would require a treatise on the general evolution of farming that would address the questions of why woman the gatherer became woman the gardener (that is, why low-intensity horticulture tends to be female farming) and why widespread polygyny came to be associated with this mode of subsistence.

Such a treatise is beyond the scope of this book, and since we are chiefly concerned here with how cultural selection works on mating behavior under plow agriculture, I will only briefly mention a few points to set the stage for our discussion of that phenomenon. For fuller treatments of the transition from food collection to food production (and in many instances, at least, to female farming) and of the organization of horticultural societies, I direct the reader to Harris (1979) and to Martin and Voorhies (1975).

The general points I would note are these. First, polygyny was probably not a common mating pattern prior to the domestication of plants. I suggest this less because polygyny is not widespread among many modern food collectors than because the demographic and environmental conditions of the Paleolithic did not favor widespread polygyny. Populations were so sparse that finding any mate may have been a problem. The elaborate marital alliance systems generally found with commonplace polygyny would have been hard to manage. Moreover, climates were colder then and large game was abundant, which meant, if modern cold climate food collectors serve as a model, that women and children relied rather heavily on the hunting of men. Polygyny would have been hard for a man to afford and contrary to his wives' reproductive interests. One may also note that Lovejoy (1981), in what strikes me as the most plausible sociobiological accounting for human evolution to date, argues that monogamy, coupled with intensive parenting by both sexes, was the reproductive strategy most likely to select for distinctly hominid/human traits. If monogamy was the strategy of choice for protohumans, why would it cease to be for early humans?

Second, a likely reason simple horticulture so often became female farming lies in the maxim that if the men won't work, the women will. The women will work because of the biological and social circumstances created by maternity. Child bearing and the nursing bond create a situation in which women are highly susceptible to models for nurturent, responsible behavior, a susceptibility that may be heightened by the hormonal changes that occur in birthing mothers as well as by the social responses of infants to maternal care. Models for such behavior are likely to be present because women (indeed, people) who internalize them are likely to be reproductively successful, which means that girls are reared in intimate contact with such women, their mothers. Thus, women tend to do whatever is necessary to support their children's welfare, which allows men to rely on them to do so. The male reproductive function does not of itself create a situation in which intimacy with children and responsiveness to their welfare is so likely to occur. The biological circumstances of human reproduction, therefore, establish conditions for the cultural mimicking of natural selection noted earlier: maternal investment tends to be high across populations; male investment tends to be variable. If women can feed their families by farming, they will. Male contributions to farming tend to be prompted by conditions that limit women's capacity to feed families.

Third, a florescence of polygyny appears to have occurred in horticultural populations as an element in a complex of traits associated with warfare. Warfare, like farming itself, may have been favored by migrant selection. Farmers could move to landscapes that were marginal for food collectors, and organization for warfare may have enhanced the capacity to acquire and hold garden sites, though, once established, warfare became a highly redundant activity pursued by participants for a variety of aims not directly related to this adaptive advantage. These derivative reasons for fighting often seem to be part of the mechanisms employed to maintain military organizations. Polygyny tends to create a pool of young bachelors on whom much fighting devolves and among whom militance is stimulated by using women as rewards. The older polygynists who do the stimulating enjoy a benefit sexual biology denies the polyandrous woman: they can, through multiple marriage, increase the number of their children and thus the scope of their cultural influence in the sons they rear and the daughters' husbands they gain as allies. And if the women are producing much of what people eat, the material base of the polygynist's prestige is enhanced by feasting funded by the work of his wives.

A large number of such warlike horticultural tribal societies, together with a smaller number practicing pastoralism or a combination of herding and farming, have persisted to modern times. Most of these societies are quite small in comparison to long-established agricultural populations, but because they display great cultural diversity, even within limited regions, anthropologists have filled the ethnographic record with their customs. This has sometimes conveyed the misimpression that polygyny is a highly typical human mating pattern, a notion often supported by the textbook datum that the great majority of recorded societies allow it. In fact, it is better viewed as a passing phase of cultural evolution that is now approaching relict status except in areas sequestered from incursions of state-level societies. Indirectly this has occurred because man the polygynous warrior and his harem have been outreproduced by man the agriculturalist and his wife by a stupendous margin. And this in turn happened as a result of cultural selection for plow agriculture, our chief topic of interest.

Male Farming

Under horticultural regimes the contribution of men to farm work seems to be responsive to at least three factors. One is population density. Martin and Voorhies (1975) note that as dependence on cultigens increases with increased population density, the contribution of men to farming tends to increase as well because women do not have enough time to do all the farm work that subsistence requires. Second, in forested regions, where gardeners are vulnerable to attack by hostile neighbors, men may undertake most farm work as a defensive measure. Third, men tend to perform tasks for which their strength is genuinely advantageous. Among horticulturalists the task most commonly performed by men is land clearing, especially where large trees are felled or pollarded, an undertaking favored by migrant selection since it speeds the establishment of new gardens.

Plow agriculture is usually male farming because its technology favors the exploitation of the male strength advantage. This occurs not because women are necessarily incapable of such work, but more likely for the following reason: if an activity enhances the material security of a population and if increased proficiency in it occurs with increases in muscular strength or aerobic work capacity, marital selection tends to favor those who cultivate their proficiency at the task. Men are typically the courting sex; women have high social value even where they have low social status, which is to say that marital selection tends to mold the economic behavior of men more vigorously than that of women. Marital selection among males also creates hypergamy: a woman who marries up the social order in some sense is marrying a man who is relatively fit in that same sense. Wealth is one criterion of fitness in husbands, and proficiency in work is another. If men can perform an important task more proficiently than women, women (or their families) will favor men who will do this work for women, and they will especially favor those men who can do it well, because such men offer benefits to wives and children.

Boserup (1970) describes an African case in which a direct transition from female to male farming took place. Apparently this group was under pressure from the government to take up plow agriculture, and the men were reluctant to do so, perhaps because they regarded farming as women's work or simply because it was arduous (either view would be regarded as positively unmanly in Yaavahalli). But if this pressure from the government were in response to population pressure or environmental degradation, it seems probable that the transition would occur rather rapidly. For as it became evident that male farmers were better able to support their families (or could pay better bride prices) than other men, they would soon become the favored grooms and other men would modify their behavior accordingly.

I suspect this kind of transition was uncommon in the past. Most likely plow agriculture originated in areas where men were already doing a good deal of farm work. Draft animals simply provided a more powerful means to carry out the land clearing and preparation that men were already doing. Once introduced, plow agriculture was favored by cultural selection because it allowed more extensive cultivation of marginal lands that would not support gardeners very well and more extensive cultivation in areas with short growing seasons. Draft animals also eased the removal of stumps and tree trunks, a great asset in forested regions.

Under plow agriculture fallowing periods could be shortened, allowing the support of ever denser populations, a matter related to the decline of polygyny. Polygyny declined for two reasons related to farming. The large proportion of farm work requiring the use of draft animals meant that women contributed only a small proportion of farm labor and that the labor costs for men of providing for women and children were high; and as populations grew, so did these costs. Thus, fewer men were polygynous because fewer could afford to be. Moreover, it was generally contrary to a woman's reproductive interests to share a husband with another woman, so that marital selection favored unmarried men.

Second, marital selection also favored young men with most of their working lives ahead of them. For polygyny to be widespread, it is often necessary for most men to spend a portion of their adult lives unmarried; otherwise the spouse pool that allows polygyny to be common will not be available. Therefore, as girls and their families increasingly turned to young grooms, older men searching for second or third wives found that fewer young women were available.

The decline of polygyny was often associated with a change in the character of marital selection among men. In humans, as in other species, it may be difficult to distinguish intrasexual competition from epigamic display, since behavior that charms a potential mate may threaten a rival at the same time. Bride price, however, is primarily a matter of intrasexual competition in that the bride's kin rather than the bride are its recipients, and in that it serves to drive away rivals: he who gets the wife is he who can best afford her, not he who most attracts her. As polygyny declines under plow agriculture, the chief economic determinant of a groom's fitness comes to be his capacity as a provider. Therefore, epigamic displays of wealth and proficiency, factors that directly bear on a woman's reproductive interests, become a prominent part of marital exchange.

This may be closely tied to the role of marital selection in the socialization of farm boys. If one asks which of the basic subsistence strategies employed by men is easiest to convey to boys and which the most difficult, given the social and biological circumstances of male development, the answers appear to be hunting and agriculture respectively.

The weapons used by hunters are readily miniaturized for the use of boys in hunting small game, and the wide-ranging activities of the hunt, characterized by bursts of energy followed by periods of rest, canalize rough and tumble play. Thus, boys can be relied upon to begin mastering hunting competence with little or no adult supervision, and if they do so in peer groups, so much the better, for the relationships and social skills they develop in these activities are directly applicable to adult behavior.

The tools used in agriculture are not so readily miniaturized, if only because there are no miniature animals to pull minature plows. Moreover, with the possible exception of land clearing, farm work has little resemblance to rough and tumble play, and the peer group is inimical to getting routine, repetitive work done. Nor is the peer group nearly so useful a unit for production in adult life, since much work is organized within households, rather than among them, and is hierarchically organized with the senior generation telling the junior one what to do. The managerial expertise of the senior generation is important because the economic consequences of a technological error in a long-term process like cultivation can be far more grievous than an error in hunting strategy.

The developmental experience of agricultural boys contrasts sharply with that of girls under female farming. In the latter case, girls intimately associated with their mothers from birth may be gradually introduced to women's work from an early age. Farm boys, however, may be subject to the marked discontinuity in their socialization discussed earlier, which stems from their inability to perform men's work until mid-adolescence. This discontinuity is perhaps compounded by the fact that the father is literally a distant figure; he is away in the fields much of the time.

Male culture everywhere seems to display ways of dealing with sexual bimaturism and the association of boys with women in early childhood. It is harder to make men of boys than it is to make women of girls. Men's culture often responds with some test of manhood that prompts rapid socialization in boys, and often this test is a condition for marriage. In agricultural societies the most important test is often one of whether an individual can work like a man so that he may be regarded as a fit husband for someone's daughter. As population grows, the standards by which this judgment is made become stricter: other things being equal, the more intensive a man's cultivation, the better the husband. Thus, by tying productive effort to reproductive opportunity, growing agricultural populations goad their young men to more strenuous effort, which enhances the intensification fitness of the population in the course of mitigating the developmental disability imposed by bimaturism.

Men's culture in such populations often displays organizations of older men that enhance their joint capacity to secure compliant behavior in sons to ensure adequate social maturation. Whether one looks at the Mediterranean coffeehouse, or the civil-religious sodalities of Meso-

America, or the village councils of rural India, one sees older men construing themselves and one another as authorities and portraying men's society as offering special benefits to younger men who can meet its standards.

Thus, I view the patriarchal character of men's culture under male farming as a phenomenon that developed chiefly to allow men to exert symbolic control over younger men's behavior in a complex technology that taxes their physical abilities and for which the social and biological circumstances of their development do not well suit them. However, the unrelenting patriarchy of men's culture has a major impact on the status of women in agricultural society, for not only are women obliged by circumstances to be economically dependent on men, even to the extent of being relegated to the legal status of children, but they are often excluded from the prestige economies men create, as indeed they are in many tribal societies. I have found that this deludes some Western intellectuals into the belief that women in these societies really are children—that men somehow brainwash women into accepting subordinate status. It has been my experience, however, that careful ethnographic inquiry into women's lives in agricultural communities usually reveals that women are not really so subordinate as they may first appear, though they may pretend to be with outsiders, and it invariably reveals, of course, that they are not children, that they have an adult culture of their own.

Investigation of women's culture may be crucial to the study of agricultural intensification because as populations become extremely dense, further intensification may be achieved only by increasing the portion of farm work done by women. Moreover, the maintenance of social harmony in domestic groups, which one suspects is always essential to the allocative efficiency with which work may be organized, may become increasingly important. Thus, any domestic policy or practice that fosters the ease with which women's farm work may be increased or allows a more efficient use of human effort in households will be favored by cultural selection. Those who employ such policies will intensify their agriculture more readily and so increase the size of the population they can support without sharp declines in real per capita income. One way or another, those who, for whatever reason, display less fit customs will find themselves under pressure to change them. They will find themselves increasingly discriminated against as mates and immigrants by more successful populations, unless they change their ways, which means that the most prosperous of their children will be those who have most abandoned their parents' culture. Or such populations may simply stop growing, as children emigrate to urban places for nonagricultural employment and the adoption of an urban lumpen proletariat culture.

This brings us finally to Yaavahalli, for I believe that the culture of its women, especially the control they exert over marital alliance, has been as important a factor as any other in the rapid agricultural growth the village has experienced. However, the reintroduction of women to agriculture is best understood in light of selective mechanisms that created earlier stages of agricultural development.

Cultural Selection for Intensification Fitness in Yaavahalli

Yaavahalli's is a famine-stressed culture because the tragic vagaries of the monsoon weather system have recurrently subjected rural populations to droughts. Just as the partial extinction of a species due to environmental perturbations may select for biological traits that improve an individual's chances of surviving them, those farm people who were best able to survive famines, and to reorganize their agriculture and reintensify their cultivation practices as population density returned to prefamine levels, left their mark on the culture of future generations.

Thus, though the origins of Dravidian domestic practices such as those encoded in the teachings of the elders may be impossible to find in the documented history of South India, it is reasonable to postulate that they developed and persisted in part because they aided the survivorship of those who employed them. They may also have supported their practitioners' fertility, for though famines diminished populations, the long-term secular trend was upward. The political and economic conditions under which villagers carried on agriculture changed as well, and therefore cultural selection would favor those groups who were able to avail themselves of new opportunities and who organized themselves in ways that allowed them to sustain denser populations through the intensification of agriculture. As population grew, the proportion of it that followed favored practices also grew because of the greater natural increases their behavior would allow them to sustain.

As we have seen, the *taluk* experienced rapid growth in both population and agriculture in this century; Yaavahalli is distinguished from most other villages by its extremely rapid growth in both respects. Yaavahalli is also distinguished by a rather high frequency of joint households and of consanguineous marriage. Thus, if we can find a connection between Yaavahalli's growth and its domestic practices, it is possible that we will have discovered factors in the growth of the region generally.

Perhaps the best way to begin is with a case that provides concrete examples of several ways in which cultural selection has occurred in Yaavahalli. It is an interesting case because it combines elements of domestic turmoil and failure with the story of a couple who turned out to be, in a way, the most successful people in the village at the time of my stay.

The case of Big Rama and Venktamma is irregular in that Big Rama came from a village some miles away to live matrilocally in a household with three sons. Here is how it happened. Big Rama was in school and looking forward to a life as something other than a village farmer when his father died. Since his mother had died earlier, his father's death left him under the authority of his father's elder brother, who withdrew him from school, while continuing the education of his own son. Embittered by this and by a later land dispute, Big Rama, like Kenchanna, eventually became a *satyagrahi* and experienced a strong dose of Gandhian patriotism along with a term in jail. On his return to his village, a Congress Party leader who had been a mentor tried to help him patch things up with his family. This process included a bridal search that seems to have more or less coincided with the failure of his attempted reconciliation with the father's brother. Eventually, the bridal search led to the house of Little Hanumappa, who had a marriageable daughter and three sons, one a little younger than Big Rama, another a boy of twelve, the other an infant, and two little girls. When I knew him the eldest of these sons was a frail man with a poor reputation as a worker, which, according to the accounts of people who were bystanders during the marriage negotiations, had a good deal to do with the offer that Little Hanumappa made. Big Rama was simply the strongest person anyone had ever met, and Little Hanumappa promised to make him a coparcener of his estate if he would become a matrilocally residing son-in-law. Here is what then occurred, according to Big Rama himself:

> When I came to my father-in-law's house, they had nothing. They were not working hard; their fields were badly cultivated. They were feeding silkworms, but they were stingy [that is, they were not investing enough in their farming]. See, their fields were not level, and I worked two years to get them even up and down. See, I worked day and night; I dug one well and put the pump set on it; I got a lot of the gardens planted in mulberry and got the silkworm feedings up to eighty feeding trays. I bought sixty of those with my own money. I was feeding the silkworms with no one to help me, and I worked in the gardens, the paddy fields, and in the *raagi* fields. . . . Some people in the village told me, "Look, your father-in-law's a very stingy man; you have worked for him for ten years and he has given you nothing."

After detailing the various promises Little Hanumappa made and broke over these years, Big Rama continues:

> See, my father-in-law thought I was his servant and did not give respect to me, and I began to think, "There is no value in this." Then the women began to quarrel [the eldest brother was widowed and remarried by then], and I began to think, "See what has happened to my life." Often I would

stop working in the house after that. . . . Some days later I received a wound [he does not explain how], and I was thinking of ending my life. I did not hope to live. But my wife saved me. If she had not saved me, I would not be alive, because this wound did not heal for months. [After he recovered, he says,] my wife began to quarrel more with her brothers' wives, and one day my wife said to me, "There is no value in this, it is better that we leave this house and live in a tree. I am not going to live here. You should try to separate from my father."

I made no reply, but I went to my father-in-law in the garden and sat down near him. I said, "See, *maava*, I have served you for ten years, since your sons were small; now they are married, and we cannot live as a combined house any longer. Therefore I ask your permission to become separate." But my father-in-law said, "See, you came with nothing and now you can go with nothing." That is what he told me. Then tears came to me like rain as I remembered the people's words of warning. Then I made *namaskaar* [the praying-hands gesture of greeting and leave taking] and began to walk down the road. But my father-in-law ran after me crying. And he stopped me and said, "Don't think these are my last words. I will give you a house and some lands. But you won't go; you and your family will live here in Yaavahalli."

At this point a narrative running to about a thousand words describes a sequence of promises and deceptions by the father-in-law, leading finally to the intervention of Karagappa, the severely puritanical father of the present headman. With his aid, Big Rama and his wife secured a house and about three acres of land.

Consider this account in terms of the reproductive interests of the parties involved. Little Hanumappa salvaged a valuable piece of a broken family, Big Rama, and thereby not only secured a husband for his daughter, but renovated his farm and funded the marriages of his sons as well. The statistical data on the economic performance of the two households in 1966 lend credence to Big Rama's description: he had the highest yields in the village; Little Hanumappa's household was one of four joint families misclassified as a single-man farm in Chapter 6 by the discriminant function analysis. I do not think it farfetched to suggest that Big Rama produced almost as must useful work during his ten-year servitude as Little Hanumappa and his eldest son combined.

By any standard one cares to name, Big Rama's labor and managerial skills were so egregiously exploited that it seems a wonder that he tolerated the situation so long. He is a first-born son, and in his decisive economic behavior, he acts like one. But he was the son of a younger brother, who died when he was an adolescent, leaving him under the control of his father's elder brother, who was the head of the household in any case, and so he was in a disadvantageous position. Because no land had ever been legally registered in his father's name, the uncle succeeded, through a series of machinations, in depriving Rama of all but a small share of the family estate. After his father's brother's betrayal, Big Rama shifted his allegiance to the Congress leader mentioned earlier. Not only did the Independence Movement provide an exciting and purposeful escape from his troubles, but I also suspect that, given the prominence of same-sex hierarchies in village life, it was quite difficult for any boy of his age to live purposefully without some sort of trusted social father. It was on this honored individual's advice that Rama finally decided to cut his losses and conclude a matrilocal marriage. The mating was negotiated under the auspices of Ramakka, the wife of Little Hanumappa's elder brother, Big Hanumappa. She was from a respected family; her husband was a respected man in Yaavahalli, a prosperous village. What is more, Little Hanumappa's resources were, on paper so to speak, ample. What Rama did not know was that Big Hanumappa and Ramakka viewed his marriage as a way of helping Little Hanumappa to put his agricultural house in order. After his arrival, Rama had little choice but to attempt just that: he renovated and modernized the farm, with his father-in-law's repeated assurances that he would eventually provide for "all that your family will need."

Venktamma, Rama's wife, is really the crucial figure at this point in the affair, for she was the initiator of household partition. Venktamma bore children in 1950, 1952, 1954, 1957, and 1960. Her eldest brother's wife had children in 1956 and 1959 and died in childbirth in 1960 (the baby survived). Later, her brother married his first wife's younger sister, who became pregnant shortly afterwards and bore a child in 1962. Her second brother had married in 1956, and his wife died in childbirth in 1958. He then married a poor girl from a village no one had ever heard of, and she bore a child in 1960, just after the eldest brother's wife had died. In short, while Big Rama was laboring in the fields, Venktamma was trying to cope with reproductive chaos. From 1958 to early 1963, when she delivered her ultimatum to Big Rama, Venktamma, with the help of her curiously hapless mother, had to do the following things in addition to her farm work, dairying, and routine housekeeping:

bear one child;

help to deliver five others;

deal with the emotional upheavals of two maternal deaths and one stillbirth (her second brother's child);

look after eight children, five of her own and three of her eldest brother's, for a year and a half;

try to arrange a *modus vivendi* with two new sisters-in-law, one of whom insisted on instantly becoming the mother of her deceased sister's three children and criticized Venktamma's care of them;

nurse a physically ill and chronically depressed husband back to health;

assist in the marriages of her two younger sisters.

It is no wonder that she said she would rather live in a tree than continue in such a madhouse, particularly when it is noted that another younger brother and an elderly and cantankerous bachelor uncle were also members of the household through all of this. But it is also pertinent to the issues at hand that Venktamma was somehow willing and able to do a very great deal to help her relatives, up to a point. This breaking point was reached when what was perhaps the household's most valuable productive asset, her husband, almost wasted away; when the household was increasingly crowded with her brothers' families and her third brother was approaching marriage; and when her own elder children were on the verge of adolescence. To have continued in her father's house at that point would have jeopardized the interests of her own children. Rama had almost died once; might he not leave her an early widow if obliged to continue to live under the pressures of their current life? If her father did not keep his promises to Rama, what property rights would her sons have in competition with her brothers' sons? What resources in money and effort would be devoted to her children's marriages in such a situation? So Venktamma concluded that an independent household, under almost any circumstances, would be preferable to the existing situation.

Venktamma and Rama emerged from the physical and emotional exploitation of her family as cultural victors. Victory was marked by the intervention of Karagappa, who stood, ironically, in the relation of classificatory father's elder brother to Big Rama through marriage. Little Hanumappa had been criticized in the village for his treatment of Rama, and though I have no notes on the subject, it seems likely that Venktamma's benighted condition may have been pitied by others also. In any case, it appears that Karagappa was expressing widespread public opinion when he went to Little Hanumappa and said (according to reports), "You *will* go to town with me tomorrow to register some land in Big Rama's name!" To this land Karagappa added two acres from his own large estate, one of three outright gifts of land the old man made toward the end of his life. Big Rama and Venktamma were cultural victors because they were held up as models of conduct for the village, while Little Hanumappa was denounced as lazy and dishonest. As Karagappa said, "When this man Rama came, you were nothing; now you are a rich man [a bit of hyperbole], but you have done nothing for him." Karagappa selected for Big Rama's behavior; he rewarded it.

Little Hanumappa had fourteen acres of land and three sons. This means that had Big Rama and Venktamma been given an equal share, the best they could hope for, they would have ended up with only slightly more than three acres. In the meantime she and Big Rama also had three sons and two daughters to think about. When they separated from Little Hanumappa, their ratio of land to people became a bit less favorable, but they and their elder children were the best part of the household work force, and after two years their per capita income was substantially better than the parental household's, and double that of Venktamma's eldest brother, who had by then hived off as well. Thus, as Venktamma said, "We had five children; what were we to do for these children?" She clearly decided in favor of the interests of her own children. Big Rama concurred in her judgment, and we have seen what followed. Still, the couple faced the prospect of dividing their tiny holding among three sons unless the holding could be expanded. Big Rama's immediate plan was to begin another well as soon as the second son reached adolescence. Unless they managed to purchase further dry lands in the interim, they would become the first household in the village to cultivate only gardens.

Big Rama and Venktamma were exemplary people in the eyes of their neighbors. Big Rama was a strong, smart, workaholic farmer who tried to stay out of trouble with other people and get on with his work. Venktamma was a good household manager who always seemed able to find time to work in the fields in the afternoon. Indeed, she was able to keep a milk buffalo fed largely on the huge quantities of weeds that she and her children gathered daily in her father's fields. She was also a gifted manager of people, including Big Rama, which leads me to my next topic, for we see in this case instances of cultural selection at work, all of which involve the management of people.

Migrant Selection

Big Rama is a migrant in a village established by migrants less than a century and a half before my stay and further increased in size by immigration. The circumstances of Big Rama's immigration were, to my knowledge, unique: I know of no other case in which a family with three sons took in a son-in-law. Venktamma was an attractive, competent woman who, one suspects, would have been welcomed as an in-marrying bride by many families. Thus, it would ordinarily have been inimical to the reproductive interests of both the daughter and her brothers to crowd resources by keeping her at home. But the arrangement would probably never have occurred had circumstances been ordinary. Little Hanumappa's affairs were in a parlous state, and Ramakka, his elder brother's wife, who had been his friend and confidante before his marriage, saw a way to set them straight. She came from Big Rama's village, and she knew of his situation, one that might make him susceptible to the arrangement she proposed. She might never have proposed it had Big Rama been an ordinary man, but his feats of strength (and rather lugubrious temperament) set him apart. Thus, Big Rama's personal attributes favored his selection as a migrant. In spite of the heavy costs that Little Hanumappa was so reluctant to pay, the work Big Rama did led to net benefits for Little Hanumappa's household.

Big Rama's agricultural yields per standard acre, Rs. 472, were the highest in the village in 1966. There were only three other male heads of household who immigrated to Yaavahalli as adults. Like Big Rama and Venktamma, they eventually formed multiple-male households and enjoyed the benefits that accrue from having around a strong young man who will do what the experienced male household head tells him to do. Even so, their yields are above average for households of this sort: Rs. 304, 311, 317, as against Rs. 276 for all multiple-male households. These data become more interesting when we note that of the three *nuclear* households misclassified as joint by the discriminant function analysis discussed earlier, two are headed by men who migrated to Yaavahalli as boys with their families. Before considering what it is about migrants that might make them especially productive, we should note that all of these people were *selected* migrants. For one thing, access to house sites is under the practical control of the village headman: without his consent you cannot immigrate. But these people were, like Big Rama, recruited, in one way or another, by someone who already lived there.

Returning to the village's founding, we find brothers, the ancestors of the village headman's lineage, settling on what was at the time (sometime in the first third of the nineteenth century) uncultivated land. According to the village headman, they came "because their household in that village [called Tippenahalli] had grown too large." They were joined by their sister and her husband, and later by a Naayk, who came to serve as a "guard" and who founded the lineage to which all but one of the present Naayk households belong.

As you will recall from the last chapter, the founders of Yaavahalli were followed by several groups of immigrants who established the other lineages that came to constitute the village I studied. The first were, according to oral history, refugees from the great famine of the 1870s: those who were Vokkaligas took brides from the *patel*'s lineage either before or after immigration. A second large group arrived following the severe droughts that occurred in the early part of this century. Like earlier immigrants, they came from old, large villages. The Vokkaligas of this group intermarried with descendants of the refugees from the great famine. Later immigrants, whose agricultural performance I have just noted, came after World War II.

The way in which these migrants were selected may have been a factor in the village's unusual agricultural growth. As a place of relatively low population density, Yaavahalli was in a position to pick and choose among refugees from famine, crowded conditions, or domestic trouble at home. A number of migration stories in life histories recount two or more changes of residence prior to final immigration to Yaavahalli, and practically all report a period of *kuli* labor in Yaavahalli or a neighboring village prior to the family's taking up lands to cultivate on its own in Yaavahalli. This suggests two likely possibilities. First, most immigrants were accustomed to hard work and relatively low incomes when they came; second, the total number of individuals and families that came to live and work as *kulis* in the area during the latter part of the nineteenth century and the early part of the twentieth may have been much larger than the number who settled there. Thus, established villagers could choose among candidates for settlement whom they had had a chance to know and observe.

Moreover, Yaavahalli was, as I have said, in a peculiarly good position to choose. Established on a long stretch of otherwise uninhabited land about a mile from one large *joodidar* village and a bit over half a mile from the next, the village was closer to many of the fields controlled by the two *joodidars* than the *joodidar* villages were. While the *joodidars* were largely unwilling to invest in the improvement of their lands, they were certainly interested in any measure that would increase their incomes at no cost to themselves. They also relied on village leaders among the cultivating castes, the people who were to become the *sovkaars*, to run the villages and administer their agricultural holdings. To become a permanent resident of a village, one had to ingratiate onself to established residents in order to gain the intercession of the *patel*, on whose recommendation lands and a house site could be obtained.

Thus, there appears to be little doubt that new immigrants were deliberately chosen, and there were several reasons villagers took an interest in selecting immigrants. In some instances immigrant families included returning daughters so that, by taking them in, established families were helping out relatives. Yaavahalli has a long history of this practice. I recently heard that a daughter of the village, an eleven-year-old when I knew her, a mother of four now, has returned to the village with her family to live. Second, under the *joodidar* system immigrants could be recruited at no cost in land to current residents. All of the land left uncultivated or lightly cultivated after the famine would eventually be more intensively cultivated by someone. Why not fill it with immigrants of one's choosing and build a village and a political base? In the process one could also acquire fit husbands for one's daughters and keep the daughters at home into the bargain.

These arrangements were not matrilocal at the level of the household, since the daughters of the village lived in the immigrant households. Nor were they serious or readily avoidable violations of the preference for hypergamy. Family fortunes change in unanticipated ways; girls who had married well in their youth sometimes experienced a series of reversals on ever more crowded holdings in their conjugal villages and returned with their families in middle age, seeking better prospects for their children. Girls who married into immigrant families might be marrying down the economic order somewhat, but they would still be marrying into households with better per capita holdings than many families in neighboring villages.

In the event, oral history indicates that downward mobility was mostly temporary, for most immigrants seem to have done well by themselves, and the Vokkaligas among them increased the size of their holdings as time passed. We do not know, of course, whether earlier migrants displayed greater agricultural productivity than established residents, as recent migrants like Big Rama, Kenchanna, and Gangappa did. But it does seem as though established residents were careful to choose good farmers for their immigrants. And if they did, they raised the standards of the agricultural behavior to which their children would be exposed.

I saw this phenomenon occur during my stay. Among the Vodda workers who came to construct the well and the tank discussed in the last chapter were a man and his family whose diligence and intelligence caught the *patel*'s eye. The cultivation of his gardens had grown so intensive that he had to import a good deal of labor from other villages at some inconvenience, and so he decided to add these people to his staff of tenants. But like the *joodidars* before him, he did not wish to disturb the tranquility of his establishment by imposing unwelcome immigrants on longtime residents, which was a problem because the newcomers might be regarded as depriving other tenants of work. He handled this problem with a subtle propaganda campaign in which he frequently praised this family's character and industry and pointed out that they would be needed to cultivate lands irrigated by the new well. They, in turn, were at pains to be congenial with their new neighbors and to live up to the reputation the *patel* had made for them as workers. Earlier immigrants may have had a similar experience. And it may be that the status of being an immigrant, as much as or more than any previous experience with privation or hard work, stimulates industry in an effort to gain acceptance in a new village.

But for either reason or both, the fact that Yaavahalli was built by immigrants may have been a major factor in the village's much more rapid than average agricultural growth; these industrious, risk-taking migrants may have created a cultural heritage that prompted exploitation of new economic opportunities as they became available.

Immigration also seems to have been a factor in the kind of political community Yaavahalli became. The village was constituted almost entirely of people who came looking for more land. Moreover, because immigrants intermarried with established residents who assisted them in obtaining land, this quest was a joint venture that may have laid the basis for the strong collective action displayed by villagers later on. Just as Karagappa gave away land to people, like Big Rama, whom he regarded as highly deserving and helped them in other ways, the *patel* helped many people to obtain loans for wells and led the village in acquiring the other public goods that gave it its reputation for technological modernity and enterprise, a reputation that benefited individuals in trying to get loans. This reputation also gave the village a decided advantage in marital selection.

Marital Selection Among Men

The scheme to bring in Big Rama to set Little Hanumappa's agricultural house in order was embedded in the choice of a groom for Venktamma. In Yavahalli marital selection for productive behavior in men is vigorous and overt. Under the conditions of village life, men who did not work hard would imperil the lives of the women and children with whom they lived, and so a demonstrated capability for hard work is made an explicit condition of marriage to the extent that men who do not prove themselves may be denied access to the roles of husband and father. Men who cannot endure the male role in South Indian villages, and there are some, have two courses open to them. A few of them become *sanyasis*, wandering mendicants. In a way the *sanyasi* is, for this work-oriented society, an analogue of the *berdache* among the warlike Plains Indians. People provide a ritual specialist role for men who do not do men's work and accordingly are supposed to have no wife or children. But being a *sanyasi* requires either a special vocation for poverty or an excellent tenor voice to be used in singing *bajana* for alms. Thus, the more prevalent course of action for the male drop-outs of village life is migration to cities, where they join the ranks of a casual, unskilled labor force. In either case, these men have no impact on the men's culture passed on to the next generation of boys, because they have no village-bred sons themselves and are not present to influence anyone else's.

There are occasional migrants, like Marappa, who return to their natal villages in order to get married, only to find themselves used by their neighbors as examples of whom not to marry, for girls, and whom not to imitate, for boys. Marappa was in his mid-twenties when I knew him, the youngest of three brothers and a man who loathed farm work. For a time he worked in a shop in a nearby town that repaired irrigation pumps and motors. Whether Marappa quit that job or was fired is not clear, but he began to return sporadically to the village for periods of a few weeks at a time to live with his parents. It is also not clear whether he left each time because his feelings were hurt or because he tired, once again, of the village work routine. When Marappa would idly mention that the time had come for him to get married, relatives and neighbors would simply give the phatic nod of South India and fall silent. In private they would say that no one wants a man who never sticks to anything. Marappa would have had sufficient land to marry; it was his behavior that troubled people.

Cases such as Marappa's constitute empirical evidence that marital selection, the cultural variant of sexual selection, is an ongoing process in which socially reproductive success is tied to economic behavior. Moreover, we have seen this process at work in other ways as well. Recall that the age of marriage for males tends to be highest among the land-poor. This generalization must be qualified to the extent that per capita land wealth is lower for some castes than others. Therefore, the standards of wealth employed in selecting a groom for a Holeya girl will be quite different from those used by the parents of a Vokkaliga bride. But within one's own breeding population, the poorer a man is, the poorer his chances on the marriage market. It might be supposed that this principle mitigates the impact of marital selection on male work performance in determining socially reproductive success among men, but this is not the case.

First, it must be noted that land wealth in one generation of a family depends substantially on the productive success and fertility of previous generations. Second, poor men try to make up for their lack of land with hard work, to improve their existing holdings, to acquire new land, and to show that they may be fit husbands in spite of their land poverty. Such men are the avant-garde of intensification, displaying in their current behavior courses of action that may become the standard for future generations of families presently more prosperous than their own.

Consider Mudrayappa and his younger brother. Their father, a collateral member of the village headman's lineage, was regarded as a bit of a dunce, and his sons were also considered rather dull-witted. Their land holdings were quite poor, chiefly because they as yet had no well, but both men were good workers who had no difficulty in finding labor as tenants. In his late twenties Mudrayappa married a poor girl who bore a son a few years later. At age five this child could not walk due to some undiagnosed malady that seems to have plagued him from birth. He had become something of a scandal in the village because the negligent infanticide sometimes practiced by poorer villagers in such situations did not work in his case. He lived on in an increasingly debilitated state in spite of poor diet and lack of medical care. Mudrayappa's gaunt, unhappy wife did not conceive again. Meanwhile, the younger brother, increasingly anxious to marry, indentured himself to wealthy relatives in order to avoid draining household resources for his own subsistence. He and his brother planned to dig a well in their spare hours, with the understanding that Mudrayappa would help his brother find a wife. Whether they succeeded or failed in this venture is less important than the fact that these men responded to reproductive failure with work. The younger brother would not get a wife and Mudrayappa's wife would not get any less gaunt, which is to say more fertile, unless something was done to improve their material circumstances.

Thus, poor men may get a double dose of the incentive to intensify labor, in part because their ancestors failed to avail themselves of opportunities to intensify production through well construction earlier. The use of sexual access to women and to the roles of husband and father as a goad to stimulate productive behavior in young men may accumulate power over generations. In the same way, the individual who has a large number of sons decreases the estate that each will inherit and increases the burden upon them to make up the deficit in hard work.

A feature of the domestic cycle in Yaavahalli is pertinent here. Recall that a decline in the crowding of household resources due to the early marriage of daughters occurs fairly often; at the same time one or more sons of a family are past or passing puberty and joining the male work force. This temporary advantage is usually invested in agricultural improvements. Because it is almost inevitable that further crowding will occur with the marriage of sons, this investment amounts to a process of preintensification. Poor men, who must work in order to qualify for marriage, set a competitive standard to which fathers, however well off, may call attention to stimulate productivity in sons. These "you're not going to let that other fellow show you up" comparisons introduce a note of intrasexual competition into male culture.

But the process of marital selection also involves a series of reciprocal epigamic displays by the families of both prospective mates. On the groom's side, arrangements must be made for a visit by the bride's parents and perhaps a whole retinue of other relatives as well. This will occur even if the families are related because it provides a warrant for the bride's kin to examine the groom's circumstances in detail. Having satisfied themselves, the bride's family return to their village after a date has been set for the betrothal ceremony in the bride's village.

The groom's family bears the brunt of the costs of the marriage, and these include a bride price. A small sum of money is presented to the bride's parents, but the central prestations at a betrothal are gifts, chiefly of clothing and jewelry, made to the bride. Shortly after these gifts are presented, the bride retires with a younger sister, or some girl who stands in that classificatory relationship to her, and the two girls emerge from the bride's house decked out in the new finery, whereupon the remainder of the ceremony is concluded. Here a ritual statement of the meaning of husbandhood is made: a man must provide for his wife. The jewelry is of particular significance, for at a practical level it constitutes insurance on his life and on his fidelity to her. It is, in short, a prepaternal investment.

The ceremony also provides a chance to display the bride and to showcase her younger sister. With the sister's aid, she serves a meal, putatively prepared by her, to the visitors. The demeanor of the girl during this play at being mother of the house is important. It is best to be gay and relaxed, satisfactory to be demure, dangerous to be nervous, and potentially disastrous to put on airs. But looking like a goddess and serving a good meal gracefully is not enough. Women too are subject to selection for intensification fitness, perhaps because Yaavahalli has gone beyond male farming of the extensive sort found in many areas in India and embarked on a form of labor intensive farming in which employment opportunities for women have greatly expanded. We shall turn to this matter presently.

But the role of marital selection among men in enhancing the intensification fitness of villagers is simple enough. Digging wells increases the value of one's estate; it is the practical equivalent of acquiring more land. As population grew, therefore, those men who dug wells were favored as grooms over those who did not. Digging wells became the fashionable thing to do, in part because it increased a man's prestige and the attractiveness of his sons.

The famine-stressed character of village culture also played a part in well digging. Life histories of older villagers are filled with stories of drought and privation in times past; droughts are, like hurricanes in my native Florida, chronological markers. As we have seen, the real growth of garden cultivation began after the drought of 1923 that so frightened villagers, some of whom must have been survivors of the great famine of the 1870s. Following the drought, the government began to offer loans for digging irrigation wells, and though this program was quite modest in comparison to that available to villagers later on (to my knowledge none of the older wells I saw were financed with these loans), it may have had a demonstration effect. The extent to which wells drought-proofed agriculture must have soon become evident to villagers.

At any rate, by the time of my stay, parents of daughters tended to place heavy emphasis on gardens in evaluating the estates of potential grooms. This became an issue in the marriage of Subanna, the shorter of the two men shown in the bridal photographs in Chapter 4. His father was a laconic man who, with the rest of his family, had an excellent reputation as a farmer except for one thing: he had not dug a well. I never understood why. The girl Subanna married was his mother's older brother's daughter, and people said that the marriage never would have occurred if Subanna's mother had not pulled the emotional strings that tie brother and sister. The girl was a first-born and proved to be the capable, responsible sort of person first-born daughters often are. And though she showed a pronounced lack of the fluent gaiety village women like in one another, people covertly speculated about the better matches she might have made.

Subanna's father had allayed the fears about his gardenlessness, which were in the forefront of everyone's speculations, by promising to dig a well. Although he had not secured a loan for one, by the time of the wedding he and Subanna had managed to gouge a modest pit in the laterite as an earnest on the promise. The gossip that attended this marriage revealed to me a criterion people employ in the selection of grooms: a man with ample acreage but no well, like Subanna, may be a less desirable groom than a man with less land some of which is irrigated by a well, because of the advantage well irrigation provides in years of low rainfall. Subanna could marry only because his parents had saved for some years, and they kept those savings only because they were able to work as tenants on the gardens of others during the drought of 1965.

Group Selection in Male Culture

Now, if you believe that common sense alone, and not selective sanctions applied by other people, would be sufficient to prompt well digging, you have probably never dug one. The amount of effort entailed in hacking a huge tube out of hard laterite is stupendous. People who do a lot of this work for money generally have little or no land, which explains why they do it. Prior to the government's loan program, many wells were dug entirely by families, or with large amounts of family labor. And while some were dug by the fathers of young nuclear families, most were dug by families containing two or more men; that is, they were largely dug by sons under the direction of fathers. Moreover, once a well is dug, the opportunities it offers can be exploited only with greatly increased amounts of *kashta kelsa*. In such circumstances, any cultural practice that increases older men's ability to get work out of younger men enhances intensification fitness. Marital selection does this. So do the patterns of interaction one observes among older men in everyday life.

Yaavahalli had no formal village *panchayat* when I lived there; nevertheless, male heads of households met from time to time in the *patel's* courtyard to settle disputes. When I spoke of this as a *panchayat* men would chide me, saying that the real *panchayat* was the group *panchayat* recognized by the government, but there was little doubt that in organizing themselves to settle disputes the male elders of the village construed themselves as authorities. In Chapter 2 we encountered Gangappa, whose dispute with his father over the allotment of a portion of family land to his sister and her husband was heard by such a council. You will recall that the *panchayat* told Gangappa to obey his father. *Panchayats* also enforce what they regard as correct paternal behavior. The Yaavahalli *panchayat*, for example, told a man that he should not sell a parcel of land against his son's wishes. But in demanding correct behavior of its members, the *panchayat* serves notice to the young that in cases such as Gangappa's where the father behaves appropriately, in their view, they will always support him.

We have already seen how patrilocal residence and patrilineal inheritance bolster the authority of senior men and favor the effective exploitation of young men's strength through the expertise of an experienced farm manager. Now we see that, in addition to this, men negotiate likemindedness concerning the *dharmas* of men in alternative roles, including the reproductive interests of a father, and in so doing foster the perpetuation of models for behavior by enforcing them.

One of the principles they systematically endorse is the moral value of work. The father may demand the son's obedience because he has worked for him; the son may demand his share of the patrimony because he has worked for his family and obeyed his father. When the *patel* praised his new Vodda tenant as a hard worker, it was with the presumption that this trait would legitimize his immigration (though he may also have pursued the exploitative motive of serving notice on some of his aging tenants that standards of productivity were going to be raised). And when Karagappa gave land to Big Rama, it legitimated his insistence that hard work must be rewarded by Little Hanumappa as well.

The recurrent public definition of paternal authority and hard work as admirable devolves the greatest prestige on him who has best exemplified them. When the experts on farming gather to discuss what they are experts about, they are listened to and never, in my experience, contradicted by juniors who have not won their status. Their conversation contains comments about the work that they or others are doing, wells that are being dug or renovated and, occasionally, disdainful remarks about the laziness or improper cultivation of others. They may do this, as I have said, for the sake of setting an example for their sons. Having set high standards for them, fathers do not like other people exposing sons to low ones. But what may be the pursuit of their reproductive interest in their sons' socialization has a communitywide effect, for no one's poor farming is allowed to go unnoticed.

And so by reciprocally supporting one another's authority (and thus one another's reproductive interests) and by creating through symbolic interaction a prestige economy based on the intensity and skill of cultivation, men enhance the intensification fitness of the community as a whole. The more such men a village contains, the more it is likely to have in the next generation who will continue to build upon the resource base bequeathed to them by the efforts of their predecessors.

This process of group selection for intensive effort, like migrant selection, may help to account for the curious character of Yaavahalli as a village. On the one hand, cultivation practices were more labor intensive in Yaavahalli than elsewhere; this seems apparent in view of the larger than average proportion of land under well irrigation in the village. On the other hand, the village also had more land per capita than most villages. Thus, we might expect men of Yaavahalli to be less intensive in their cultivation, on the average, than men elsewhere, but they are more intensive. This apparent contradiction must be resolved if we are to account for the concentration of agricultural growth in Yaavahalli. I believe the contradiction is more apparent than real for the following reasons.

First, it should be borne in mind that the mechanisms of cultural selection prompting labor intensification often have to do with the means by which the senior generation attempts to *prepare* its children for the economic consequences of population growth. In a sense village fathers simultaneously lie to their sons and tell them the truth when they urge young men to work hard in preparation for marriage. If a family has a well, it is not really true that a son will severely jeopardize his chance to marry if he does not help to dig another or work hard with existing resources to save to buy more land or make agricultural improvements. For all the father knows, the boy might get a bride with whom he would be well satisfied if things were left alone. But it really is true that if there are two or more sons, or if a single son has two or more sons himself in the future, the resources of the household will become more crowded unless measures are taken to mitigate the impact of family growth. And since the parents of prospective brides know this too, it is also true that the young man who works hard to increase household productivity increases the scope of his marital prospects.

Second, the ability of older men to prompt effort in junior men is influenced by the role models young men observe around them. As we have just seen, the most salient models for young men, and those to which their fathers most often call attention, are those of their village mates. Thus, it does not matter much if men elsewhere with as much land or less do not work as hard as a boy of a particular household is asked to, for he does not know how hard they work. What he knows about is the prestige economy around him, and that around him in Yaavahalli was erected by tough immigrants. Nor are parents of prospective brides likely to tell him that the standards of marital selection among men elsewhere are not as high as he supposes, for even if the agricultural resources, jewelry, and so on his father offers them are better than they anticipated, the bride's father who negotiates the contract will, in an effort to do as well as he can for his daughter, insist that they are barely enough.

Thus, it is entirely possible for greater agricultural intensification to occur in a community of lower population density, provided that population has experienced a substantial increase, because the standards used to judge its response to population growth are internal ones.

Through the development of their resources, the men of Yaavahalli have, on the average, achieved an advantage over many men elsewhere, and villagers take pride in the quality of the brides they attract. They have also created for themselves an incentive to acquire brides who can easily take part in the more complex organization of labor that garden cultivation requires.

Marital Selection Among Women

Hypergamy and consanguineous marriage, two factors that influence the migratory and marital options of women, may have been favored by cultural selection in the past largely because of the advantages they conveyed to those who practiced them in coping with environmental problems. The famine-management strategy villagers employed in 1965 laid heavy stress on the prevention of conflict. People under stress were especially liable to quarreling, which made matters worse. Families therefore prefer brides who are, like Venktamma, capable of enduring and dealing responsibly with family crises. One way to obtain such brides is to choose a girl from a family poorer than one's own, one accustomed to more hardship. Families may also enhance their stability in times of crisis by cultivating relationships with known and trusted kin that may lead to consanguineous marriages, for a girl who has been treated as a future family member over a period of years and who is

genealogically linked to a family is less likely to have difficulty in forming stable relations with the other family members, so that a crisis is less
likely to provoke quarrels leading to household partition. This might be
a matter of some importance, since household partition could seriously
impede the restoration of normal cultivation following a drought. Moreover, those who cultivate affinal ties with old-relationship marriages
might, as one informant noted in an earlier chapter, be able to borrow
money or food from them in time of need. Indeed, affines might offer
one a place to migrate to if conditions became too crowded at home.

When population grows rapidly and becomes extremely dense, however, these marital policies take on an added importance. The highly
labor intensive cultivation I observed in Yaavahalli was made possible by
increases in the amount of farm work done by women. By digging wells,
villagers provided themselves with many more cultivation opportunities,
including many more opportunities for men to employ themselves and
one another in *kashta kelsa*. But these efforts would have been fruitless
unless the women had provided the time and effort the men could not
provide to take advantage of the additional opportunities to do productive work.

How much has the average woman's contribution to farming increased as a result of garden cultivation? This question cannot be
answered accurately because we have no data on the allocation of women's
effort in times past. A rough idea of the increase may be gained, however,
from an examination of women's work in 1966. Had the garden lands of
the village been left unirrigated and cultivated in the same fashion as other
unirrigated land, the total hours contributed to farm work by women
would have approximately halved. This does not necessarily mean that the
total contribution of women to farm work has doubled as a result of garden
cultivation, and it certainly does not indicate that the hours contributed
per woman have doubled. Time later spent working in gardens might have
been employed in the past to weed unirrigated fields more thoroughly.

But it is extremely unlikely that unirrigated farming could have
absorbed anything remotely close to the total effort women now expend
in gardening. Women's work on unirrigated land is, as you will recall,
largely restricted to weeding and harvesting. Crop failure is more frequent on unirrigated than on irrigated land. When crop failure occurs
late in the cultivation process, the only harvesting task is cutting straw
for fodder, a job that proceeds much faster than cutting stalks of grain
and picking avare beans, tasks that must be followed by efforts to thresh,
winnow, and store the crop. Moreover, when crop failure occurs early in
the cultivation of unirrigated land, but too late to plant a new crop,
harvesting work disappears, and weeding ceases as well, though much of
the effort may be diverted to improving the chances of fields that have

not failed. By contrast, gardens, which are less prone to failure anyway, are prepared for a new crop the moment crop failure is evident. As a result, the average contribution of women to the cultivation of unirrigated fields, including those that failed and the seldom weeded ones at some distance from the village, came to only about 150 hours per acre per year. By contrast, the annual contribution of women to gardens in which grains were grown averaged about 1,100 hours per acre.

But even if women's total contribution to farm labor before gardening was much less than their present contribution, might not the average hours contributed per woman have been as great when there were, say, half as many women? Perhaps, but I doubt it simply because about all those women could have done was more weeding. If women of years past had spent as much time in the fields on the average as women were to spend later, and if they had used the portion of their time that was later employed in gardens in the more thorough weeding of unirrigated lands, we would be talking about an extraordinary amount of weeding, roughly eighty-six full eight-hour days per woman and adolescent girl each year. We saw earlier that the weeding efforts of women on unirrigated land, which are rather unevenly distributed over plots, probably yielded rather low average returns in terms of crop yields. Had women in the past devoted the equivalent of an additional eighty-six eight-hour days to weeding, it seems likely that the marginal product of their effort in terms of crop yields would be very low indeed.

What is more, two other factors may have reduced the likelihood that women would engage in this effort. Bear in mind that prior to garden cultivation men would have had substantial slack periods in their other work, which would have allowed them to do more weeding too, though they may have been less proficient at the task than women. Perhaps more important would have been a decreased incentive to weed for fodder in the past. Over the years the number of draft animals increased with the number of men to drive them. I do not know how much, if at all, the sheep and goat population declined at the same time. Villagers' recollections of diets past and present certainly indicated a decline in meat consumption per capita, and villagers reported their ancestors as owning many more animals than they themselves owned, though these reports may be exaggerated, as their reports of ancestors' land holdings appear to have been. But even if herds have declined, it appears that the amount and quality of pasturage available on uncultivated wasteland some distance from the village declined as well. Some of these areas were planted in casaurina trees, and much of the remaining land was severely eroded because, according to local agricultural officers, of overgrazing. As a result, the capacity of the village to support its livestock with cultivated fodder, chiefly the by-products of human food production, and from pasturage has probably declined over the years. Perhaps the decline has been rather substantial, since gardens are often planted in crops that yield little or no fodder. If so, villagers had to make up the difference by gathering wild plants on farm land, where they grow better than they do on eroded wasteland.

If women before gardening had little reason to weed enough to spend as many hours in the fields as the women I knew, how great an increase in the per capita contribution of women to farming had occurred by the time of my stay? Obviously nothing better than a somewhat educated guess is possible. My guess is that it increased by at least a half.

What is virtually certain is that important qualitative changes occurred in women's contribution to farming. So long as women's farm work was restricted to unirrigated cultivation and to paddy cultivation before the uniform adoption of the transplantation technique, women's time was subjected to the regimented constraints imposed by farm technology only at harvest time. Weeding, as we have seen, can be done as time permits and is thus rather easily coordinated with domestic work. With the growth of garden cultivation, however, women were increasingly employed in transplanting, irrigating, a number of harvests, and a variety of minor tasks, all of which had to be carefully coordinated and carried out on a fairly precise schedule. Moreover, the women I knew had to cope with the crises that sometimes arose in farming. If parasites are eating the cabbage leaves in the garden, the only readily available way to get rid of them is to pick them off by hand, which must be done immediately lest the crop be irreparably damaged. Likewise, if a man became ill or was needed elsewhere during a peak demand for labor, it was often necessary for a woman to replace him in the fields.

In the meantime domestic work had to be done, children cared for, and livestock tended to, which further complicated women's lives. Thus, in all but the richest households, village women were very busy people, and rather often there was no convenient way to manage the varied and competing demands on women's time and attention. Still, some women appeared to manage better than others, and any policy of marital selection for women who managed well would enhance a household's capacity to carry out intricate and labor intensive cultivation procedures well at minimal cost to domestic comfort. As we have noted, villagers endorse hypergamy on the grounds that girls from poorer families tend to be willing workers who appreciate their new surroundings. They also prefer brides from known and trusted kin because such girls may be relied upon to adapt easily to their conjugal family's ways. Both sorts of brides are said to foster joint household stability, and this is important, not only because of the deleterious consequences of dividing the males of a household, but also because, as you will recall, households that contain two or more women get their housework done more efficiently than those containing only one and are able to participate more proficiently in other activities.

I cannot show that hypergamous and consanguineous marriages actually yielded the benefits claimed for them for a number of reasons. Not the least of these was the fact that many of those marriages that were not consanguineous were said to be hypergamous, though I cannot confirm the extent to which they were because I failed to gather data on the size of the parents' estates at the time of the marriages. Thus, while some marriages that violated villagers' marital preferences had clearly worked out badly, no statistical evaluation of the matter could be made even if I had some way to quantify success in marriage. The only such quantifiable measures I can think of are the time between a marriage and a household partition and the extent to which particular women were blamed for household partitions in life history texts. The first of these is suspect because many circumstances, such as the deaths of founding parents and differences in the fertility of couples, seem to influence household partition. Thus, teasing out the proportion of variance accounted for by the kinds of brides people selected would be difficult at best. It is fruitless to employ the second measure because where women are blamed for household partition they are simply said to have argued; they are not accused of specific acts of aggression as men are. Moreover, the fact that one woman is said to have initiated partition does not necessarily mean she is the villain of the piece; Venktamma demanded the partition of her household, but she was regarded as an admirable woman.

But even if the benefits claimed for the standards of marital selection applied to women must remain a non-disconfirmable postulate, the assumption that the benefits occur may account, in part, for the concentration of agricultural development in Yaavahalli because the village's households were, as a group, in a peculiarly strong position to get the brides they wanted.

The advantage many households of Yaavahalli enjoy in obtaining brides from poorer families stems from the fact that most of those households own more land and a good deal more garden land than the average for their caste mates elsewhere. It might appear that this situation should create difficulties in finding grooms for village girls, but this is rarely the case, for the only women in the region whose marital prospects in village society are really limited are those from *sovkaar* families. Just as bachelors tend to be concentrated at the bottom of the economic order, spinsters are concentrated at the top. This occurs, or so it is said, because no one wants a bride accustomed to a life of leisure, except perhaps other *sovkaar* families. One solution to this problem is to marry rich girls out of village society altogether to urban, educated men, a measure *sovkaar* families saw as improving a daughter's life chances, though I suspect that they had little appreciation of what it might be like to be the country wife of an urban husband. Note that such women, upon leaving, abrogate any influence they might have on village women's culture, which will be molded by the practical, hard-working women who remain behind. In Yaavahalli only the *patel*'s family considered choosing urban grooms; most villagers were in the enviable position of having a wide range of prospective brides to choose among and having a fair to excellent chance of marrying daughters further up the economic order because most were, for lack of better terms, middle to upper-middle class by regional standards.

In order to clarify the role of hypergamy in marital choice, it is well to provide a more precise description of the policy. First, it is often stated in a negative form: one should not marry daughters down the economic order or take brides from those wealthier than oneself. As one man said, "See, my elder brother's wife came from rich people, whereas my wife and I came from poor people; she could not understand our difficulties and would not cooperate with us." Thus, the policy could just as well be described as the avoidance of hypogamy were it not for the fact that villagers say they look for girls who have had to become accustomed to a good deal of work. Second, rarely do women marry out of poverty into wealth. Rich families do not want poor girls because such alliances convey no prestige or political influence. Rather, most families intermarry with people whose means are fairly close to their own.

As a matter of fact, wealth differences between families at the time of a marriage seem to stem more from family size than from the size of their holdings. This fact is tied to an interesting feature of village demographics. So far as I could tell, the culturally standard rule for family planning among village couples was to have at least one son; once a couple had a son or two, they were rather likely to try to limit further pregnancies, whereas those who had a run of daughters might continue to have children in hopes of having that one son. As a result, sons tend to predominate somewhat in small families, whereas large families tend to run to daughters. Parents with three or more daughters did not worry a great deal about the crowding of family resources because it was only temporary: girls high in the birth order might have to work hard to support younger siblings, but the chances were excellent of finding good matches for such hard-working girls. By contrast, parents with many sons were quite worried by the prospect of having to divide their estate among them.

This association between sex ratio and family size is germane to two points. First, it is entirely possible for reciprocal exchanges of brides between families to be reciprocally hypergamous. A girl with several sisters but few brothers might well marry into a relatively small family, and thus up the economic order, and then send a daughter back to marry her younger brother or her brother's son after her natal family's per capita land wealth had increased due to the marriages of her sisters. Second, the practical reality of hypergamy in Yaavahalli had much to do with birth order in the families from which villagers chose brides. Almost half of in-marrying brides in recent generations were first-born daughters, many of them first-born siblings, and many came from relatively large families. The advantage enjoyed by many households in Yaavahalli in acquiring such brides did not stem from having smaller families; in fact, couples tended to be somewhat more fertile than couples elsewhere, and the sex/birth order composition of families showed distributions comparable to those of other villages. The advantage derived from the fact that the average groom in Yaavahalli stood to inherit a better estate than competitors elsewhere.

If villagers were actually choosing first-born daughters of big families, why, one might ask, did they not state that policy instead of the hypergamous one? In fact, they did regard first-borns as desirable brides, but the stated policy subsumed a variety of choices. One might choose a girl from a family with substantially less land than one's own, or one might choose a late-born daughter of a family with many sons. In any of these cases villagers would have rather regularly chosen girls who had had to cope early in life with the practical consequences of population growth for women's work. Many of them had done a good deal of *kuli* work as well as work on family land and thus brought with them the competence to deal with the farm work that intensification requires. The rapid pace of intensification in Yaavahalli, then, may be due in part to the heavy concentration of such women in the village.

Here, as elsewhere in South India, population growth occurs fastest among rural people of middle to upper-middle income. Thus, the practice of hypergamy may tend to increase the propensity of this sector of the population to respond to growth with further intensification by providing it with women who have already learned to cope with more crowded circumstances.

Consanguineous Marriage and Group Selection in Women's Culture

The stability of the joint households depends, as we have seen, on the ability of women to get on well and work proficiently together. Like hypergamy, consanguinity is a criterion of marital selection that is said to increase this ability. I have described the benefits accruing to this practice as a self-fulfilling prophecy largely created by the visiting of women.

Women who engage in this behavior reciprocally increase their joint capacity to form stable households by assisting one another in the marriage cultivation process.

There may be other ways of fostering harmony among women, but cross-cousin and uncle/niece marriage has a peculiar characteristic: it is sensitive to population growth. When large sibling sets in one generation are followed by large sibling sets in the next generation of two or more bride-exchanging groups, the chances of having a cross-relative of suitable age to marry to a given child of either group dramatically increase because this specialized breeding population has grown larger. Thus, consanguineous marriage serves people best when they need it most, when families are growing quickly and agricultural measures must be taken if declines in per capita income are to be averted. For example, the *patel*'s lineage, which had grown rapidly, had concluded half a dozen marriages over two generations with another lineage that had also grown rapidly in a village a few miles away. The density of the social networks thereby created was a prominent element in relations among members of the *patel*'s group. When I asked them how they were related to one another, they would jokingly remark that they were related in a number of ways. These ties between as well as within households were the basis of a good deal of reciprocal help. The *patel*'s wife frequently exchanged goods and advice with her classificatory elder sister across the street, who was married to the *patel*'s classificatory father's younger brother by blood, and thus his classificatory older brother by marriage.

The cultural practices that foster repeated marital alliances between groups may be said to be favored by group selection. Leaving aside the question of how formal rules of Dravidian marital alliance arose in the first place, we may observe that they occur in the cultural repertoire of a population as a set of instructions specifying certain classes of relatives, including rather close ones whom one knows well, as appropriate spouses for one's children. Because they do, people cultivate these relations on the grounds that prior ties may be used to establish successful marriages. To the extent that such marriages foster joint household stability and thus long-term prosperity, people pursue them further. In the course of doing so, families provide benefits for one another, chiefly through the reciprocal exchange of brides, but also through the information networks created by the women. Thus, a woman who wishes to cultivate one match with a family but not another may tactfully suggest an alternative for the prospective spouse she does not want and may even help to bring the parties together.

These practices will be most prevalent among people who remain in the same general area for some time and who intermarry with people relatively short distances away, because they will be able to cultivate affinal ties more readily than those who do not. And as we have just seen, the development of marital alliance may be most elaborate in those groups that have grown the fastest because of the larger spouse pools created by rapid growth. If consanguineous marriage actually fosters joint household stability, it also fosters the intensification fitness to sustain a population increase because such households are able to organize human effort more proficiently. Note too that this means that the women who have the most daughters convey to these girls the protocols and social skills they have developed, creating a condition conducive to the persistence of these behaviors in the population.

If this is the case, we might expect to find rather high frequencies of consanguineous marriage in areas that have experienced rapid growth in both population and agricultural intensification. This appears to be true of Yaavahalli. I suspect, moreover, that the circumstances of the village's development may have placed villagers in a particularly strong position to arrange consanguineous marriages.

How do we know if the frequency of consanguineous marriage was higher in Yaavahalli than in other villages of the region? The 40 percent frequency I found is certainly higher, often much higher, than the rate reported by ethnographers in other parts of South India. These differences must be viewed cautiously, however, because the techniques used in tabulating such data may vary from one ethnographer to the next. In this and many other matters, I employed elicitation techniques taught to me by Alan Beals. He too has reported higher frequencies of consanguineous marriage than most other ethnographers. Some ethnographers appear to count only first cross-cousin marriages and those between a man and his "real" (in contrast to classificatory) elder sister's daughter, whereas the techniques used by Beals and taught to me turn up all sorts of more distant marital connections.

At any rate, the apparent fact that consanguineous marriage is more common in Yaavahalli than in other parts of South India does not mean that it is less common in other villages of the *taluk*. Perhaps not, but without putting too fine a statistical point on the issue, it seems unlikely that the frequency elsewhere in the region could be any higher. For even if one counts marriages with second and third cousins as old-relationship marriages as villagers did, it seems improbable that demographic circumstances would permit people to push consanguineous marriage a great deal higher than the figure of 40 percent that I recorded; and they certainly could not do so without taking a good many brides from households substantially wealthier than their own. Thus, it seems warranted to suppose that the frequency of consanguineous marriage in Yaavahalli was relatively high. Moreover, I see no reason to doubt villagers' word in claiming that most of these marriages were carefully arranged, even though one might anticipate that a certain number of such marriages would occur by chance, given the relatively small spouse pools from which mates are selected and the rule of moiety exogamy noted in Chapter 3.

Why did this rather high rate of consanguineous marriage occur in Yaavahalli? I can offer no conclusive answer to this question, but there is some circumstantial evidence indicating that the affinal networks of Yaavahalli's Vokkaligas, at least, were highly developed.

A village that grows solely by natural increase does not increase the number of its exogamous lineages, whereas one that grows through immigration will, especially if established residents systematically pick affines or potential affines. As a result, average lineage size will be much smaller than that in a village of comparable population that grew by natural increase. That fact would not of itself influence the proportion of consanguineous marriages people in the two villages could arrange. But let us suppose that the immigrants to one village came from another, which grew by natural increase, and that they brought with them affinal ties that they or their kin had established back home. If we assume further that the immigrants eventually increased their land holdings over those of their kin who remained behind, we can see that these newly established lineage segments might be favored as bride receivers over kin who stayed behind by those to whom their lineage had given brides in the past. Whether this really happened or not is hard to say, but circumstantial evidence suggests that it may have: on a number of occasions earlier in this century, Vokkaliga immigrants or their sons married girls from the immigrants' natal village who were the daughters of kinswomen. Apparently these kinswomen came to visit the immigrants, were impressed by their new opportunities, and married their daughters to sons of the immigrants instead of marrying them to their husbands' sisters' sons or sending them elsewhere. Other immigrants gave brides to other villages shortly after they came to Yaavahalli, when they were still working as *kulis*, and then took brides back from these families once they had obtained land to cultivate themselves.

This immigrant advantage would be only temporary, and it may have been countered by the disadvantage of having moved further away from affines. But migration was taking place elsewhere as well. As population grew denser, new villages cropped up in the interstices between older established ones, from which they drew immigrants, either because people wanted to be near the newly irrigated land that they had to cultivate regularly or because, as in Yaavahalli, people were seeking less crowded conditions.

There are other villages in the area whose history and demography are like Yaavahalli's, and the Vokkaligas of Yaavahalli have intermarried with these people, some of whom were immigrants from the same villages the ancestors of Yaavahalli's population left, establishing new segments of affinally related lineages nearby. Like Yaavahalli, these villages seem to have experienced a rapid natural increase in population. The relatively large sibling sets produced by groups with prior marital alliances created many opportunities for consanguineous marriage, and these were duly exploited.

Thus Yaavahalli was established and began to grow under the economic conditions that favored consanguineous marriage on the part of migrants. Later, as it and similar villages began to exhibit the spurt of natural increase that seems to be typical of areas of lower density that have been populated by persons from areas of higher population density, demographic circumstances favored the continuation of a high frequency of consanguineous marriage.

However, the fact that Yaavahalli's high rate of consanguineous marriage is accounted for in part by demographic circumstances should not lead us to ignore the social interactional aspects of the question, for the fact of consanguinity itself does not create the benefits attributed to consanguineous marriage. Those benefits stem from a socially constructed reality, the self-fulfilling prophecy created by the visiting of women. Circumstances gave villagers many chances to employ this ancient Dravidian marital policy, but perhaps these opportunities would not have been exploited so fully had not the policy provided real benefits. The more village women implemented this policy through their visits, the more they found that consanguineous marriage provided the harmony among the women of a household that their increasingly complicated lives and their desire to hold joint households together made so useful. How much the policy has facilitated the gradual change in women's agricultural roles and how much it increased the stability of joint households is impossible to say. Since most marriages were either hypergamous or consanguineous, we have little basis for comparing households that followed recommended practice in recruiting brides with those that did not. But the highly suggestive fact remains that the villages, such as Yaavahalli, in which the greatest agricultural growth took place were not ones in which traditional Dravidian domestic practices were withering away but ones in which they were most highly cultivated. And since these were also places where population had grown most rapidly, one might conclude that the practices and doctrines endorsing them were becoming, if anything, more widespread in the regional population.

I have portrayed the *dharmas* of the sexes and the teachings of the elders as a reproductive strategy that persists because it succeeds. It succeeds because it provides a proficient and reliable way of organizing agriculture, a villager's way of creating more villagers, and of increasing the intensity of cultivation in response to population increase. Ecological arguments of this kind are often criticized for providing no examples of adaptive failure. It is fitting, therefore, that I conclude this chapter with just such an example: Bedapur.

A Reproductive Failure

Bedapur is one of two villages I censused in which villagers had taken virtually no steps to intensify their agriculture and which had not grown in population in recent years. One is a Harijan community in which toddy is made, a village denounced for enticing Harijans of other villages into the evils of alcohol. The other, Bedapur, is a community composed entirely of Naayks.

Bedapur had seventeen households at the time of my census, four of them polygynous. Located on high ground north of Yaavahalli, the village had no irrigation, and the soil of its fields was poor and rocky. I became acquainted with the people of Bedapur initially through their women, who routinely came to Yaavahalli to work as *kulis*. Sometimes a few young men would come too, but I did not encounter the senior men until I visited the community. In taking the census I discovered that about a dozen young men had moved in recent years to urban areas in search of wage labor. Apparently this was not the result of family decisions; the young men simply started going to nearby towns and then to the city of Bangalore, and the more often they went the longer they stayed. When I remarked on the number of polygynous households (three men had two wives, one had three), a possible reason for the defection of these young men emerged. Yes, one informant responded, polygyny was frowned upon in places like Yaavahalli, but there were many things done in Bedapur that were frowned upon by such stuffy villages. This meant, I came to understand, that premarital sexual activity also occurred in Bedapur. I also discovered that Bedapur had been largely endogamous for some years and that affairs had reached a point at which the proper Naayks of Yaavahalli, at least, would not contemplate sending brides to such profligates. The hamlet was divided into two lineages, and it turned out that two polygynous men in each had exchanged daughters with two in the other to acquire junior wives.

These few details are about all I can empirically attest to concerning Bedapur, but perhaps we can surmise something more from them. First, the village's population problem, if indeed it had one, was dealt with through migration: daily migration for wage work in nearby villages, mostly by women, and emigration to urban areas by a large segment of the community's young men. Second, no effort had been made to intensify the village's own farming through irrigation: while the local topography would have made well digging difficult, the presence of ample water in the drinking water well suggests that some irrigation wells could have been successfully constructed. Third, no attempt appears to have been made to construct cohesive, productive joint families. With the exception of the polygynous ones, all households were nuclear or were composed of pieces of nuclear families through remarriage. To all appearances, *laissez faire* prevailed. I was left with the impression that, so far as the four older men were concerned, unrestricted premarital (and perhaps extramarital) sexual activity was somehow a *quid pro quo* for polygyny, and vice versa. As long as the senior men had young wives, the young people could have each other.

Perhaps Bedapur's problem was that hard work organized within households would not have readily produced conditions appreciably better than those they achieved through the measures I observed, simply because farm resources were so poor. Hence, there was little reason to employ the regulation of sexual behavior as an incentive to hard work or to establish strong economic bonds between women and men.

I doubt that there was a Bedapur at the time of the great famine, since, given the population density prevailing at the time, there would be little reason to locate a village in such a barren place. If I am correct, the settlers of Bedapur may have come from areas of lower rainfall to the east. That is the source of most of the recent immigrants who came looking for *kuli* work, and so far as I could tell the people of Bedapur had always relied on finding such work in richer villages. Indeed, they may be descendants of rejected immigrants, for while many Naayks managed to settle in more favorable surroundings, their *jaati* in the past was regarded as a criminal caste. Perhaps finding themselves subject to discrimination, these people settled on a bit of landscape nobody wanted, but close enough to better areas to allow daily commuting for wage work. They would still have been too far away to become tenants in richer villages, however, because landowners like their tenants to live nearby, where they can be called upon to watch standing crops and to provide the various extra services tenants are asked to perform. Tenancy, as we have seen, tends to go to households with two or more men and so favors joint households. The availability of *kuli* labor is not much influenced by household composition, unless you are a tenant, which provides the lever for you to acquire additional work from your patron. But the men may have been better off staying at home and scratching what crops they could from the land nobody else wanted (how they gained title to it I do not know) while the women went to work as *kulis*. Thus, emerging sex roles constituted rather separate economies, with little need for coordinated activity between the sexes. During the years of poor rainfall, the women may have contributed substantially more to family income than the men. The productivity of the men's agriculture could have been increased by digging wells, as people elsewhere were doing, but the effort of digging through sixty or seventy feet of rocky soil, as they had had to do for their drinking water well, may have seemed so enormous compared to the prospective benefits that no one thought it worthwhile.

Moreover, I suspect that the village had experienced out-migration for a long time before I censused it. The houses were built all in a row, were of similar design, and appeared to be of the same age, exactly what one might expect of a hamlet constructed all at once by a group of colonists whose later growth was siphoned off through emigration. If over several generations young men had been leaving to find work elsewhere with no one making an effort to stop them, it would be all the harder to set them to the long period of back-breaking and unpaid labor entailed in digging wells. With the emigration of young men, the sex ratio was skewed towards females, and while some women must have married out of the village, the sex ratio was still slightly skewed, providing wives for polygynists. Why should the older men exchange daughters as second wives? Why not? Bedapur women were not popular as brides elsewhere; one presumes that the older men found one another's daughters attractive; and women produced a substantial portion of family income anyway. Moreover, the women were either very infertile or they experienced a very high rate of infant mortality or both, so that in taking a second wife the polygynous men were not taking on much added responsibility, especially since the first wife's eldest children were nearly grown by the time they took the second. There were also three nuclear family households formed by a widow's remarriage to a younger man, suggesting the possibility that these women were formerly second wives who had taken up with another man, perhaps previously a lover, after the death of an elderly husband.

By their own rights—or those of the male elders, anyway—the people of Bedapur were doing badly but the best they could do in the circumstances. Still, theirs was a dying culture. Their major problem was one of material resources; yet the domestic practices they employed in response to this situation were not ones that could have reliably created the basis for their own repetition in a growing population even if they had had better resources, nor were they conducive to acquiring better resources. The people of Bedapur would not have been welcomed as immigrants in places like Yaavahalli, and even if they had been given better land to work with, it seems to me that they would have had to substantially revise the way in which they organized their lives in order to use it effectively to support any population growth.

They would have had to become more like the people of Yaavahalli in their behavior. As it was, they had produced something rather like a culture of poverty. I dislike this term because the matter of which I speak has nothing to do with being poor. The Voddas are very poor, but they are the most highly organized people I observed, mobilizing groups of descent groups under a single leader to construct irrigation works.

The difference between the Voddas and the people of Bedapur stems from the fact that the Voddas have economic opportunities in which a high level of highly coordinated effort pays off. Though it is poorly paid, there are abundant employment opportunities in the work they do, and the best and largest opportunities go to those who can put together a large group of disciplined workers under expert leadership. Those who are best able to do this not only support their children, but also convey to them a body of competence that can be utilized in the next generation to exploit the same resources in the same settings. The Voddas can reproduce their culture in apparently growing numbers of people. The people of Bedapur cannot; many of their children, who are small in number in the first place, move away and come to adopt the cultural practices of heaven knows who.

The complex patterns of Vodda social organization recur not because they make anyone wealthy or happy—the evolution of culture has woefully little to do with the pursuit of happiness—but because the women and men who join together in producing them jointly increase the likelihood that their children will survive, mate, and behave as their parents behaved. The work ethic that keeps them hacking away at the earth year after year for a pittance persists because it has produced more Voddas; it is an effective way of continuing life.

The same is true of the Vokkaliga farmer and his wife and their patrilocal joint family household. The household persists because it allows them to withstand the environmental perturbations to which they are subject and because this unit of production and the mechanisms used in forming it prompt rural people to increase their level of effort in response to a growing population.

Anthropological Materialism with a Human Face

There is nothing Panglossian about the materialist approach employed in this study. The adaptation of the people of Yaavahalli to the conditions of their lives was achieved only through struggle, and by their own standards it remained highly imperfect. Nor were their solutions in any sense final. At the time of my stay the block development officer feared that soon the number of wells would exceed the number the aquifer could support. If that happened, and loans for wells ceased, the employment opportunities of the Voddas would decline rapidly, the farming population would have to find a new technological fix for any further population growth, and class conflict would be exacerbated, because benefits already offered to some, namely loans for wells, would be denied to others. The world of Yaavahalli was not optimal; it was merely a workable world in which conventional wisdom proved continually sound, for the time being.

There is also nothing mechanical about the materialism employed in this study. On the contrary, an actor-centered approach conveys a human face to cultural ecology. In acknowledging the role of the decisive human actor in achieving cultural adaptation, the political economist of everyday life does not, however, suggest that people know precisely what is happening to them or exactly what they are doing. He or she simply recognizes that people pose and attempt to solve practical problems, and then sets out to understand how they do so.

Recognition of the role of human competence in achieving adaptation—a recognition (entailing no presumption that all behavior is in any sense adaptive) of a competence that includes, among other matters, the human capacity for creative self-deception—has a number of interesting implications. One of these is the further recognition that a peoples' response to the conditions prevailing at a given time must be undertaken from the perspective of their extant cultural heritage. This does not deny primacy to the material conditions of social life as influences on social action; it merely denies that a full account of cultural adaptation can ignore the deliberations and interaction of those who achieve it, for to do so would be to ignore that which is most cultural about the behavior. And if the cultural heritage of a people at a given time influences their responses to given conditions, it follows that one should not expect to predict the details of their response from the conditions alone. One only predicts that they will have to live with the consequences of their behavior, consequences that will condition subsequent responses.

If this is so, we should not be at all surprised that peoples of distinctly different cultural heritages achieve analogous cultural adaptations to similar conditions while continuing to display, symbolically, quite different presumptions about the world. The people of Yaavahalli, for example, resemble, in their emphasis on the collective security provided by the family and in their gerontocratic way of organizing it, intensive agriculturalists elsewhere in Asia. The rural Japanese family displays a sexual division of domains of activity similar to that found in Yaavahalli, stipulates a head for each domain, and recruits an heir for each. But the Japanese ways of managing this process and the semantic structure of the rhetoric used in managing it are strikingly different from those found in Yaavahalli.

If we should not be surprised that there is more than one path to similar ends, we should be even less surprised that there is more than one path from similar beginnings. The adaptations of the Voddas and the people of Yaavahalli are homologous; they entail quite different interpretations of a common Dravidian rhetoric of kinship and marriage used in organizing responses to different opportunities within the political economy. The kinship terminologies of the two groups display only minor structural differences from one another and from many others found in South India. Both groups trace descent patrilineally and allow the same kinds of marriages between groups. There are marked differences, however, between the social realities the two groups create with these rhetorics of kinship and marriage.

The Voddas who dug the *patel*'s well, for instance, were divided into six lineages. These in turn were grouped into moieties of three lineages each, such that each group of three regarded the other as marriageable. A ridge of earth was maintained across the diameter of the well to represent this distinction. Organized in this way, these Voddas resembled nothing so much as a kin-based labor union. On payday a steward or headman received the money due his lineage from the overall foreman, and these stewards constituted the leadership who negotiated wages, hours, and working conditions, such as access to shelter, with employers. The people of Yaavahalli displayed no such elaboration of patrilineal descent in the organization of their work. For them it was the extended farm household that mattered.

There is nothing mystical about this homologous process of divergent adaptation. One would expect the Voddas to approach labor organization with the symbolic resources and social relations at hand. As it happened, the symbolic resources at hand shared a common historical origin with those of their employers.

Comparisons such as the foregoing oblige one to attend to the role of problem solving in human adaptation elsewhere, an interest which inclines one to regard as specious much of the debate between anthropological materialists and those who profess cognitive or structuralist views. Ethnography should teach the materialist the mistake of treating the things people say as epiphenomena of the things they do, a mistake that is clear the moment one observes people trying to do anything more complicated than brushing their teeth. In admitting this mistake and in apprehending the obvious—that any people must begin an adaptive process using available symbolic resources—the materialist does not become unscientific; he or she merely admits a more complex reality to the field of scientific inquiry. Likewise, the structuralist or cognitivist should be disabused (if this has not occurred already) of the notion that the symbolic heritage of a people can somehow be divorced from their competence to cope with the practical problems of a world that will never abrogate its laws to please them. The study of the political economy of everyday life leads us, then, to see others as we see ourselves: as interested actors whose reason is evidenced in countless imperfect and, in the end, evanescent products, such as the teachings of the elders or this book.

Notes on the Social Sciences, Sociobiology, and the Sexual Miasma

> The first adherents of a movement are no argument against it.
>
> —Nietzsche

My argument concerning Yaavahalli is now complete. But because it deals with a controversial subject, relations between sexual biology and behavior, I would like to add this brief appendix dealing with the approach I adopted toward this subject and its implications for the work of others.

In the course of constructing this theory of my field notes, I concluded that no sense could be made of the organization of work and domestic life in Yaavahalli without considering sexual biology as a context in which social learning occurs. After reading a great deal in the field of sex differences, I have concluded too that this is true of the behavior of women and men everywhere. The contrasting doctrine of biological arbitrariness is widely held: the notion that because sex-role behavior is learned and variable across (and within) societies, biological factors, apart from the impact of child bearing on women's cultures, can be disregarded in explaining it. This doctrine is empirically untenable and methodologically fatuous. The fact that sex-role behavior is learned has no bearing whatever on the question of whether biological factors influence the learning process. And though sex-role behavior varies, it varies in rather predictable ways, as we saw in the case of the division of farm labor. There are, moreover, a number of cross-cultural uniformities in sex-role behavior. If these patterns and uniformities are not to be ex-

plained in terms of the cultural amplification of biological sex differences, how are they to be explained? The alternative appears to be an
indefinite and increasingly obscurantist regress of causation based on
social learning theory alone.

The scholars who appear to agree with this conclusion fall into two
general groups. The first is composed of social scientists (mostly psy-
chologists, such as Maccoby and Jacklin, whose work I cited earlier, and
anthropologists, such as my former classmate Naomi Quinn [1977]) and
a few biologists. The work of this group is characterized by inferential
empiricism. In some cases the starting point is a reliable pattern of
behavior, such as the sex difference in aggression. By a process of elimi-
nation it is concluded that biological factors must be implicated in the
behavior, and this conclusion leads to an effort to identify those factors.
In other cases the point of departure is a study of some feature of sexual
biology, such as the hormonal changes that occur in birthing mothers,
which leads to an inquiry into associated behavior such as mother/infant
bonding. My argument was strongly influenced by this group in style as
well as in substance; I have tried to adhere to their take-nothing-for-
granted empiricism. For while they and I regard it as absurd to suppose
that the physical differences between the sexes play no part in differenti-
ating the behavior of women and men, it is also unwarranted to prejudge
the part they play. Caution is all the more in order in view of our limited
knowledge of biocultural interactions and in view of the moral and political implications others may draw from one's work.

The second group adopts a deductive, evolutionary approach to the
study of sexual biology and behavior. This group is composed of the
sociobiologists, in whose ranks I include sociobiology's social scientific
converts, and a few individuals like Lovejoy who construct essentially
sociobiological arguments without labeling them as such. The work of
this group is diverse. At one extreme there is Symons (1979), whose
work strikes me as a brainstorming expedition advancing the proposition
that differing determinants of male and female reproductive success have
produced human male and female biograms so different that men and
women are forever destined to experience mutual antagonism and exploitation. On the other hand, the position taken by Wilson (1978) is far less
deterministic. On reading his chapter about sex after writing the first
draft of this book, I was interested to find not only that he spoke of the
cultural amplification of biological sex differences much as I had, but
that he too noted the way in which cultural selection mimicked natural
selection through the amplification of these traits.

It is important to note this diversity, for the works of different
authors lead to radically different conclusions. For instance, Lovejoy

argues that the suppression of visible estrus and the capacity for continual sexual activity that emerged during hominid evolution led to a con-
vergence in the determinants of male and female reproductive success.
Deprived of information indicating that a receptive female was ready to
conceive, the promiscuous male no longer enjoyed a reproductive advantage over the individual who routinely copulated with a single female; on
the contrary, the supportive monogamist won the balance of selective
advantage through the provisioning and protection he offered his mate
and offspring. Lovejoy argues that natural selection favored suppressed
estrus and the capacity for continuous sexual activity, because these traits
conveyed a faculty for intersexual cooperation promoting the high rate of
juvenile survivorship that is a hallmark of our species.

Despite these differences, however, scholars of this group are united
in the view that the study of human biology and behavior should be
undertaken as a specialty in the theory of evolutionary ecology. Behavior
should be examined in the light of its impact on the genetic fitness of
individuals and therefore on that of the genetically programmed biology
that underlies the behavior. The other group, the biocultural empiricists,
ordinarily make no such presumption.

At the outset I said that I did not propose to settle any of the
differences separating sociobiologists and their critics. But perhaps the
outlines of a potential *rapprochement* may be noted. The sociobiologists
challenge the biocultural empiricists to regard the aspects of human sexual biology they study as features of an adaptive biologic system, the
human biogram, that has persisted relatively unchanged because of the
fitness it conveys, and to deal with the question of how natural selection
may have favored those features. However much one may disagree with
particular extant sexual sociobiologies, it is difficult to deny the legitimacy of this challenge.

Reciprocally, the biocultural empiricists challenge sociobiologists to
desist from the distressingly frequent tendency to treat the human body
as a genetic black box containing postulated genes for common behaviors, and to treat it instead as an observable anatomical and physiological
system whose polygenically regulated properties may be studied in a
behavioral context.

I have tried to treat the matters of being male and female in Yaavahalli in this way, though my observations were simple and my conclusions modest. But when one makes similarly simple observations about
the ethnographic record concerning sex-role behavior as a whole, fundamental conclusions may emerge. One is that sexual dimorphism increases
the range of cultural behavior and thus the scope of cultural adaptation
of which a population is capable. That is, women and men could not do

all of the things that they do so well if they were physically just the same apart from reproductive functions. At least they could not so long as biological sex differences involved biological trade-offs inhibiting the combination of all secondary traits in a single individual. Second, one observes a strong tendency towards productive proficiency and reproductive security in the divisions of labor and domestic relations that the sexes construct. This is scarcely all one observes—there is no gainsaying, for instance, the occurrence of male privilege and dominance in a variety of forms in many societies—but proficiency and security seem to account for such persistent patterns as the tendency for women to undertake tasks compatible with and related to child care and for men to undertake heavy work and tasks incompatible with child care.

Therein, it would appear, lies the evolutionary significance, biological and cultural, of human sexual biology. It is most fruitfully regarded not as a set of biological imperatives that limit the behavioral alternatives of women and men, but as a source of adaptive flexibility that confers the facultative capability for a wide range of alternatives.

To appreciate the scope of these alternatives, consider the South Indian farmer and the South American Indian warrior. To the South Indian farmer, male strength is meant for hard work; to the South American Indian, it is meant for war. For the latter aggressiveness is cultivated with strength as a virtue; for the former, male aggression is culturally amplified in institutions that suppress it. The South Indian would regard the South American's behavior as boorish at best and at worst, and more likely, as criminal. The South American would regard the South Indian as a drudge at best and at worst, from his perspective, effeminate. The South American treats women as weak and cowardly; the South Indian worships powerful mother goddesses and regards maternal love as superior to a god's. Neither man could get a wife in the other's society, which is, in large measure, why each behaves as he does. Both men share the same basic male biogram but attribute entirely different meanings to features of it, meanings that have been molded by and have reciprocally molded the material conditions under which the two societies live.

Likewise, maternity means very different things to the South Indian woman and the American professional woman. To the former motherhood is a career that she can pursue for her entire lifetime; to the latter a family is a source of emotional satisfaction, but it is also difficult to reconcile its demands with those of her work. Where the one cultivates contacts with babysitters and day care centers, the other cultivates contacts with cross-cousins. If the American mother were to treat her grown children as the Indian mother does, the neighbors would regard it as maternal meddling; if the Indian mother allowed her children to choose their own mates, the neighbors would be scandalized. Yet the two women could find a good deal of common ground because the biological circumstances of their lives are similar despite the cultural differences.

Examples of this sort suggest a principle of differential amplification. Biology-as-destiny doctrines, such as the Freudian one, appear to imply that the physical traits of each sex form a gestalt, a bundle of inseparable features that exert a uniform influence on feminine and masculine experience. As the comparison of our hypothetical South American and South Indian suggests, this is not necessarily so. Both cultures explicitly magnify the sex difference in physical strength but in separate ways. And where one society deliberately cultivates male aggression, the other deliberately suppresses it. The symbolically managed experiences of being male in the two societies would appear to be utterly different. Thus, particular physical attributes of each sex may be subject to separate and differential cultural amplification. The principle of differential amplification provides a systematic way to account for the commonplace observation that while definitions of masculinity and femininity differ, all societies seem to have them. This notion suggests another. If one looks at men and women as organisms, rather than as culture-bearing human beings, there is no doubt that we are male and female animals. Morphological differences resemble those found in other species, notably other primate species, and the social relations between us have been heavily influenced by our reproductive behavior. The fact that we mate with one another means that the physical differences between us have a significance that is entirely different from the significance, say, of physical differences between human breeding populations. That is why it may be seriously misleading to derive the notion of sexism from that of racism, or to take literally Engels's analogy between women and men and proletarians and capitalists. Unlike social classes, women and men mate and rear children, and because they do, criteria of joint reproductive success, over the long-term experience of a society, mold their behavior in the most intimate of groups, families.

When one adds, however, the further observation that men and women share a specialized faculty for language and culture, our character as male and female animals is utterly transformed. This faculty confers upon us the capacity to attribute varied meanings to biological sex differences and to regulate the impact these have on nonsymbolic aspects of our behavior. As a result we have the ability to act like a variety of male and female animals who mimic in their cross-cultural differences variations in male and female behavior across other species.

Wilson (1978) agrees, for, as he says, "Societies mold their customs to the requirements of the environment and in so doing duplicate in totality a large fraction of the arrangements encountered throughout the remainder of the animal kingdom." An observationally adequate human sociobiology must concern itself with the human biological ability to produce this pattern. In so doing, it must recognize as well that attributions of value and meaning are invariably elements in its production.

In the meantime, further empirical studies of biocultural interactions in sex-role behavior may serve to dispel in some measure the miasma now surrounding discussion of relations between the sexes. A reflorescent feminist movement aimed at addressing women's authentic dissatisfaction with the *status quo* has generated a prolific literature in which two themes are recurrent: one is the notion that women almost everywhere have been oppressed, at least in historical times; the second is a radical revival of the doctrine of biological arbitrariness. Contemporaneously there has emerged a popular literature of scientific male chauvinism, which argues that the sexual *status quo* is either inevitable or to be altered only at unconscionable social cost. The authors of these works go on to point out the paradox of the two feminist themes I have just mentioned: if women have everywhere been oppressed, how can it be that men enjoy no biological advantage as oppressors; if they enjoy no biological advantage, how can they systematically oppress women?

The findings of this study and others like it render the premises of both camps specious. Political and economic relations between the sexes are more variable than either camp appears to suppose them to be. And while it appears that sexual biology and conditions of society interact to produce the variation we observe, these conditions and interactions are, in principle, subject to intentional change. There is, in short, not the slightest reason to believe that it is impossible to be distinctively male and female and at the same time to be the people we would like to be, for there is not the slightest reason to believe that the alternatives of the past dictate the outlines of all possible futures. Conditions change, and as they do new alternatives emerge.

References

Astrand, Irma
   1967   "Aerobic Work Capacity: Its Relation to Age, Sex and Other Factors." In *Physiology of Muscular Exercise: American Heart Association Monograph Number Fifteen*, ed. C. B. Chapman. New York: American Heart Association.

Beals, Alan R., G. Spindler, and L. Spindler
   1967   *Culture in Process*. New York: Holt, Rinehart and Winston.

Boehm, Christopher
   1978   "Rational Preselection from Hamadryas to *Homo Sapiens:* The Place of Decisions in Adaptive Process." *American Anthropoligist* 80: 265.

Borg, G.
   1971   "The Perception of Physical Performance." In *Frontiers of Fitness*, ed. R. J. Shephard. Springfield, Ill.: Charles C. Thomas.

Boserup, Ester
   1965   *The Conditions of Agricultural Growth*. Chicago and New York: Aldine Atherton.
   1970   *Women's Role in Economic Development*. London: G. Allen and Unwin.

Bronson, Bennet
   1972   "Farm Labor and the Evolution of Food Production." In *Population Growth: Anthropological Implications*, ed. Brian Spooner. Cambridge and London: MIT Press.

Brown, Judith K.
   1970   "A Note on the Division of Labor by Sex." *American Anthropologist* 72: 1074.

Burke, Kenneth
   1969   *A Grammar of Motives*. Berkeley, University of California Press.

Burton, M. L., L. A. Brudner, and D. R. White
   1976   "A Model of the Sexual Division of Labor." Manuscript. University of California, Irvine.

Census of India 1961
   1964   *Volume XI: Mysore*. Bangalore: Government Central Press.

Digby, William
  1878   *The Famine Campaign in Southern India 1876–1878*. London: Longmans, Green.
DuBois, Cora
  1944   *The People of Alor*. Minneapolis: University of Minnesota Press.
Durham, William H.
  1978   "Toward a Coevolutionary Theory of Human Biology and Culture." In *The Sociobiology Debate*, ed. Arthur L. Caplan. New York and London: Harper and Row.
Epstein, T. Scarlett
  1962   *Economic Development and Social Change in South India*. Manchester: Manchester University Press.
Geertz, Clifford
  1966   "Religion as a Cultural System." In *Anthropological Approaches to the Study of Religion*, ed. Michael Blanton. A.S.A. Monographs No. 3. London: Tavistock.
Harris, Marvin
  1979   *Cultural Materialism*. New York: Vintage Books.
Hayavadana Rao, C.
  1930   *The Mysore Gazetteer*, vol. 5. Bangalore: The Government Press.
Indian Council of Agricultural Research
  1960   *Indigenous Agricultural Implements of India*. New Dehli: Indian Council of Agricultural Research.
Intrilligator, Michael D.
  1971   *Mathematical Optimization and Economic Theory*. Englewood Cliffs, N.J.: Prentice-Hall.
Loveday, A.
  1914   *The History and Economics of Indian Famines*. London: G. Bell and Sons.
Lovejoy, C. Owen
  1981   "The Origin of Man." *Science* 211: 341.
Maccoby, Eleanor E., and Carol N. Jacklin
  1974   *The Psychology of Sex Differences*. Stanford: Stanford University Press.
Martin, M. Kay, and Barbara Voorhies
  1975   *Female of the Species*. New York and London: Columbia University Press.
Meade, J. E.
  1952   "External Economics and Diseconomies in a Competitive Situation." *The Economic Journal* 62: 54.
Miller, G. A., E. Gallanter, and K. H. Pribram
  1960   *Plans and the Structure of Behavior*. New York: Holt, Rinehart and Winston.

Money, J., and A. A. Ehrhardt
  1972   *Man and Woman, Boy and Girl.* Baltimore: Johns Hopkins
          University Press.
Osgood, C. E.
  1964   "Semantic Differential Technique in the Comparative Study
          of Cultures." *American Anthropologist,* Special Publications,
          vol. 66, no. 3, part 2, p. 171.
Quinn, Naomi
  1977   "Anthropological Studies on Women's Status." In *Annual
          Review of Anthropology,* ed. B. J. Siegel, A. R. Beals, and S.
          A. Tyler. Palo Alto: Annual Reviews Inc.
Rohmert, W., and P. Jenik
  1971   "Isometric Muscular Strength in Women." In *Frontiers of Fit-
          ness,* ed. R. J. Shephard. Springfield, Ill.: Charles C. Thomas.
Sahlins, Marshall
  1972   *Stone Age Economics.* Chicago: Aldine.
Scitovsky, Tibor
  1971   "Two Concepts of External Economies." In *The Economic of
          Underdevelopment,* ed. A. N. Agarwala and S. P. Singh. Lon-
          don: Oxford University Press.
Selby, Henry A.
  1975   *Social Organization: Symbol, Structure, and Setting.* Dubuque,
          Iowa: Wm. C. Brown.
Symons, Donald
  1979   *The Evolution of Human Sexuality.* London: Oxford Univer-
          sity Press.
Tanner, J. M.
  1955   *Growth at Adolescence.* Oxford: Blackwell Scientific Publica-
          tions.
Wilson, E. O.
  1978   *On Human Nature.* Cambridge: Harvard University Press.

Index

Aerobic work capacity, 81
  defined, 84
  and manual labor, 94
  of physical education students, 85–86
  studies of, 85–87
  See also Kashta kelsa; Sex differences
Age at marriage, 43
Aggression, 39, 160–171, 187–189.
    See also Men, disputes among;
    Sex differences, agression;
    Women, disputes among
Agriculture, sequential nature of, 110, 113
Agricultural implements, 122
  carts, 148
  Chandrankies (silkworm spinning frames), 153
  gudali (digging implement), 96
  guntive (thinning rake), 98
  kapile (irrigation device), 175, 214
  plow, 97, 98, 123
  seed drills, 148
  silkworm feeding trays, 247
Agricultural tasks (specific)
  bunding, 122
  digging, 96, 137, 158, 180
  harrowing, 122
  harvesting, 119, 152, 263
  irrigating, 120–121, 155, 199
  leveling land, 122, 247
  manuring, 122, 123
  planting, 122
  plowing, 98, 121–122
  rated by difficulty and urgency, 95–100

thinning, 98–99
  transplanting, 114–116, 120–121, 152, 158
  weeding, 120–121, 124–127, 172, 263, 264
Agricultural proficiency, 11, 12
Anubha vastaaru (appraisers), 150, 156
Astrand, Irma, 85–86, 88, 103
Avunculocal residence, 186

Bajana (religious songs), 183
Beals, Alan R., 270
  and G. Spindler and L. Spindler, 136
Bedapur (village), 273–276
Biological predispositions, 232–234
Biological sex differences. *See* Sex differences
Birds, crop damage by, 124
Block development officer, 7, 200, 276
Boehm, Christopher, 237
Borg, G., 95
Boserup, Ester, 16, 200, 201–202, 218, 225, 229, 238, 242
Boys
  adolescent, estimating ages of, 102
  at age 8, 175
  at age 12, 175, 178
  at age 15, 181–182
  conspiracies among, 183–184
  control of rough play among, 176–178
  discontinuities in socialization of, 181–182
  education of, 163, 175, 176
  first-born, 248

289

Boys (*continued*)
    as indentured servants, 175–176
    kashta kelsa done by, 181
    parental attitudes at birth of, 169
    peer groups of, 175, 181–184, 244
    socialization of, 160, 175–185
    technology as influence on socialization of, 243–244
    tests of manhood for, 244
    variation in lives of, 176
Brahmin, 4
Bride price, 258
Bronson, Bennet, 201
Brown, Judith K., 71
Buchannan, F. H., 73, 208
Burke, Kenneth, 190
Burton, M. L., L. A. Brudner, and D. R. White, 71

Caste. *See* Brahmin; Holeya; *Jaati;* Naayk; Vodda; Vokkaliga
Chayanov's rule, 202
Children
    age of, at weaning, 171
    dependence training of, 172
    food sharing among, 170
    infants treated as androgynous, 171
    language acquisition of, 172
    men's care of, 171
    mother surrogates for, 171
    nursing of, 171
    play of, 166–167
    practice of elderhood by, 78
    work of, 101, 174, 175–176, 177–178
    See also Boys; Girls
Class consciousness, 209, 213, 221, 276. *See also Joodidars; Sovkaars*
Collective rationality, 22, 77–79
Crops
    avare, 111–112, 122, 125, 131
    damage to, 124
    dry land, 111
    elicitation of, 25
    failure of, 116–117, 263
    haaraka, 111, 118
    honge, 126
    joLLa, 111–112, 122, 125, 131
    onions, 154
    potatoes, 155
    proportion sold, 111

    raagi, 111–112, 119, 122, 124, 125, 131, 154
    rice, 112, 212
    selection of, 118–119
    See also Yields, agricultural
Cultivation opportunities, 110–112, 113, 115–117, 118, 152, 206, 214, 230, 263
    defined, 110
    opportunity costs of, 117, 124
    variable intensification of, 115–116
    See also Employment opportunities; Labor; Land
Cultural adaptations, 199, 232
    analogous, 277
    homologous, 277–278
Cultural selection, 19, 245–246, 250, 261
    compared to natural selection, 236–238
    defined, 236
    See also Group selection; Kin selection; Marital selection; Migrant selection

Decision making
    analogic, 135–138
    interactive, 149, 154–157
Dharmas of the sexes, 11–15, 21, 25–26, 77, 80, 164, 234, 235, 272.
    See also Men, *dharma* of; Women, *dharma* of
Diet, 226–229. *See also* Famine; Food shortage, management of; Women, domestic work of
Digby, William, 199, 208, 209
Discriminant function analysis, 140–142
Domestic mode of production, 201
Drought
    effects of, on irrigation tanks, 212
    of 1870s, 8–9, 199, 203, 207, 212
    from 1891 through 1914, 215
    of 1923, 215, 229
    of 1965, 8–9, 199, 212
    See also Rainfall
DuBois, Cora, 63
Durham, William H., 232–233

Economies of scale, 145–148
Elders, 15, 27, 29, 159, 164, 171,

182, 186, 192, 198, 228. *See also* Men, as fathers; Mother of the house; Teachings of the elders; Women, as mothers *and* as mothers-in-law; *Yajaman*
Employment opportunities, 112–115, 118, 147
  defined, 112
  management of, 113–115, 118
Epstein, T. Scarlett, 226
Estrus, suppression of, 233, 281
External diseconomies, 50–60. *See also* Male dominance
External economies, 113, 145

Factionalism, 5
Facultative traits, 233, 282
Famine, 9–10, 138
  concealment of food during, 210
  disruption of families by, 210
  effect of, on composition of population, 210
  effect of, on livestock, 209
  effect of, on workers, 208–209
  forgiveness of taxes during, 209
  government response to, 9, 207–209
  gratuitous relief during, 209
  relief work during, 208–209
  stocks of food in, 208
  See also Diet; Food shortage
Farm management
  as dynamic control process, 112
  as folk engineering, 136
  See also Cultivation opportunities; Decision making; Men, work of
Farm managers
  experience and effectiveness of, 149–158
  quick adoption of new technology by, 224–225
  See also Men, *dharma of and* work of
Female farming, 200, 238, 239–241
Fieldwork techniques, 24–26
Food shortage, management of, 226–228

Gangappa (villager), 26–29, 156–157
Geertz, Clifford, 12–13

Gerontocracy, 77
Giffin commodity, 138
Girls
  adolescent, estimating ages of, 102
  at age 7, 171
  at age 12, 172–173
  at age 15, 174
  behavior of, as brides, 53, 194–195
  child care of, 170
  discontinuity in socialization of, 181–182
  domestic work of, 168–170, 173
  earlier marriage of, 43, 102, 185
  education of, 176
  first-born, 268
  friendships of, 53, 173–174
  holistic learnings of, 173
  as *kulis*, 174
  parental attitudes toward birth of, 169
  relations of, with kin, 53–54
  socialization of, 172–174
  in *sovkaar* families, 175, 266
Golden Grain, story of, 187–188
Government, rural development programs of, 9, 216, 218–226
Graft, 221–224
Group selection, 237–238
  among men in Yaavahalli, 259–262
  among women in Yaavahalli, 268–272

Harris, Marvin, 79, 232–234, 240
Holeya, 4, 166, 178, 211, 256
Homans, G. C., 22
Hormones
  progestin, 161
  testosterone, 160
Hosadevaru Puja (ritual), 63–66
Households, 20–41 *passim*
  composition of, 143–144, 148, 267
  crop yields of, 140–143
  developmental cycles of, 22
  female-headed, 36, 141
  incomes of, 140–143
  joint, advantages of, 13, 26–42, 81, 140–158 *passim*
  in life histories, 32–39
  as measures of village size, 28
  partition of, 30, 36–40, 189–192, 249

Households (*continued*)
  sexual dimorphism in, 92
  sizes of, 141
  struggle to maintain, 21
  terms for, 35
  villagers' views on, 32–39, 157
  wealth as influence on labor in,
    113, 130
Hypothalamus, 162

Immigration. *See* Migrant selection
Inclusive fitness, 237. *See also* Natural
    selection
Income
  changes in, 204, 225–229
  dietary, 226–229
  inequality in, 225–226
  in manufactured goods, 226
  per capita, defined, 141
  residual, defined, 142
  See also Diet; Wealth
Indian independence, villagers' par-
    ticipation in, 188, 247, 249
Indivisibility problems, 148–149
Informed consent (of villagers), 24
Inheritance, 44. *See also* Teachings of
    the elders
Intensification, 16–18, 98–99, 121, 126
  in anticipation of population
    growth, 217
  Boserup's theory of, 16–18, 200–
    202
  effects of, on income, 204, 225–229
  fallowing periods as measure of, 201
  maximizing food in bad years and,
    202
  men's work and, 201
  variable, 116
Intensification fitness, 18, 231, 244–
    272
Interpersonal comparisons of produc-
    tivity, 153–154
Intrilligator, Michael D., 138
Irrigation works, 3
  construction of, 109, 169, 182, 203,
    219, 274
  famine relief work on, 208–209
  fathers' role in construction of, 258
  and gardens in nineteenth century,
    212–213
  on *joodidar* land, 213

joodidars' unwillingness to invest in,
    212
  labor costs of, 213–214
  labor of women on, 109, 213–214
  loans for, 219–223
  marital selection and construction
    of, 258–259
  migrant labor used on, 213–214,
    219–220
  tanks, in efficiency of, 212
  wells, 10, 118, 148, 169, 202, 205,
    214, 217, 230, 258–259, 274, 276
Isometric muscular strength
  defined, 84
  role of, in work, 94, 96
  studies of, 85–87
  See also Aerobic work capacity; La-
    bor; Sex differences, physical
    strength

Jaati (caste), 4–5
  and food sharing, 170
  and girls friendships, 173
  and marital selection, 256
  See also Brahmin; Holeya; Naayk;
    Vodda; Vokkaliga
Jiita (indentured servitude), 129
Joodidars (landlords)
  abolition of, 6, 215
  class hatred toward, 209, 213
  establishment of, 205
  farmers' deception of, 210
  farmers' relationships with, 206,
    207, 211–212, 254
  indemnification of, 128
  reliance of, on *sovkaars*, 253
  See also Land, tenure

Kasta jiivigaLu (hard workers), 150
Kashta kelsa (difficult work), 11, 14–
    15, 26, 69, 71–72, 74, 80, 83–
    106 *passim*, 108–135 *passim*, 140,
    158, 178, 181, 259, 263. *See also*
    Aerobic work capacity; Agricul-
    tural tasks; Isometric muscular
    strength; Labor; Men, *dharma* of
Kin selection, 237. *See also* Cultural
    selection; Natural selection
Kuli (wage) workers, 113, 127–134,
    147–148, 149, 151, 155, 174,
    189, 228, 253, 268, 271, 273–274
  compliants about, 97–98

difficult work by, 105–106
employment, conditions of, 128
in joint households, 147
wages of, 131–132
women as, 129–132

Labor
of adolescents, 106
allocations of, 110, 112, 116–124,
 135–137, 146–149, 151–152
bottlenecks in demand for, 116
children's, 101
difficult. *See Kashta kelsa*
domestic, 146, 193–194
intensification of. *See* Intensification
measuring difficulty of, 93, 95–100
men's, 25–26, 66–77, 108, 118–
 120, 126, 135, 140, 147, 201
of older villagers, 103
as parental investment, 238
preparatory, 108, 119–120, 122–
 124, 126, 131, 133, 140, 206, 229
in prime of life, 104
productivity of, 80, 108, 113–127
risk, uncertainty in employment of,
 116
urgency of, 99–101
varada kelsa (weekly work), 6
wealth as influence on, 129–130
withdrawal of, 115
women's, 55–56, 80, 119–121, 126–
 127, 129, 133–135, 193, 200
Land
areas under cultivation, 110
dry (unirrigated), 111–112, 118,
 121–127, 140–141, 263
equity in, 207
garden, 3, 111, 116, 118–119, 134,
 140, 155, 199, 206, 213, 251,
 258, 263–264, 265
kinds of, 110, 118
not treated as commodity, 113
per capita holdings of, 141–142
size of holdings of, 140–142, 148
tank irrigated (paddy), 140–141,
 206, 265
tenure, 6
waste, 125
yields of, 110–111
See also Cultivation opportunities;

Irrigation works; *Joodidars; Sov-
 kaars;* Yields
Least-effort strategies, 233
Life histories, 32–39
Lineages (*gumpus*), 45, 205, 211, 269
Livestock, 127, 152
bullocks, 94, 104, 108, 122, 123,
 156, 264
effects of drought on, 209
income from, 111, 144–146
overgrazing of, 264
Loans, 139, 219–223
Loveday, A., 9
Lovejoy, C. Owen, 240, 280
Lusk coefficient of consumption, 141

Maccoby, Eleanor, and Carol N. Jacklin, 136, 160–162, 177, 280
Maclachlan, Caryl A., 17
Male dominance, 48–60
Male farming, 238, 239–240, 241–246
Marital selection, 211
and incest taboo, 237
among men in Yaavahalli, 255–259
under plow agriculture, 242–245
and polygyny, 239–243
and socialization of boys, 243–245
among women in Yaavahalli, 262–
 268
Marriage
age at, 43
behavior of brides in years following, 51–53
bride price, 169
consanguineous, 44–48, 51–55, 61,
 192–196, 262–268, 270–272
dowry, 169
formal rules of, 45–46
hypergamous, 44–45, 192–196,
 254, 262–268
and immigration, 211
lineage size and, 269
and sexuality, 61–62
uncle/niece, 46–47
women's role in, 47, 51–55
See also Monogamy; Polygyny
Martin, M. Kay, and Barbara
 Voorhies, 240, 241
Marx, Karl, 22, 127
Material interests, 235–236. *See also*
 Motive; Reproductive interests

Materialism, 79–80, 276–278
Matrilocal residence, 22, 185, 254
Men
    age of, at marriage, 43, 81, 102,
        159
    aging and personality change in,
        171
    dharma of, 15, 25–26, 69–77, 81,
        156, 164, 259
    disputes among, 74–76. *See also*
        Aggression
    as fathers, 29, 71, 139, 150, 155–
        157, 167, 182, 186–192
    as fathers-in-law, 51–52, 54, 186–
        187, 247–248
    views on farm work among, 71–73
    views of women of, 76–77
    womens' views of, 57–58
    work of, 25–26, 66–77, 108, 118–
        120, 126, 135, 140, 147, 201
Migrant selection, 241, 242
    in Yaavahalli, 251–255
Miller, G. A., E. Gallanter, and
    K. H. Pribram, 136
Milpa (Meso-American farm land),
    202
Money, J., and A. A. Ehrhardt, 161
Monkeys, crop damage by, 124
Monogamy, 200–201, 238, 240. *See
    also* Marriage; Polygyny
Mother Goddesses, 63–64
Mother of the house, 34, 36, 38. *See
    also* Elders; Women, as mothers
    and as mothers-in-law
Motive, 43, 196
Mysore wars, 204
Mysoreans, British view of, 208

Naayk(s), 4, 37–38, 173, 211
    Bedapur (village), 273–276
    discrimination against, 165–166,
        274
Natural selection, 232, 237–239. *See
    also* Cultural selection
Nepotism, 237
    teachings of the elders as, 78. *See
    also* Group selection; Reproduc-
    tive interests

Opportunity costs, 117, 124
Osgood, C. T., 92

Panchayat (village council), 29, 56,
    167, 189, 260
Panglossian functionalism, 20, 276–
    277
Parental investment, 196
    farm work as, 238
    maternal, 238, 240
    paternal, 238–239
Patriarchal anecdote, 190
Patriarchal rhetoric, 75
Patriarchy, 74, 185–192, 245
Patrilocal residence, 44, 159, 185–192
Patron/client relations, 127–133. *See
    also Joodidars; Kuli* workers; *Sov-
    kaars;* Tenancy
Political economy of everyday life,
    the, 10–11, 277
Polygyny, 200, 238–241, 243, 273.
    See also Marital selection; Mar-
    riage; Monogamy
Population, density and growth, 2–3,
    200, 203, 206, 214, 229, 263
    and dependence on cultigens, 241–
        242
    and male farming, 241–243
    and standards of marital selection,
        244
    See also Intensification
Price controls, 216
Production functions, 115–116

Quinn, Naomi, 280

Rainfall
    average, 2
    influence of, on crop yields, 123
Regions, terms of trade between, 219
Reproductive interests, 235, 236, 248,
    250–251
    joint, 237–238, 261–262
Reproductive success, 16, 237
    determinants of, 239–240
Rhizomes, 120, 121
Ricardian principles, landowners' im-
    position of, 225
Risk aversion in cultivation of land,
    122, 153
Rohmert, W., and P. Jenik, 85

Sahlins, Marshall, 201
Sanyasis (wandering mendicants), 255

Satyagrahis (nonviolent demonstrators), 188, 247
Scitovsky, Tibor, 145
Selby, Henry A., 145
Sericulture, 111, 146, 152, 153–154, 215
Sex differences (behavioral, biological), 196–197
  aggression, 159–171, 239, 282
  cognitive, 136
  cultural amplification of, 13–15, 82, 234, 280
  determinants of reproductive success and, 239–240
  dexterity, suppleness in women, 105, 130
  differential amplification of, 282
  endocrine, 160–161
  hemoglobin loss in women, 86, 88–89
  later maturation of males (bimaturism), 13, 81, 159, 160, 179, 244
  neurological, 161–162
  physical strength, 80–82, 83–93, 106, 160, 196, 239, 242, 282–283. *See also* Aerobic work capacity; Isometric muscular strength
Sex roles, 11–15, 36, 235, 274, 279, 281, 284
  defined, 11
  See also Cultural selection; Labor; Men, *dharma* of; Sex differences; Sexual division of labor; Women, *dharma* of
Sexual antagonism, competition, 59, 60
Sexual biology and behavior, theories of, 13–15, 79–80, 234–235, 279–284
Sexual bonds, 233, 239
Sexual dimorphism
  in households, 92
  in India, 87–88
  in Western populations, 84, 87–88
  See also Sex differences
Sexual division of labor, 11–15, 36, 71–73, 77, 81, 95–107, 169, 175, 196, 200, 235, 238, 277, 282
  defined, 11
  See also Cultural selection; Labor;

Men, work of; Sex differences; Women, work of
Sexual selection, 237, 239. *See also* Marital selection
Shambog (village accountant), 33
Sociobiology, 18–19, 233, 279–284
Soils, 3
  effects of manure on, 123, 152
  moisture of, 122–123
  quality of, 123, 125
Sovkaars
  class consciousness toward, 221, 222
  labor relations of, 113, 129
  land reform, beneficiaries of, 128
  leadership of, 203–204
Spirit possession, 181–182
Sustu (anemia), 88, 181
Symons, Donald, 280

Tanner, J. M., 87
Teachings of the elders, 12, 15, 19, 21, 28, 42–48, 78–79, 190, 196–198, 231, 235, 246, 272
Tenancy, 105, 127–128, 130–132, 134, 138, 139, 147, 151, 155, 207, 254, 274
  income from, 132
  joint household monopolization of, 147–148
  landowners' view of, 131–132
  men's work and, 130
  widows resort to, 68
Tippu Sultan, 204
Topography, 1–2. *See also* Land; Soils
Transportation, improvement of, 215

Udy, S., 22
United Temple. *See* Household, joint, advantages of

Vamsharuksha (genealogy), 73
Village product, 110–111. *See also* Yields
Vodda, 213–214, 217, 254, 275–278
Vokkaliga, 3–4, 37–38, 165, 173, 211, 252, 256, 276
  dominance of, 4
  ritual of, 63–66

Wages, 134, 141, 147
  of *kulis,* 132
  power of landowners to dictate,
    131–132
  of tenants, 132
  See also Kuli; Tenancy; *Sovkaars*
Wealth
  access to loans influenced by, 221–
    222
  differences between joint, nuclear
    households in, 143, 147, 148
  increase of inequality in, 226
  influence of, on organization of
    work, 113, 127–133
Wells. *See* Irrigation works
Wilson, E. O., 280, 283
Wodeyar Rajas, 205
Women
  attributions of inferiority of, ab-
    sence of, 76
  aging and personality change in, 171
  as brides, 51–53, 195
  dharma of, 11, 15, 62–69, 168
  difficult work done by, 109
  disputes among, 65–66
  domestic work of, 146, 193–194
  esthetic elements in activities of, 173
  livestock care of, 144–145, 170, 194
  marital preferences of, 47
  menopausal depression, low fre-
    quency of, 66
  men's views of, 76–77
  as mothers, 36, 51, 58, 65–67, 164,
    174, 191, 193, 240, 268–269
  as mothers-in-law, 51–52, 63–66,
    181, 193

  political participation of, 56–57,
    59–60
  proverbs about, 59
  sustu (anemia) among, 88, 181
  turn taking in farm work of, 193
  "uppitiness" among, 45
  views of men of, 67–70
  visiting of, 53–54, 268–269
  wealth as influence on work of,
    129–130
  as widows, 36, 67–70
  as wives, 77
  work of, 55–56, 80, 119–121, 126–
    127, 129, 133–135, 193, 200
Work. *See* Labor

Yaavahalli
  concentration of agricultural growth
    in, 231, 246, 253–255, 261–262
  famine-stressed culture in, 246, 263
  founding and growth of, 204–206,
    252
  migration to, 211
  past farming practices of, 115, 206
  selection of, for research, 200
Yajaman (male head of household),
    34–38 *passim. See also* Elders;
    Men, as fathers
Yields (per acre), 120, 124, 140–141,
    143, 151–152
  declining, 116
  among immigrants, 252
  single and multiple male households
    compared, 143–144, 147
  village product, defined, 110–111